Lie Detection
and
Criminal Interrogation

BY

Fred E. Inbau

Professor of Law, Northwestern University
Former Director, Chicago Police
Scientific Crime Detection Laboratory

AND

John E. Reid

Director, John E. Reid and Associates
Former Staff Member, Chicago Police
Scientific Crime Detection Laboratory

THIRD EDITION
Revised and Enlarged

BALTIMORE
THE WILLIAMS & WILKINS COMPANY
1953

Made in United States of America

First Edition, September, 1942
Second Edition, June, 1948
Third Edition, September, 1953
Reprinted, August, 1954; April, 1957; May, 1958; February, 1959

Composed and Printed at the
WAVERLY PRESS, INC.
Baltimore 2, Md., U. S. A.

DEDICATED TO

Mrs. A. P. Perrin

—from F. E. I.

AND

Mr. and Mrs. Thomas Reid

—from J. E. R.

PREFACE TO THIRD EDITION

The present publication represents an extensive revision and enlargement of the previous 1948 edition.

Part I, dealing with the lie-detector technique, is almost entirely new. This major change was made necessary by the development and refinement of a better test procedure than the one previously described and discussed. That fact also constitutes the reason why I invited my good friend and former colleague, John E. Reid, to join me as co-author, for it was his research and experimentation that effected this advancement in the lie-detector technique. In fact, the "control question" test procedure he devised and developed should render obsolete the conventional "relevant-irrelevant question" method of conducting a lie-detector test.

Another very material revision of the second edition is contained in the discussion of the law concerning criminal confessions. Since 1948 a considerable change in the law has resulted from several decisions of the United States Supreme Court. These decisions are all analyzed and discussed in the present edition.

The material in Part II on interrogation tactics and techniques is essentially the same as in the previous editions, although it too has been enlarged and re-arranged to some extent.

Acknowledgments

In addition to reaffirming my own debt of gratitude to the friends whose advice and assistance on the previous editions were so helpful to me then, Mr. Reid and I are greatly appreciative of the cooperation we received from several others in the preparation of the present edition.

Richard O. Arther, of the staff of John E. Reid and Associates, was of great assistance, particularly with regard to some very valuable original ideas and suggestions.

For the photographic reproductions of the many lie-detector records contained in the present edition we are greatly indebted to Ray Heimbuch of the Chicago Police Scientific Crime Detection Laboratory. We are also appreciative of the cooperation of the Director of that Laboratory, Lieutenant John Ascher, in making available a number of the Laboratory's lie-detector case records.

George W. Harman, of the staff of John E. Reid and Associates, rendered valuable assistance in the preparation of the manuscript. Harry T. Mahoney of Washington, D. C., and Charles A. McInerney of Pittsburgh,

Pa., cooperated with us in checking the final copy of the manuscript. In addition, Mr. Mahoney assisted in some of the legal research regarding the law on confessions.

The typing of the various drafts of the manuscript was the responsibility of our respective secretaries, Norah Goudy and Mildred McGuffie. They carried on this task very efficiently and in a spirit of enthusiastic cooperation.

Fred E. Inbau

Chicago, Illinois

PREFACE TO FIRST EDITION

One of the most difficult tasks confronting a law-enforcement officer is the determination of whether a criminal suspect is telling the truth regarding the offense under investigation. Another problem of comparable difficulty is that of obtaining a confession from a suspect after his guilt has been established or indicated with reasonable certainty. Occasionally a problem of a somewhat similar nature is presented in cases where a witness or other prospective informant is in possession of helpful information which he is reluctant or unwilling to disclose.

Although far from offering a complete solution to the detection of deception phase of the interrogator's task, the relatively recent development and increasing use of a so-called "lie-detector technique" has proved to be of much practical utility. Likewise, with respect to the interrogation methods used in obtaining confessions or other helpful information, there has been a decided improvement, due largely to recent advances in police training and education. There remains, however, a need for greater efforts in both directions.

It is the writer's desire that this book will serve not only as a practical and useful manual for criminal interrogators but that it will also serve to stimulate further interest, research, and progress in the art of lie detection and criminal interrogation.

The first part of the book—*The Lie-Detector Technique*—is an illustrated discussion of the methods used in the detection of deception from recordings of physiological phenomena such as changes in blood pressure, pulse, respiration, and electrodermal responses. The second part—*Criminal Interrogation*—consists of a discussion of various tactics and techniques which may be used by any law enforcement officer for the purpose of eliciting confessions or other helpful information. Each part is supplemented with a treatment of the legal aspects of the subject matter.

In presenting the material on *The Lie-Detector Technique*, the writer had in mind three principal objectives: (1) to offer to criminal investigators, and particularly to those interested in utilizing the technique, a detailed yet simple and concise explanation of the application of the technique in actual case examinations; (2) to create among academic psychologists, physiologists, and other scientific groups an interest in a method of detecting deception which has already proved itself practically useful, and which is replete with possibilities for further exploration; and (3) to present to the legal profession a frank analysis and appraisal of this much debated and misunderstood subject.

Although the tactics and techniques described in the part on *Criminal*

Interrogation are of practical utility to the lie-detector operator, they were prepared primarily for the average police interrogator who does not have the aid of such an instrument. With that purpose in view, a special effort was made to minimize theoretical considerations and to concentrate on the practical aspects of the interrogator's problems. It was upon the basis of the actual criminal case experiences of the writer and his former colleagues that these various tactics and techniques were formulated. They are offered, therefore, with the utmost confidence in their practical merit to anyone engaged in the practice of interrogating criminal suspects and witnesses.

Acknowledgments

From the very inception of the idea up to the time of the book's publication I received much valuable advice and assistance from M. Edwin O'Neill of the Chicago Police Scientific Crime Detection Laboratory. I am deeply grateful for his suggestions, criticisms, and encouragement, and also for the many hours he spent with me in the preparation of the illustrations of the lie-detector tracings.

To Ordway Hilton, Editor of the *American Journal of Police Science*, and a member of the staff of the Chicago Police Scientific Crime Detection Laboratory, I wish to express my appreciation for his many helpful suggestions and criticisms during the preparation of the manuscript, and also for his painstaking efforts in editing the final draft.

For their valuable comments on the manuscript, I am indebted to Dean Emeritus John H. Wigmore of Northwestern University School of Law, Dean Charles T. McCormick of the University of Texas Law School, Dr. Harold S. Hulbert, Dr. C. W. Muehlberger, Rosella Hart, and John E. Reid.

During the preparation of the manuscript, some particularly helpful suggestions regarding various phases of the subject were offered by Charles M. Wilson, Director of the Chicago Police Scientific Crime Detection Laboratory, and Paul V. Trovillo, formerly of the same institution.

I also wish to acknowledge the assistance of Joseph Albaum in collecting some of the material used in the section on the legal aspects of criminal interrogation, and to express my indebtedness to Northwestern University for the frequent use of its law school library.

As with any book of this type, the writer did not act upon all of the suggestions and criticisms offered by the many friends whose advice or assistance he had solicited, however much their cooperation was appreciated. For this reason, therefore, the responsibility for the book as it now stands, with its inevitable shortcomings, rests upon the writer alone.

FRED E. INBAU

Chicago, Illinois
August, 1942

TABLE OF CONTENTS

PART I
The Lie-Detector Technique

Everyone has at least a partial understanding of the psychology of lying and lie detection. Since lying is such a commonplace occurrence, most of us are personally acquainted with the inner sensations that so often accompany the telling of a lie. We also have learned from personal experience in the everyday affairs of life that it is sometimes possible to detect a lie in others simply by observing their facial expressions or their general conduct and behavior.

In endeavoring to conceal the truth, have we not on occasions felt a thudding increase of the heart beat, or the rush of blood to the face, or an uncontrollable impulse to swallow, or other such phenomena resulting from fear over the possibility that the lie will be detected? Have we not also experienced a sigh of relief—ordinarily manifested by heavier breathing—after the lie has been told with apparent success? And have we not encountered many occasions when we have been able to detect lies by various indications such as blushing, twitching of the lips, squinting of the eyes, failure to look the inquirer "straight in the eye", a peculiar monotone of the voice, a "forced laugh", a counter inquiry of "who, me?", an unnecessary request for a repetition of the question, movements of the hands and feet exhibiting a state of uneasiness, increased activity of the "Adam's apple", and many other reactions of a similar nature?

It is a fact, of course, that some persons are better liars than others. They are more successful either because they are not very much disturbed over the telling of a lie, or because they are better able to control the emotional disturbances produced by lying and thus avoid a display of the outward indications exhibited by persons less fortified with these essentials of successful lying. Nevertheless, even among the best of liars there are a considerable number who experience certain internal sensations of uneasiness or fear of detection, and this is particularly true as regards matters of a serious nature, as in the case of a criminal offense.

In view of the many years of experience human beings have had in lying and in detecting lies in others on the basis of various outward indications,

1

such as the ones previously mentioned, it was inevitable that eventually someone would conceive the idea that it might be possible to detect deception scientifically—by obtaining indications or recordings of physiological phenomena such as blood pressure, pulse, respiration, etc. Certainly there was a basis for the idea, and, moreover, there obviously was a practical need—particularly in the field of criminal investigation—for a method which would render it possible to detect lies more often and more accurately than when considering outward or observational indications alone.

Historical Development

The first attempt to utilize a scientific instrument in an effort to detect deception occurred about 1895. In that year Cesare Lombroso published an account of several experiments he had conducted on actual criminal suspects whose guilt or innocence he sought to determine on the basis of the presence or absence of blood pressure-pulse changes when the suspects were questioned about the offense under investigation.[1] The instruments which Lombroso used had been invented and developed by other scientists for medical purposes and originally were not intended for use as instruments for detecting deception. Since these instruments were in existence at the time Lombroso conducted his experiments in detecting deception, he cannot be considered as a "lie-detector inventor", but at the same time he must be accorded the distinction of being the first person to utilize an instrument for the purpose of detecting lies.[2]

Although Lombroso reported successful results in his experiments,[3] his research in the field of detecting deception was not very extensive, perhaps because of his widespread interest in so many other phases of criminology. Apparently he did little or nothing more with deception experiments than is reported in his 1895 publication; and it was not until 1915 that any

[1] Lombroso, C., *L'Homme Criminel* (2d ed., 1895) 1: 336–346. The first (Italian) edition of this book appeared in 1876, but it was not until the second (French) 1895 edition that mention was made of the use of an instrument for testing a person's veracity. No English translation has ever appeared.

[2] Lombroso used a "hydrosphygmograph" for obtaining recordings on a smoked drum of changes in pulse patterns and blood pressure. The instrument consisted essentially of a small water filled tank into which the subject's hand was placed. The immersed fist was then sealed across the top of the tank by a rubber membrane. Changes in pulse pattern and blood pressure in the fist were presumably transferred to the water and changes in the water level were carried over into an air filled tube leading to a revolving smoked drum.

A reproduction of an original sketch of the water tank of Lombroso's "hydrosphygmograph" appears in Trovillo, P. V. "A History of Lie Detection", J. Crim. L & Criminology 29 (6): 848, at p 864 (1939).

[3] Lombroso, C., *L'Homme Criminel* (2d ed., 1895) 1: 336–346, and particularly plates 17 and 18 of the book's *Atlas;* also see Lombroso, C., *Crime, Its Causes and Remedies* (translated by H. P. Horton, 1911) §137, and Ferrero, G. L., *Criminal Man* (1911) 223–225.

further experiments with blood pressure changes were conducted by anyone else. This was the year that William Moulton Marston began his research. His technique consisted essentially of the use of an ordinary sphygmomanometer—the same type of instrument as is commonly used by physicians in determining a patient's blood pressure—by means of which he obtained periodic, discontinuous blood pressure readings during the course of a subject's examination. With this technique Marston reported some very successful results.[4]

In 1914 Vittorio Benussi, another pioneer in the field, published an account of his research on respiration changes as symptoms of deception. In test cases he measured recorded respiratory tracings and found that if the length of inspiration were divided by the length of expiration the ratio was greater before telling the truth than afterwards, and greater after lying than before lying.[5] Harold E. Burtt later partially confirmed the results obtained by Benussi and improved upon his technique. However, Burtt considered this respiratory method of less diagnostic value than the blood pressure technique.[6]

Encouraged by the reported successes of his predecessors, John A. Larson, in 1921, constructed an instrument capable of continuously recording all three phenomena—blood pressure, pulse, and respiration—during the entire period of the deception test. With his instrument Larson conducted a number of tests on criminal suspects and reported a high percentage of accuracy in his results.[7]

[4] Marston, W. M., "Systolic Blood Pressure Symptoms of Deception", J. Exper. Psychol. 2 (2): 117 (1917); "Psychological Possibilities in the Deception Tests", J. Crim. L. & Criminology 11 (4): 551 (1921); "Studies in Testimony", ibid. 15 (1): 5 (1924). Also see Marston's book, The Lie Detector Test (1938).

Marston began his work while a student of Professor Hugo Münsterberg, author of On the Witness Stand (1908), in which book, in the chapter on "The Traces of Emotions" Münsterberg discussed the effects of emotional changes upon blood pressure, respiration. psychogalvanic skin reflex, etc., and pointed out the possibilities of utilizing such reactions in detecting deception.

[5] Benussi, V., "Die Atmungssymptome der Lüge", Archiv. f. die gesamte Psychologie 31: 244 (1914).

[6] Burtt, H. E., "A Pneumograph for Inspiration-Expiration Ratios", Psychol. Bull. 15 (10): 325 (1918); "The Inspiration-Expiration Ratio During Truth and Falsehood", J. Exper. Psychol. 4 (1): 1 (1921); "Further Technique for Inspiration-Expiration Ratios", ibid. 4 (2): 106 (1921).

[7] Larson, J. A., "Modification of the Marston Deception Test", J. Crim. L. & Criminology 12 (3): 390 (1921); "The Cardio-Pneumo-Psychogram and Its Use in the Study of Emotions, with Practical Applications", J. Exper. Psychol. 5 (5): 323 (1922). Also see his book, Lying and its Detection (1932).

Much of Larson's interest and success in the field of detection of deception can be attributed to the encouragement and support he received from Chief of Police August Vollmer of Berkely, California, under whom Larson was then serving as a police officer. Larson is now a psychiatrist.

In 1926 Leonarde Keeler constructed a more satisfactory instrument than the one used by Larson.[8] Later on Keeler made additional changes in the instrument, and at the time of his death in 1949 the "Keeler Polygraph" included, in addition to units for recording blood pressure-pulse and respiration changes, a galvanometer for recording what is known as the psychogalvanic skin reflex or electrodermal response (generally referred to as the G.S.R.). However, as in the case of the blood pressure-pulse and respiration recorders, the G.S.R. unit was not a lie-detector invention. Instruments for measuring and recording the G.S.R. have been in existence a long time and were only adapted or modified for lie detection purposes.[9]

In 1945 one of the present authors found that by various forms of unobserved muscular activity a subject's blood pressure could be changed in such a manner as to seriously affect the accuracy of the examiner's diagnosis. He then devised an instrument (the "Reid Polygraph") for recording muscular activity along with changes in blood pressure, pulse, respiration and psychogalvanic skin reflex.

Generally overlooked in the history of the lie-detector technique is the fact that the so-called "Polygraph" was in existence at least as early as 1906. Its invention, however, was not for lie detection purposes but rather for use in medical examinations. Nevertheless, it did contain the essential features of present day instruments and its construction was based upon precisely the same principles. Its inventor was Sir James Mackenzie, a famous English heart specialist. He first described the instrument in an article entitled "The Ink Polygraph", which appeared in a 1908 number of

[8] See Keeler, L., "A Method for Detecting Deception", Am. J. Police Sci. 1 (1): 38 (1930).

[9] In 1791 Galvani, an Italian for whom the modern galvanometer was named, published the results of his study and experiments with this phenomenon. In 1897 Sticker's experiments with the galvanometer indicated that the response resulted from "exciting mental impressions." Veraguth (1907) was apparently the first to use the galvanometer in connection with word association tests, although about the same time Münsterberg was pointing to the possibility of its application in criminal cases. Marston reports that in 1917 he used a galvanometer for lie detection purposes. (For a detailed discussion of the history of the G.S.R. see Trovillo, P. V., "A History of Lie Detection", J. Crim. L. & Criminology 30 (1): 104, etc. (1939). The same article, in two parts, also contains a comprehensive and interesting history of lie detection up to 1939. The first part appears in Vol. 29, No. 6, p. 848 of the same Journal.)

In 1935 a G.E. photoelectric recorder was adapted for use as a lie-detector unit by Charles M. Wilson at the Scientific Crime Detection Laboratory of Northwestern University. Keeler, in 1939, incorporated a galvanograph into his blood pressure-pulse and respiration polygraph. Several of the polygraphs which have appeared since then also include a galvanograph unit. Some examiners have attempted to rely solely upon the G.S.R. for lie detection purposes. (An evaluation of the G.S.R. as a criterion of deception appears *infra* pp. 99–106.)

the British Medical Journal. Dr. Mackenzie's article, including his sketch of the "Polygraph", is reproduced in the Appendix of the present publication.[10]

A number of instruments are now available for recording most of these various physiological phenomena for deception test purposes. Although the quality of mechanical structure and function possessed by certain polygraphs may warrant the preference of some instruments over others, the most important factor involved in the use of any such instrument is the ability, experience, and integrity of the examiner himself.

The Instrument

In popular fancy, a lie-detector is often thought of as an instrument that is supposed to ring a bell, or flash a light, or produce a dial indication or some other quick and positive indication of a lie when one is told by the person being tested. Unfortunately, however, there is no instrument in existence at the present time that will detect deception so simply and effectively.[11] Nevertheless, it is a demonstrated fact that there are available such instruments as those already mentioned which are capable of producing a record of physiological phenomena that may be used as the basis for the application of a reliable *technique* for diagnosing deception.

The instrument which was used in obtaining most of the records illustrated and discussed in this edition is the Reid Polygraph. The other records, which were used in the earlier editions, were obtained with an early model of the Keeler Polygraph. Both instruments, as well as practically all other dependable polygraph instruments used for lie detection purposes, are essentially pneumatically operated mechanical recorders of changes in blood pressure, pulse, and respiration, supplemented with a unit for recording the G.S.R. (psychogalvanic skin reflex). An additional unit in the Reid Polygraph permits a recording of certain muscular activity, particularly muscular pressure exerted by the subject's forearms, thighs, or feet.

The Reid Polygraph, illustrated in Figures 1, 2, and 3, is attached in the following manner to the person being tested: a pneumograph tube, with the aid of a beaded chain, is fastened on to the subject's chest or abdomen; a blood pressure cuff, of the type used by physicians, is fastened around

[10] See p. 233. This interesting historical information about the "Polygraph" was not previously known to the author of the earlier editions of this book. He first learned of it from reading an article entitled "The Search for the Truth", by William O. Gay, in a 1948 number of the English Police Journal 21: 4, 284, in which the statement was made that "the Polygraph is really a modification of a device invented by Sir James Mackenzie, the famous heart specialist".

[11] See in this connection Keeler, L., "Debunking the Lie-Detector", J. Crim. L. & Criminology 25 (1): 153 (1934).

one arm; and a set of electrodes is attached to the palmar and dorsal surfaces of the hand of the other arm. No attachments are required for the muscular activity recording unit, the details of which will be subsequently explained and illustrated.

The pneumograph tube (Fig. 3-B) consists of a ten-inch corrugated rubber tube, one end of which is sealed and the other end connected to the instrument proper by a rather thick-walled rubber tube considerably smaller in diameter than the pneumograph tube itself. During a test, as the circumference of the subject's chest increases with each inspiration of air, the pneumograph tube stretches; as the subject exhales, it contracts. This movement produces pressure changes inside the pneumograph tube, which changes are transmitted through the smaller tubing to a tambour consisting of hollow metal stacks, or bellows, constructed of thin metal and situated below the panel of the instrument (see Fig. 4). These pressure changes cause the tambour to either contract or distend, and the motion of its free end is transmitted to a pivot shaft, the upper extremity of which carries the recording pen arm (Fig. 3-E).

A similar mechanical arrangement is used for the blood pressure-pulse recording system. When the rubber cuff (Fig. 3-A) is inflated, the alternating distention and contraction of the tissue of the subject's arm, due to the action of the heart and the changes in blood pressure (and probably blood volume as well), cause an increase or decrease in pressure within the cuff and in the associated tambour (Fig. 4). These varying pressure changes within the tambour cause it to expand or contract, and, just as in the case of the respiration tambour, the motion of the free end is transferred to the blood pressure-pulse pivot shaft and pen arm (Fig. 3-G).

By means of the passage of an imperceptible amount of electrical current through the hand bearing the attached electrodes (Fig. 3-C), a galvanometer unit provides a recording of the variations in the flow of that current, which is known as the G.S.R.—the psychogalvanic skin reflex or electrodermal response. (The details of the galvanometer system are later discussed and illustrated on pages 99–106.)

The blood pressure-pulse, respiration, and G.S.R. are recorded simultaneously and continuously on the surface of moving graph paper driven by a small electric motor.

Because of the fact that blood pressure changes can be induced by certain types of unobserved muscular movements, a lie-detector should be equipped with a unit for recording such muscular activity. The examiner may thereby properly evaluate blood pressure changes resulting from muscular movements. (The details of the muscular activity recording unit will be discussed and illustrated on pages 88–100.)

FIG. 1. LIE DETECTOR (REID POLYGRAPH) IN OPERATION

Observe the pneumograph tube around the subject's chest, the blood pressure-pulse cuff around his arm, and the electrodes attached to the hand. (It is advisable to attach the electrodes to the opposite hand from which the blood pressure is recorded.) The chair is equipped with metal bellows under the arms and seat for the purpose of recording muscular contractions and pressures. (Figure 67 illustrates and describes the chair itself more fully.)

The subject is placed in a position so that he looks straight ahead while the instrument and the examiner are to the rear and to the side. The examiner should be in the position, however, to at least observe the subject's profile while operating the instrument.

The examiner in this picture is John E. Reid; the subject is posed by Richard O. Arther, of the staff of John E. Reid and Associates.

FIG 2. REID POLYGRAPH RECESSED INTO SUPPORTING TABLE

View of examination room in laboratory of John E. Reid and Associates, with George W. Harman of the staff posing as a subject. The examiner is Fred E. Inbau.

7

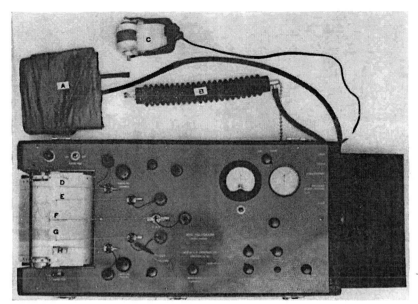

FIG. 3. TOPSIDE VIEW OF REID POLYGRAPH PANEL SHOWING BLOOD PRESSURE CUFF, PNEUMOGRAPH, ELECTRODES AND RECORDING PENS

A. Blood pressure cuff
B. Respiration or pneumograph tube
C. Electrodes for psychogalvanic skin reflex
D. Muscular movement pen for arm recordings

E. Respiration recording pen
F. Psychogalvanic skin reflex recording pen
G. Blood pressure recording pen
H. Muscular movement pen for thigh recordings

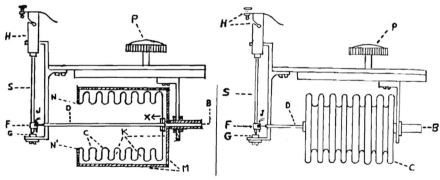

FIG. 4. DIAGRAMMATIC SKETCHES OF THE BLOOD PRESSURE-PULSE AND RESPIRATION BELLLOWS

Left. The "Housed Bellows" for Blood Pressure-Pulse Recordings:
   The rubber tubing from the blood pressure cuff is attached to the hollow rod inlet B. As the cuff around the subject's arm is inflated, the air pressure (about 90 mm.)

Test Procedure

EXAMINATION ROOM

Lie-detector tests should be conducted in a quiet, private room. Extraneous noises, such as the ringing of a telephone or the conversation of persons outside the examination room, or the presence of arresting officers or other spectators in the room itself, will probably induce disturbances

equalizes itself in the cuff and bellows and circulates within the enclosed area K between the housing M and the rim of the bellows C. The bellows (.005″ thick) is sealed airtight at N and N^1.

As the air pressure enters area K, the bellows partially contracts, forcing forward drive shaft D. D is attached to a clevis, F, near the base of pivot shaft S, which rotates on jeweled bearing G and on a similar bearing within pen cradle H. The fluctuating movement of D, actuates S in a semi-circular movement, which in turn produces the pen recording of pulse and blood pressure changes. (A crank, J, hinges D with F in such a way as to allow the half-circle movement of shaft S.)

When the air pressure system is sufficiently inflated for recording purposes the bellows collapses approximately to point X, and with each pulse beat the bellows contracts or releases slightly and abruptly. As the subject's blood pressure increases or decreases there is a greater and steadier contraction or relaxation of the bellows. At no time during the operation, however, does the bellows relax completely as shown in the above diagram until the blood pressure cuff is deflated by the examiner.

P is an adjusting knob which permits a sliding of the bellows assembly forward and backward by means of a rack and pinion system so as to manually center the recording pen on the recording chart.

Since the blood pressure recording is operated on a forced air system with an inflator bulb it is necessary to use the housed bellows, rather than an open bellows, becaused otherwise the bellows would be stretched beyond normal limits.

Right. The "Open Bellows" for the Respiration Recording:

Contrary to the "housed bellows" required for the blood pressure-pulse recording, the "open bellows" is more suitable for the respiration recording because the respiration system requires no forced air inflation. It operates upon a principle of "dead air" displacement.

P is the adjusting knob for manually centering the pen. B is the hollow rod inlet for the rubber tubing leading to the pneumograph tube itself; C, the thin-walled brass metal bellows (.005″ thickness) which contracts when the air is drawn out and returns to normal when the air is replaced; D, the drive shaft, connected to the sealed end of the bellows.

As the pneumograph tube is stretched and placed around the subject's chest, additional air is required within the pneumograph tube. The air thus required is automatically withdrawn from the bellows, thereby causing it to contract slightly. As the subject inhales more air is withdrawn from the bellows, and when he exhales the air automatically returns to the bellows. The resulting alternating contracting and expansion of the bellows pushes shaft D forward and backward. This action actuates S and ultimately the respiration pen itself by means of parts F, G, S, H and J, and in the same manner as previously described for the "housed bellows" blood pressure-pulse system.

(This same type of "open bellows" is used in the subsequently described unit for recording muscular activity.)

and distractions which will distort the recording and interfere with a satisfactory diagnosis of deception.

Whenever it is feasible to do so, a specially equipped and furnished room should be set aside for lie-detector examinations. Such a room should contain no ornaments, pictures, or other objects which would in any way distract the attention of the person being examined. If ornaments, pictures, or other decorative objects are desired, however, they should not be placed in any part of the room faced by the subject during the course of the test. The lighting fixtures of the room should be arranged in such a way as to provide good but not excessive or glaring illumination.

PRELIMINARY PREPARATIONS

In order to conduct a satisfactory lie-detector examination, it is advisable for the examiner first to obtain from the investigators interested in the case all the available facts and circumstances forming the basis of the accusation or suspicion directed against the person to be examined. This will include, of course, the details of the case itself. Such information is essential to the examiner so that he can properly conduct the interview and thereby ascertain which questions should be asked of the subject during the test. It is also helpful for the examiner to know as much about the subject and his background as circumstances permit.

PRELIMINARY OBSERVATIONS

Although the lie-detector records themselves will usually permit a reliable diagnosis of deception, much can be gained from preliminary observations of the subject from the time he enters the examiner's office or reception room until he is escorted into the examination room. The recorded observations of a competent secretary or receptionist as to the subject's general conduct and behavior while in the waiting room will be very helpful to the examiner. They will furnish him with a clue or guide to the most effective handling of the subject, and particularly with regard to his possible resentment toward the test or other attitudes which should be understood and perhaps alleviated before the actual administration of the test.

THE PRE-TEST INTERVIEW

The examiner's interview with the subject prior to the test is of considerable importance, both for the purpose of conditioning the subject for the examination and also in order to provoke and observe the helpful indications of guilt or innocence which are often forthcoming at this time.

Following is a detailed outline of the pre-test interview which has been found to be the most effective of any the authors have employed or observed. (We are assuming in the case illustration that the subject has already been advised of the fact that he is to be given a lie-detector test.)

As the examiner enters the waiting room to request the subject to accompany him into the examination room, the greeting which the examiner extends should be cordial but firm. Upon entering the examination room the subject should be requested to sit down in the chair alongside the instrument, and immediately thereafter the examiner should proceed to put the blood pressure cuff, pneumograph tube, and electrodes on the subject,[12] and at the same time inquire: "Have you ever been on a lie-detector before?" No further comment should be made by the examiner, but he should listen carefully to whatever the subject himself may say. Then, without any further instrument adjustment, the examiner should sit down in a chair on the opposite side of the instrument (as shown in Figs. 1 and 2) and make notes or tabulations regarding the subject's comments or questions up to this point. As long as the subject wishes to ask questions, or make statements of any kind, he should be permitted to do so and a record should be kept of what he says. Note should also be made of the subject's physical composure (e.g., uneasiness or apprehensiveness); and particular attention should be paid to the subject's expressions reflecting his attitude toward the test, and to any comments made or questions asked by him regarding his physical, mental, or emotional condition.

After all such available preliminary behavior observations have been made, the examiner should then move over to the other side of the instrument and sit down in a chair close to and in front of the subject to discuss the case with him, instruct him about the test procedure, and prepare the questions to be asked during the test. At this point it is important that the examiner discourage any prolonged discussion of the case by the subject himself.

The examiner then addresses the subject somewhat as follows. "You know, of course, that we're checking on [the disappearance of the money from the store last week, or the death of John Jones the other night, or any other such criminal case situations]. If you did this yourself, then, I'm going to know about it just as soon as this lie-detector test is run. If that's so, I suggest you straighten the whole thing out right now". Here the examiner should pause for whatever comment or reaction is forthcoming from the subject. An innocent subject of average or better than average intelligence will usually respond immediately, by making some

---

[12] If the subject has not been told of the purpose of his appearance in the testing laboratory, the examiner should, of course, explain that a lie-detector test is desired of him as part of the investigation regarding the particular loss or offense, and as much time should be spent in this preliminary interview as the circumstances reasonably warrant.

such statement as: "Look, I didn't have anything to do with it; I'm as anxious as you are to have the guilty person found out". On the other hand the person who is guilty or who has some guilty knowledge will not usually display such frankness or interest; he is rather prone to speak evasively or in generalities about not doing it himself or not knowing who did it. Many times he will, in contrast to the innocent subject, squirm around in the chair, look away from the examiner, cross his legs, use his hands as though trying to dust something off his clothes, or engage in other physical activity.

The examiner should then say to the subject: "On this test I'm going to ask you this question: 'Do you know who [took the money, etc.]'? If you have any suspicions, that will show on the test just as if you actually knew, so if you have any suspicions tell me about them now before the test. Tell me then, whom do you think did this thing?" Where the offense is of such a nature or was committed under such circumstances that the subject, even though innocent, probably has some ideas about the case, he may respond: "Well, I don't like to say if I can't prove it". At this point the examiner should make it clear to him that what he says will not later on be attributed to him or used as proof of any sort, but that a divulgence of the suspicions is necessary for the subject's own test purposes. He should then be urged to name the person he suspects. Usually the innocent subject who harbors any suspicions will name the person or persons he suspects; the guilty subject will seldom identify another person as a suspect.

If the case is one in which fingerprints might have been left at the scene of the offense, it is advisable to say to him: "Is there any reason why your fingerprints should be on the [glass, drawer, or other object]?" Except when the circumstances indicate the possibility of the innocent subject's prints being there, he will usually say: "No, there's no reason why my fingerprints should be there". The guilty person, on the other hand, is apt to offer an explanation of their presence (e.g., "Well, I may have handled the glass or leaned on the drawer when I went there for my paycheck".)

During all of this part of the interview, the examiner should make notes regarding the subject's comments and behavior. One thing for the examiner to bear in mind is that during the interview the guilty person will neglect to do whatever feigning (e.g., coughing or sniffing) he may have contemplated on the actual test itself. In other words, physical difficulties or normal nervous habits, such as coughing, clearing of throat, sniffing, deep sighing, or other bodily movements, if genuine, will be displayed during the test interview and not just during the test itself. Consequently, the presence of such difficulties, or the subject's otherwise normal behavior in these respects, should be noted during the interview. The examiner's observations and notes regarding the presence or absence of such characteristics during the interview will permit a proper evaluation of any such interfering factors during the actual lie-detector examination.[18] Moreover, if during the test the non-cooperative subject indulges in such interfering practices, the examiner can call his attention to the fact that his notes reveal that the subject did not do anything of that sort during the test interview and there is therefore no reason for his doing it during the test. A strong practical psychological advantage is gained from this revealed comparison between pre-test and test behavior.

THE TEST QUESTIONS

The preparation of test questions is an extremely important aspect of the examination. The questions must be unambiguous, unequivocal and thoroughly understandable to the subject. They should be couched in words and terms customarily used and understood by the subject. The questions must be as short as possible, stated as simply as possible, and with a complete avoidance of such double inquiries as "Did you shoot him and then run to the river?", which combines two sets of acts or occurrences, one of which might truthfully be answerable by "yes", and the other by "no".

Words like "murder", "rape", and "embezzlement" should not be used in test questions because they are not sufficiently precise in meaning and they also connote social condemnation and criminal responsibility. Instead of "murder" words such as "kill", "shoot", or "hit" should be used. For "rape", the term "forced to have sexual intercourse" is more accurately descriptive of the event and devoid of legal connotation; and the same advantages are possessed by the word "steal" over the word "embezzle". In fact, in most case situations a descriptive expression of the event is much more desirable in a test question than a single word which only generally describes the crime itself. It has been the experience of the writers that the perpetrators of criminal offenses may have sufficiently rationalized their acts so that to them their act of killing is not "murder", their excessive persuasion not "rape", and their stealing of money while working for an inadequate salary not "embezzlement".

Apart from the foregoing suggestions, the effective question preparation procedure which we here recommend can best be stated by an actual criminal case illustration. Assume, therefore, that the subject to be tested, Joe "Red" Blake, is suspected of the murder last Saturday night of John Jones during the course of a robbery in which Jones' watch was stolen.

In a case of this type, while writing down the questions to be asked, the examiner tells the subject: "On this test, Joe, I'm going to ask you: 'Do you know who shot John Jones last Saturday night?', 'Did you shoot John

[18] The tablet sheet used for the test questions can contain symbols for checking off the subject's behavior symptoms and statements, and thereby obviate the necessity for extensive note taking.

Jones last Saturday night?', and I'll ask you "Did you steal John Jones' watch last Saturday night' "?[14] Then, for "guilt complex" test purposes (the details of which will be discussed later) the examiner refers to another crime of a non-existing, fictitious nature, but in such a way as to lead the subject to believe he is under equal suspicion of its commission. This is done by saying, "Another fellow by the name of Jim Smith was fatally shot during a robbery two months ago, at the intersection of First and Main streets, not far from where Jones was shot. Did you have anything to do with that? If you did, I'll find out about it on this test, so if you had anything to do with it, tell me now". At this point an innocent subject is apt to say rather excitedly, "Is that another murder they're trying to pin on me?", whereas a guilty person is inclined, in effecting his denial, to be passive and smug in his attitude, knowing full well that only the first offense is of any importance to him.

The examiner then refers to a "control" question—the full significance of which will be subsequently described. Such a question, in this type of case, might be: "Did you ever steal anything in your life?" If the subject acknowledges that he did steal something as a child or up to a certain period of his life, he should then be told: "Well, I'll ask you, 'Besides what you told me about, did you ever steal anything else' ".[15] The purpose of this question is not to get the full truth about the "control" situation but rather to have available a question to which the subject will actually lie. This will supply a reaction for comparison with the reactions to the questions regarding the principal offense itself.[16]

At this stage of the proceedings, the examiner should leave the chair upon which he has been sitting in front of the subject and proceed to ready the instrument for the test. As he proceeds he should tell the subject rather casually: "In addition to the questions I have discussed with you I'm also going to ask you some questions such as 'Are you in Chicago now?', 'Do you smoke?', etc. I'll mix the questions in with the others we just talked

---

[14] We are assuming that the subject had been previously advised that Jones' watch was stolen; otherwise questioning about the watch would have been reserved for the "peak of tension" test, which will be subsequently described, pages 53–63.

[15] When a guilty person is asked a question about ever stealing anything he is apt to say "I've never stolen anything in my life", whereas an innocent suspect is more inclined to admit that he has stolen things as a child, or as a young man, or at various times as an adult.

[16] In some situations the examiner may be fortunate enough to have in his possession certain information about the subject concerning a less serious offense than the one under investigation, and the examiner knows or feels reasonably sure the subject will lie about it. A question based upon such information, coupled with a false reply, will serve very well to indicate the nature of the subject's deception responses, if any; and the recording at that point will afford a basis for evaluating that portion of the record obtained when he is asked questions relating to the principal offense.

about". The primary purpose of irrelevant questions of this sort is to ascertain the subject's norm under test conditions.

After the foregoing test preparation procedures, the examiner tells the subject rather emphatically, "If you're telling the truth this machine will show it; if you're not, the machine will show that, too". Then the subject is instructed to look straight ahead, sit still, and answer all the questions by just "yes" or "no". The motor driven chart is then set in motion.

FINAL INSTRUMENT ADJUSTMENT

When using the Reid Polygraph, which contains the auxiliary unit for recording muscular movement and pressure, the examiner will have to adjust the forearm boards to accommodate comfortably the subject's arms. This permits a slight wavering recording from the arm recording pen. The subject should then be instructed to place his feet flat on the floor, and then the examiner must adjust the thigh recording board to the point where a slight wavering recording is also obtained from the thigh recording pen.

To be sure of a proper adjustment of the pneumograph tube, and particularly as regards female subjects, the examiner should then inquire: "Does this tube around your chest feel all right"? If the subject gives any indication whatsoever of discomfort, the tube should be readjusted.[17]

After a satisfactory respiration recording pattern has been obtained on about six inches of the chart, the galvanometer should be balanced and its sensitivity reduced to a minimum, so that slight, rather than gross, fluctuations are recorded by the galvanograph pen. Following this, the blood pressure cuff should be inflated to about 90 millimeters of mercury pressure, as indicated on the sphygmomanometer situated on the instrument panel.

If the dicrotic notch appears at or near the top of the pulse beat, this is an indication that the cuff pressure is too low for a proper recording and the cuff must therefore be inflated about 10 millimeters of mercury pressure. On the other hand, if the dicrotic notch appears at the bottom of the pulse beat it is an indication that the cuff pressure must be lowered about 5 millimeters. On a few subjects no evidence of the dicrotic notch is obtain-

[17] On occasions, especially with obese female subjects, the examiner may have difficulty obtaining a proper breathing amplitude, in which instances it is advisable to place an ordinary 12-inch ruler or other similar object under the pneumograph tube and in an upright or vertical position. Ordinarily this will serve to double the amplitude, although there will still be occasions when even with the ruler a satisfactory respiration amplitude is unobtainable. In this latter type situation, the muscular movement recording of the arms and thighs may closely reflect the respiratory wave and give sufficient amplitude so that in effect the changes in respiration rate are observable and recorded.

able, regardless of the lowering or raising of the pressure, and in such instances the examiner must be content with only a satisfactory amplitude recording.

Upon completion of the foregoing instrument adjustments, the examiner should gently take hold of the subject's blood pressure cuff arm, straighten it out and then place it back on the chair arm in a relaxed position. This will result in a drop in the cuff pressure of about 5 or 10 millimeters of mercury pressure. If the amplitude of the pulse beat is about ¼ to 1 inch, with the dicrotic notch appearing in the approximate center of the pulse beat, then no further adjustment of cuff pressure is necessary.[18]

The purpose of the foregoing procedure regarding the lifting up and straightening out of the blood pressure cuff arm is to be certain that no muscular tension is involved, for otherwise the cuff pressure will be artificially higher than it normally should be, with the consequent risk of "masking out" deception responses in the record of a guilty subject. In other words, the artificially created high level of cuff pressure at the outset of the test may prevent the appearance on the record of specific blood pressure increases which might otherwise occur when the subject lies in his answers to particular test questions.[19]

THE "CONTROL QUESTION" TEST

After the final inflation of the blood pressure cuff the examiner should proceed, without further delay, to the asking of the test questions which by now he has down on paper in the order in which he intends to state them.[20] Following is a sample listing of the questions appropriate for the

[18] The dicrotic notch appears on the recording as a sharp deviation from the downward stroke of the heart beat tracing.

As the heart contracts (systole) and the blood is forced into the aorta, the recording pen makes an abrupt upward sweep on the chart. Then when the heart relaxes (diastole) and the force of the blood drive has been completed, the recording pen drifts downward on the chart. During the brief period of heart relaxation the blood starts to flow back into the heart but is closed off by the aortic semilunar valves. The backward-flowing blood "bounces off" the valves and starts to flow forward again. This temporary forward movement of the blood is reflected in the tracing as a very short horizontal line, which is called the dicrotic notch.

[19] The basis for the foregoing statements is discussed later, on pages 88–100.

[20] By eliminating the running of the conventional pre-question "norm" the examiner will minimize the usual cuff pressure discomfort and reasonably insure that the final question responses on the test will not be disturbed because of the subject's cuff pressure weariness.

If for any reason there is to be a delay in the asking of the test questions—for instance, if the subject inquires as to whether he may make some additional statement or comment—the blood pressure cuff should be deflated until everything is again in readiness. In other words, the time during which the cuff pressure is on should be kept at an absolute minimum—for the period of the test questioning and no longer.

previously described case situation where the subject, Joe "Red" Blake, is suspected of the murder last Saturday night of John Jones during the course of a robbery in which Jones' watch was stolen:

1. Are you in Chicago now?
2. Have you ever been called "Red"?
3. Do you know who shot John Jones?
4. Do you ever smoke?
5. Did you shoot John Jones last Saturday night?
6. Did you ever steal anything?
7. Are you wearing glasses now?
8. About two months ago, did you shoot Jim Smith at First and Main Streets?
9. Did you steal John Jones' watch last Saturday night?
10. Did you have a coat with you today?

Each one of the irrelevant questions *1, 2, 4, 7* and *10* should deal with a known fact and not with a situation based upon a probability which the examiner only assumes to be true. For instance, it is a certainty that at some time or other the subject was called "Red", but there may be no assurance that his name is really Joe or Blake. Likewise, if the examiner has seen the subject smoking or wearing a coat or glasses, questions to that effect are much better than the questions such as "Did you have something to eat today?", the correct answers to which are not definitely known to the examiner. These recommendations are based upon experiences which demonstrate that some subjects attempt to test the efficacy of the lie-detector by deliberately lying on irrelevant questions calling for answers not definitely known by the examiner. If they are not called to task about such a lie (which may well be so, since the irrelevant questions are only used for the limited purpose of establishing a "norm"), the examiner will encounter some difficulty, after the test is over, in obtaining a confession by confronting the subject with the fact of his lying regarding the crime itself.

The time spacing for the various questions should be as follows: about five seconds between *1* and *2*; about ten seconds between *2* and *3*; and about fifteen to twenty seconds between each of the remaining questions. However, if the subject moves, coughs, or sighs no question should be asked at that point until his normal recording is restored; or in some instances where the return to normal is delayed it is usually advisable to repeat an irrelevant question before proceeding with the asking of a relevant one.

The reason for the shorter time interval between questions *1–2* and *2–3* is the fact that the first two questions are essentially only conditioning questions and the responses to them are not intended to serve any diagnostic purpose. Since this is so, there should be a consequent minimization of the duration of the cuff pressure.

After each question is asked, a number should be immediately placed on the recording chart which corresponds to the number on the question sheet. Also, at the point on the chart when the subject gives his answer, the examiner should place a plus (+) or minus (−) sign or some other symbol to indicate, respectively, the "yes" and "no" answers. In other words, when the answer is given promptly the "yes" or "no" symbol should be placed under the question number on the chart, and if there is a delay in the answer the symbol should be placed at the precise point where the recording is in progress when the answer is given. Whenever the subject coughs, or moves his arm, or indulges in any activity that distorts the record, an appropriate sign or notation should be made on the chart at the point of occurrence to indicate that fact.

Immediately upon completion of this first test, the cuff pressure should be released. The examiner then tells the subject: "Here's another part of the test", whereupon the examiner shows him seven variously numbered cards, face down, and he is instructed to take one, look at it, and put it back in the group without showing it to the examiner or otherwise identifying the number.[21] After the selection is made, the examiner proceeds to shuffle the cards and instruct the subject to answer "no" to each question concerning the cards, even when asked the number of the card he selected. In other words, the subject's answer to one of the questions will be a lie The examiner then calls off each card as part of the question "Did you pick the ———"?

The card test is conducted in much the same manner as the regular test, with time intervals of about fifteen seconds between each question.

Upon completion of the card test the examiner deflates the blood pressure cuff and informs the subject of the selected card. Then following the subject's acknowledgment of the selection, the examiner states, "I know now that you're responsive to this test; therefore, in accordance with my usual practice, I'll ask you the regular test questions again, as I did on the first test".[22]

This third test is then conducted in the same manner as the first, with the same questions being used again, and usually in the same order.

Although the recorded criteria upon which the examiner bases his deception diagnosis are considered in greater detail later on, brief mention

———

[21] Satisfactory cards for this purpose are ones about 2½" x 3½"—such as ordinary "flinch deck" cards—with numbers on them like 15, 8, 3, 5, 7, 10, and 14.

[22] As will be pointed out later (p. 48), the main value of the card test is its "stimulation" effect. For "control" purposes it is far less dependable than the general control question technique as discussed herein.

must be made of some of them at this point in order to complete the discussion of test procedure. For present purposes, therefore, it may be stated that if the control question (# 6) response (e.g., increase in blood pressure, or suppression in respiration) is greater than the responses to the questions about the principal offense under investigation, the subject may be considered as telling the truth about the principal offense, particularly where there is positive evidence that his answer to the control question was a lie. On the other hand, if the responses on the principal test questions are greater than on the control question, this fact is suggestive of deception regarding the principal offense. The examiner should then proceed to interrogate the subject with respect to his control question answer. If he admits he lied to it, or if independent evidence establishes that his answer to it was a lie, then his greater response to the principal offense questions may be accepted as an indication of deception. Following this, of course, the examiner proceeds with his interrogation in an effort to obtain the truth from the subject about the principal offense itself.

In the event there is no appreciable difference between the control question response and the principal offense question response, or whenever there is no response to either question, the examiner should interrogate the subject somewhat as follows: "Joe. your records are all mixed up; so let's get some of the small things out of the way and we'll run the test again. Now, Joe, what have you ever stolen? [Or here the examiner should use whatever subject matter has been selected for control question purposes.] I'm positive you're not telling the truth on that question, at least". If the subject is hesitant or equivocates in his answer, the examiner should say to him, by way of inviting the truth at this point, "Tell me what it is and if that's all that's on your mind your next record will clear itself up, because now your responses may be running themselves into each other". If the subject admits that he has withheld the truth here, then he should be told that on the next test he will be asked, among the other questions, "Besides what you've told me, have you ever stolen anything else"?

The primary purpose of this discussion is to obtain the benefit of the stimulating effect it has in provoking a guilty person's response to the principal test questions and an innocent person's responses to the control questions. Experience has indicated that the stimulating effect thus produced has resulted in a considerable reduction in the number of indefinite reports or conclusions which previously prevailed.

After the subject's fourth test, which is usually a duplicate of the third test questions, if the indications of truthtelling or lying are not more definite than on the third test (i.e., no difference between the control question and principal offense question response; or no response on either one), the examiner, for purposes of stimulation, should accuse the subject of lying about the principal offense. When the subject re-asserts his innocence, as he ordinarily does, the examiner should then say "Well, if you are telling the truth about this [the principal offense] then straighten out these other things. Now, tell me, what about the question (# 6) regarding ever stealing anything [or anything in addition to what you already told me]. Now, Joe, what have you ever stolen [or what have you ever stolen that you have not told me about]"? At this point the subject may or may not admit lying about the control question. In either event, he should then be given a fifth test. If the fifth test record is no more indicative of truthtelling or deception than the previous test records, arrangements should be made for a re-examination the following day or at a later date. His subsequent re-examination records will sometimes become quite clear in their indications.

In contrast to the foregoing situation presented by a subject who is not responsive to either the principal offense question or the control question, or whose responses to either question are about the same, the examiner may be confronted with a subject whose first and third test records contain indications of general disturbance or else contain responses to all questions regardless of whether they are relevant, irrelevant, or of a control nature. In such instances the examiner may follow either one of the following procedures: he may conduct an interview with the subject and inquire "Is there any question, or are there any questions on this test about which you have not told the truth"? If the answer is "No, I have told the truth on all of them", the examiner should say "Well, do you understand all the questions"? (These inquiries and the attending discussion by the subject will usually serve to render the next or fourth test more specific in its indications.) Or, as an alternative, the examiner may re-word the control question (# 6) so as to imply that the subject lied in his previous control question answers. For instance, if the subject had denied ever stealing anything in his life, instead of repeating the control question "Did you ever steal anything in your life"? it should be changed to "Beside when you were a child, have you ever stolen anything?" In other words, by this substitute control question the examiner gives the subject the impression that the first and third tests indicated that he lied to the original control question.

The attending implication will often serve to stimulate the subject's responsiveness on the next test to either the control or the principal offense question, depending upon his innocence or guilt.

In instances where it appears from the subject's first and third test records that he is overly apprehensive, which is ordinarily evidenced by his anticipatory responses before a question is asked, the examiner should instruct him that on the next (fourth) test the questions will be asked in a different order than on the previous test.

Changing the order of the questions on the fourth test, and a prior instruction by the examiner regarding his intention to do so, is also an advantageous procedure with a subject who might be termed a "spot responder". A "spot responder" is a person whose blood pressure (and sometimes respiration) tracing on his first and third tests will contain a response to the same relevant question, but only to that one question on each test. In other words, the subject's record might contain a blood pressure response to question 5 ("Did you shoot John Jones last Saturday night"?) on both the first and third tests but no response to the other pertinent questions 3 and 9. Whenever this occurs the examiner should announce to the subject that on the next test (the fourth) the questions will be in a different order than on the preceding tests. Then question 8, the guilt complex question, should be asked in the position previously occupied by question 5, and the fifth question should be relegated to the ⚹ 8 question position. If on subsequent tests the only blood pressure response appears at question 8, in the former position occupied by question 5, the subject thereby reveals he is a "spot responder". Consequently, his prior responses at question 5 should be considered insignificant.

Occasionally a subject's first and third records will contain a response only to the first relevant question on each test. Here again changing the order of the questions on the fourth test and a prior instruction to that effect will be extremely helpful. With guilt complex question 8 placed in the position of the former ⚹ 3 question, the response to it as the first question of any apparent importance to the subject will render insignificant the response which appeared at 3 on the first and third tests.

In some cases where a subject gives a significant response to a relevant question other than the one concerning his actual commission of the principal offense, his own later explanation thereafter may render that particular question response an excellent one for control purposes. By way of illustration, suppose that the record contains a respiratory or blood pressure change when he says "no" to the question "Do you know who shot John Jones?", and then, after that test is over he tells the examiner "I don't know for sure who shot Jones but I was thinking it might be Pete Smith, although I can't really say". This explanation will usually establish the knowledge response as one of deception origin and thereby render as significant of truthtelling the lack of response (or the lesser response) when the subject was asked about his commission of the principal offense. Nevertheless, as a check against the possibility of the subject having any further information or knowledge regarding the actual offender, and also as a double check on the remote possibility of his own implication, the appropriate question on any additional test would be: "Do you know *for sure* who shot Jones"?

The "guilt complex" question (*# 8*), which is based upon the fictitious crime situation ("About two months ago, did you shoot Jim Smith at First and Main Streets"?), is used primarily as an additional safeguard against mistaking the pertinent question responses of an apprehensive innocent subject as deception responses. This technique of using a "guilt complex" question is particularly helpful whenever the previously discussed control question (*# 6*) technique has not already furnished a definite diagnosis.[23]

For more reliable and accurate testing, the technique of using questions *6* and *8*, which do serve as true controls, is far superior to relying for control purposes upon either the card test or the so-called "personal embarrassing question" employed by some examiners. The latter procedure consists essentially of a statement being made by the examiner, toward the end of a test record, "Now I'm going to ask you a personal embarrassing question." Sometimes no question is actually asked, or perhaps only an incomplete question such as "Did you ever go down on a . . . "?

The intended purpose of the "personal embarrassing question" is avowedly that of ascertaining whether the subject is a "reactor" or "non-reactor". As a practical matter, however, a reaction to this question is used as a basis for comparing and evaluating the response or lack of response to the questions pertaining to the offense under investigation. This has to be so, because a determination of whether the subject is a "reactor" or "non-reactor" necessarily must have some reference to his capacity or ability to react to the pertinent questions. Otherwise the use of a "personal embarrassing question" would be a completely meaningless gesture.

A subject's reaction to a stimulus question of the "personal embarrassing" type is not significant for any practical, useful purpose. Moreover, it can be misleading to the examiner using it. The factors of surprise, anticipation, embarrassment, etc., which constitute the stimulating effect of a "personal embarrassing" question, are totally different and unrelated to those involved in a question about the offense (e.g., burglary) under investigation. For control purposes the examiner might just as well set off a firecracker as to ask a "personal embarrassing" question.[24]

[23] As previously stated, the guilt complex question technique may be of considerable value merely because of the significance of the subject's verbal reaction when the fictitious crime situation is discussed with him (see *supra* p. 14). It can also be of real assistance during the post-test interrogation, for it furnishes the examiner the opportunity of advising a guilty subject that although the test showed that he did not commit the one crime (the fictitious offense), it did show that he was not telling the truth regarding the other one (the principal offense).

[24] The "personal embarrassing question" procedure is also subject to the defect

THE "PEAK OF TENSION" TEST

In addition to the previously described test procedure, another type of test may be used in instances where the subject has not been informed by the investigators (or newspapers, etc.) of all the important details of the offense in question. In cases of this nature, the examiner may resort to the use of what is known as a "peak of tension" test. This test resembles in a general way the card test, for it consists essentially of the asking of a series of questions in which only one has any bearing upon the matter under investigation. This one pertinent question refers to some detail of the case (e.g., the object or amount of money stolen) which could not have been known to an innocent person or by anyone who had not been informed previously of such a detail. The following hypothetical case is an example of the application of this type of test. Let us assume that in a certain burglary the only article of any value taken from the burglarized premises was a diamond ring; and that the suspect to be examined had not been informed of that fact, even though he knows he is suspected of a burglary at that particular place. In other words, the circumstances of this hypothetical case are such that the only way in which the subject could have known that the stolen object was a diamond ring was for him to have been a participant in the burglary or else to have learned of it from some other person involved in the commission of the offense. In such a situation as this the examiner could proceed as follows: (1) draw up a list of about seven articles of value —for example, a gold watch, a pearl necklace, etc.—including a "diamond ring" as one of the articles;[25] (2) show the list to the subject, with an

that in personnel testing it may be met with considerable resentment because of its sex implications. As a good example of this objectionable feature reference can be made to a report which Senator Wayne Morse of Oregon made in the United States Senate on January 17, 1952. He discussed a case involving the use of the lie-detector technique in the testing of an applicant for a position of trust in the Defense Department. What he found in that case, and the impression he gained of the "personal embarrassing question" procedure, induced him to state, that if the use of the lie-detector technique as an employment testing procedure was not abandoned by federal agencies he would introduce legislation to outlaw its use. See 98(7) Congressional record 261–265 (Jan. 17, 1952).

Although Senator Morse's exposure of this particular case situation and the objections he later voiced brought forth an announcement from the Defense Department that lie-detector applicant testing would be abandoned within the Department, fortunately no outlawing legislation has been proposed up to now. What happened thus far, however, is sufficient proof that a continuance of this type of abuse may ultimately result in a rejection of the lie-detector technique in the fight against crime and in the struggle for security safeguards in government and industry.

[25] For reasons which become apparent in the ensuing discussion of "peak of tension" criteria, it is advisable to place the name of the missing article somewhere between the first and the last ones on the list.

explanation to the effect that among the articles on the list is the one which was stolen from the burglarized premises; (3) inform him that on the test he will be asked, in separate questions, if, to his knowledge, the object taken in the burglary was any one of those named on the list, to all of which questions the subject will, of course, answer "no"; (4) then obtain two or three lie-detector records based upon such test questions. Depending upon the presence or absence of a subsequently defined and illustrated "peak of tension" in the subject's lie-detector tracings, the examiner may be able to determine whether or not the subject knows which object named on the list represents the one stolen from the burglarized premises. He may thereby give an indication as to his guilt or innocence of the burglary itself.

Whenever the "peak of tension" technique is used, the first such test should be repeated a second, and probably a third time, but with a few minutes time interval between each one. This rest period will provide the guilty subject with an opportunity to review the previous test experience and contemplate further the position of the relevant article among the irrelevant ones.

To insure the reliability of the "peaks of tension" test, the following precautions must be taken by the examiner:

1. Be sure that the subject has not already been informed by the investigators, or by other means such as newspaper reports, regarding the particular detail that the examiner intends to use for "peak of tension" purposes. Otherwise the test would be completely unreliable and misleading, since an innocent person so informed would very probably reach a "peak of tension" at the crucial question. To guard against this risk of error no "peak of tension" test should ever be given or relied upon until the examiner is satisfied, from his questioning of both the investigators and the subject, that the only way the subject could have acquired any knowledge of the particular detail was by his own implication in the offence or by having been told about it by someone else involved in its perpetration.

2. Use for the crucial question detail only some article or circumstance that could not possibly have been overlooked by the perpetrator of the offense. For example, if a bloody baseball bat was found alongside the crushed head of a murder victim, the killer is obviously aware of the fact that a baseball bat was used. "Baseball bat" is therefore a proper crucial question detail to use along with such non-crucial items as "iron pipe", "brass knuckles", etc. Likewise, if a ring was taken off a robbery victim's finger, the robber certainly knows what the object was and consequently "ring" is a good detail for the crucial question. On the other hand, however, a thief who steals a package of bracelets from a jewelry salesman's car may have concealed the package without having opened it by the time of his arrest. To give him a "peak of tension" test with "bracelets" as the basis

for a crucial question would obviously lead to an erroneous deception diagnosis.

3. In using as a crucial question detail the specific amount of money that the victim reported as stolen, the examiner should be on guard against the possibility of an exaggerated figure having been given by a victim whose loss is covered by insurance. Also, in using an "amounts test", consideration should be given to the possibility that the thief himself may not actually know the specific amount of money which he took. In other words, he may pocket the money and spend all or part of it without ever having counted it or remembering how much of the original sum he spent. Under such circumstances it would be foolhardy to rely upon an "amounts test".

4. The non-crucial articles should be of the same general type or category as the crucial ones. In other words, in a case involving a stolen ring, the non-crucial articles should be other pieces of jewelry and not such relatively insignificant items as pencils, cigarettes, etc.; otherwise the great difference in value and importance of the stolen ring over the other articles may create an artificial peak of tension at the "ring" question even in the record of a perfectly innocent subject.

5. The crucial question article should not be described or labeled with any greater particularity or emphasis than the non-crucial ones. For instance, when investigating the theft of a pearl necklace, an artificial stimulation will result from identifying the article as a *pearl* necklace while referring to the non-crucial items as merely a watch, a bracelet, a ring, etc. All of the articles should be described in the same manner, either as a *pearl* necklace, a *silver* bracelet, a *diamond* ring, etc., or simply as a necklace, a bracelet, a ring, etc.

FACTORS LIMITING NUMBER OF TESTS AND NUMBER OF TEST QUESTIONS

Ordinarily three to five "control question" test records are sufficient for a deception diagnosis, although where circumstances permit the use of the "peak of tension" technique several additional tests may be conducted. As a general rule, if a definite diagnosis cannot be made after this number of tests, the running of additional tests on the same day will be of no avail. The emotional fatigue and conditioning of the subject to the test situation after this amount of testing will usually result in unresponsiveness or erratic and meaningless reactions. On these occasions, however, it is advisable to conduct a re-examination at a later date.[26] A number of experiences have been encountered where a definite and accurate diagnosis was made on a subject whose earlier tests the day before or at some other time produced indefinite results.

---

[26] As to the advisability of beginning a re-examination with a card test, see p. 52.

The regular test questions asked of each subject should usually be confined to the one actual offense or incident under investigation. If questions about a number of offenses are asked during a test, a guilty subject may have a greater concern or fear of detection regarding one offense than the others, and consequently there will be relatively little or perhaps even no response respecting the latter situations. This may result in an erroneous interpretation of truthtelling with regard to the offenses about which the subject has relatively less concern.

For the purpose of determining whether a subject is guilty or innocent of a particular offense it is unnecessary and unwise to ask a number of questions respecting the various details of the offense. A guilty subject is only, or at least primarily, fearful of exposing his lie when asked about the essential facts as to whether he knows who committed the offense or whether he himself committed the act. The particular details of the offense are of little consequence to him (except, of course, on the "peak of tension" tests) and ordinarily nothing is gained by the use of test questions based upon such details. Moreover, the cuff pressure discomfort occasioned by the longer tests required for many detailed questions is a complicating factor; and the asking of so many detailed questions may also serve to over-stimulate an innocent subject. For these reasons the number of questions should never exceed twelve in number and the time limit for any test should be no longer than three and a half minutes in duration.

Deception Responses, Deception Criteria, and Diagnostic Technique

Since the most reliable deception criteria are obtainable from a continuous and simultaneous recording of relative changes in blood pressure, pulse, and respiration, the greater portion of the following discussion will be devoted to the technique of diagnosing deception from the blood pressure-pulse and respiration recordings. For that reason, in many of the following case record illustrations the recordings of changes in the G.S.R. (psychogalvanic skin reflex) and muscular activity have been omitted from the reproductions for the purpose of simplifying the discussion of the blood pressure-pulse and respiration responses and criteria. Subsequent illustrations, of course, are devoted to the explanation and discussion of the G.S.R. and muscular activity recordings.

Although the general appearance and relative positions of the blood pressure-pulse and respiration tracings on the lie-detector chart are shown in Figure 3, the diagrammatic sketch in Figure 5 illustrates blood pressure, pulse, and respiration changes which may be recorded during the course of a test. These changes, or deviations from the normal recording as the subject answers a test question, are referred to as "responses". Actual case illustrations of significant responses are shown in Figures 6 to 10.

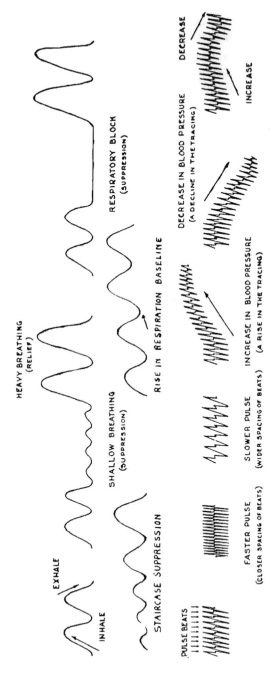

FIG 5. SKETCHES OF LIE-DETECTOR TRACINGS OF BLOOD PRESSURE, PULSE, AND RESPIRATION

The above sketches identify the types of blood pressure, pulse, and respiration responses which appear in later illustrations of actual case records.

Any change in the recording (i.e., a deviation from the "norm") as the subject answers a test question is usually referred to as a "response".

CASE ILLUSTRATIONS OF SIMULTANEOUS RESPONSES IN RESPIRATION AND
BLOOD PRESSURE

The response which is most significant and most dependable as an indicator of deception is the simultaneous occurrence of a suppression in respiration and an increase in blood pressure when the subject answers an examiner's question (see Fig. 6-A,B,C). To be significant, however, this response, as well as all the others illustrated within the next few pages, must constitute a deviation from the subject's norm which is established during that part of the record when irrelevant questions are asked and answered. Such a deviation is usually referred to as a "specific response".

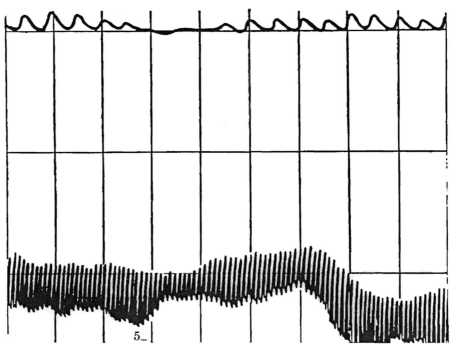

FIG. 6-A. A specific response in both respiration and blood pressure appears at question 5 as an embezzler answers "no" to the question "Did you take the missing money?" (He confessed his guilt during an interrogation immediately after his test.)

The dash by the 5 is a symbol which is used to signify a "no" answer. A plus sign is used to indicate a "yes" answer.

The ruled lines shown in this illustration are on the paper strip chart itself. The vertical ones—or rather the spaces between them—serve the purpose of timing the recording. Each space represents a five second interval, since the paper rolls off the instrument at the rate of twelve spaces (or six inches) a minute. The paper strip chart itself is six inches wide.

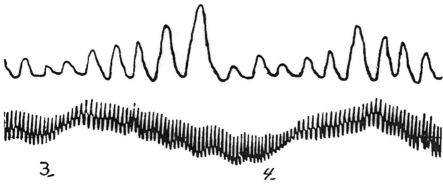

3_   4_

FIG. 6-B. A specific response in both respiration and blood pressure appears at questions *3* and *4*, when a thief answered "no" to questions pertaining to the missing money. These respiration responses, and particularly the one at 3, are describable as "staircase suppression". (This subject confessed his guilt during an interrogation immediately following his test.)

In reproducing this and many of the other case records appearing in this book, a filter was used, whenever feasible, to remove the chart lines and thereby render the tracings themselves more legible.

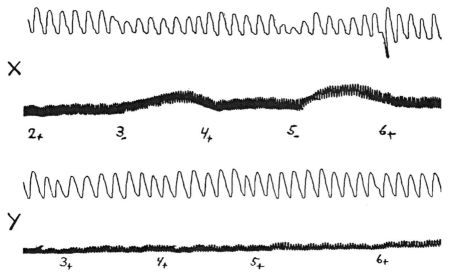

X

2₊   3_   4₊   5_   6₊

Y

3₊   4₊   5₊   6₊

FIG. 6-C. Observe on record X the dual response in respiration and blood pressure at *3* and *5* when a murder suspect answered "no" to questions pertaining to his guilt. (*2*, *4* and *6* are irrelevant questions.)

Compare record X with record Y, which was obtained after the subject's confession, when he answered "yes" to questions regarding his commission of the offense.

CASE ILLUSTRATIONS OF RESPONSES IN RESPIRATION OR BLOOD PRESSURE

The most common of significant responses is the one which appears *either* as a suppression in respiration *or* as an increase in blood pressure, rather than the simultaneous occurrence of both (see Fig. 7-A,B).

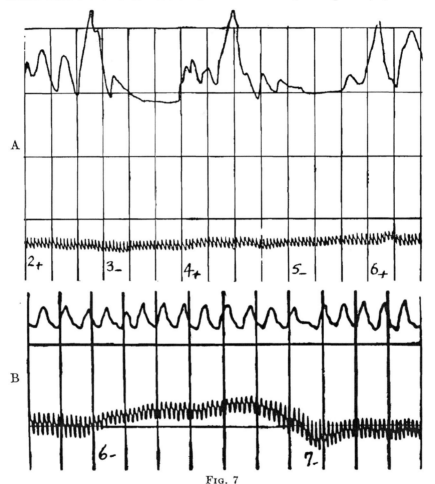

FIG. 7

A. Upper. Observe the suppression in respiration, but the absence of any deviation in blood pressure, when a robber said "no" to questions *3* and *5* pertaining to his guilt. *2*, *4* and *6* represent irrelevant questions.

B. Lower. In this record there is no deviation in the respiration recording at *6*, but the murderer gave a definite response in the form of an increse in blood pressure when he denied killing his wife. *7* is an irrelevant question.

(The interpretation of the above records was verified by the subjects' confessions following post-test interrogations.)

CASE ILLUSTRATIONS OF SIGNIFICANT
PULSE RESPONSES

A deception response occasionally occurs in the form of a decrease in pulse amplitude, as a slower or radically irregular pulse at the time of or immediately after the subject's reply to a question, or as an irregular pulse up to a particular question, followed by a regular pulse thereafter (see Fig. 8-A,B,C).

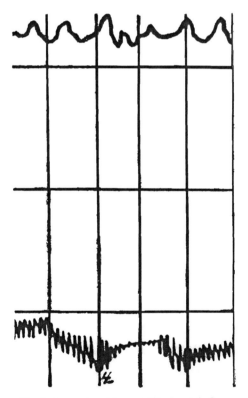

FIG. 8-A. Observe the decrease in pulse amplitude at 4 when a suspected embezzler was asked whether he had taken any of the bank's money. (Interpretation verified by the subject's confession following a post-test interrogation.)

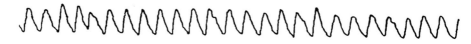

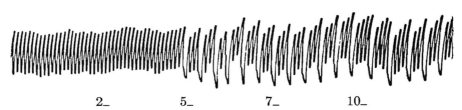

2_   5_   7_   10_

FIG. 8-B. On the above card test record, observe the slower and radically irregular pulse change, in the form of a series of "extra systoles," which occurs at *5*, as the subject said "no" when asked whether that was his chosen card.

(This subject gave a similar pulse response when he lied on his regular test, as shown in Figure 14.)

2_   3_   4_   5_   6_   7_

FIG. 8-C. On this record of a suspected arsonist, observe the irregular pulse up to question *6* and the regular pulse from that point on. At *6* he was asked a control question to which his answer was a known lie. Questions *3* and *5* pertained to the arson. *2*, *4*, and *7* are irrelevant. Also notice the "staircase suppression" at *6*.

This record was considered indicative of deception at *6* only, and the subject was reported innocent of the arson. (Another person's confession of the arson verified the foregoing interpretation of the present subject's innocence.) Apparently this subject anticipated his deception at *6*, and this anticipation is reflected in the erratic pulse pattern up to that point. This relief of tension at *6* is evident from the smooth pulse pattern thereafter.

CASE ILLUSTRATIONS OF "RELIEF IN RESPIRATION" RESPONSE

Heavier breathing, or "relief" in respiration, about twenty or thirty seconds after the subject's reply to a question, is indicative of deception (see Fig. 9).

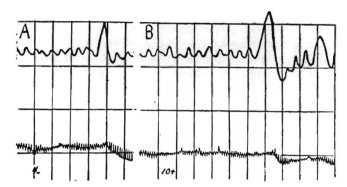

FIG. 9. In this case a rapist-murderer's characteristic deception response was his heavier breathing or "relief" in respiration about twenty seconds after his answer to a relevant question. 4 on A and 10 on B are relevant questions. (Interpretation verified by subject's subsequent confession.)

CASE ILLUSTRATION OF CHANGE IN RESPIRATION BASE LEVEL RESPONSE

A change in respiration base level is indicative of deception. It may sometimes occur as a result of a deliberate effort to "beat the machine", but it is none the less significant as a deception criterion (see Fig. 10).[27]

FIG. 10. Observe the rise in the base line of the respiration recording at 3 and 6 when the subject, a murderer, denied his guilt. Irrelevant questions were asked at 2, 4 and 5. (The dotted line has been inserted to show the normal respiration base line.) (Interpretation of guilt verified by subject's confession.)

---

[27] As regards the respiration criteria, see the excellent article by Harney, J. W., "The Analyses of Respiratory Criteria in Deception Tests", J. Crim. L. & Criminology **34** (4): 268 (1943), in which the author discusses the results of experiments which showed that pseudo-deception respiration responses might be produced by non-deception test situations, such as when a subject is given a relatively simple problem to solve (e.g., looking at three strips of cardboard and deciding upon a geometrical figure that can be made with the strips). Harney suggests the possibility that pseudo-

As previously pointed out, there are in general two types of lie-detector tests: one, the "control question" test, which involves the asking of irrelevant, relevant and control questions; and the other, the "peak of tension" test, which consists essentially of the asking of only one pertinent question among a number of irrelevant ones. The deception criteria obtainable with the "control question" type of test, and the attending diagnostic technique, differ considerably from those involved in the "peak of tension" test. For this reason, in discussing deception criteria and diagnostic techniques it is necessary to treat each type of test separately.

THE "CONTROL QUESTION" TEST CRITERIA AND DIAGNOSTIC TECHNIQUE

The deception diagnosis centers about that portion of the recording when the "control" questions are asked—in other words, question *6* in our hypothetical case, when the murder-robbery suspect is asked "Did you ever steal anything?", and question *8*, when he is asked the guilt complex question regarding a fictitious crime. Because of the importance of what happens when these questions are asked, the entire test technique is deliberately referred to as the *"control question" test*.

The selection of the control question (#*6*) depends upon the type of offense under investigation. If the basic, motivating factor in the offense was stealing—for instance, a murder for financial gain, a robbery, a burglary, and all larcenies—the control question should pertain to general stealing, regarding which it is reasonable to believe the subject will lie. An example of such an appropriate control question in the foregoing hypothetical murder-robbery situation would be, "Did you ever steal anything in your life"? Likewise, if the crime under investigation was sex motivated —for instance, the murder of a rape victim, rape, arson for sexual satisfaction, indecent liberties, etc.,—the control question should pertain to a sexual practice or indulgence of the type reasonably attributed to the subject. Examples of such control questions of this type would be: "Have you ever masturbated?", or "Did you ever commit an act of sexual perversion"?

---

deception responses might appear in the respiration recording in an actual case as a result of a mental conflict due to a misunderstanding of the examiner's instructions or test questions. This latter difficulty, of course, can be almost completely obviated by a proper pre-test interview during which the examiner adequately discusses and reads the questions to the subject before the test is begun.

No set list of control questions can be given for all purposes. In determining what control questions should be used in any given case situation, the examiner will have to rely upon his own ingenuity. At times he will be at a loss to make a selection until after the preliminary interview. A competent examiner, however, can always resolve the difficulty by use of the same facility and capacity that qualifies him for the task in the first instance.

In addition to confining this control question to the same general category as the principal offense, the following precautions must also be observed: It must be general in scope; it must be of lesser importance than the crime under investigation; it must be a question to which the subject will answer "no"; and it must be a question to which the answer will, in all probability, be a lie. Moreover, if, during the pre-test interview or at any later time, the subject admits having done what the question suggested, then it should be rephrased, for example, "Besides what you told me about, did you ever steal anything else"?

The "control question" criteria, which will be subsequently illustrated with actual case records, are as follows. In many instances they permit an accurate diagnosis to be made from the first test record alone.

1. If the control question (6) response is greater than the responses to the questions about the principal offense under investigation, the subject may be considered as telling the truth, particularly where there is positive evidence that his answer to the control question was a lie, or where the subject makes an admission to that effect during the interrogation following the test.[28]

2. If the responses on the principal test questions are greater than on the control question, that fact is suggestive of deception, provided, of course, that the subject's later admission or other independent evidence establishes the fact that the subject's answer to the control question was a lie.

3. Where there is no appreciable difference between the control question response and the principal offense question response, a specific response on the guilt complex question is suggestive of truthtelling.

4. Where there is a specific response to the principal offense question, and no response to either the control question or the guilt complex question, that fact is strongly indicative of deception.

[28] In some cases, as previously stated on page 21, where a subject gives a significant response to a relevant question other than the one concerning his commission of the principal offense, his own later explanation thereafter may render that particular question response an excellent one for control purposes.

In the rare instances where the response to the fictitious crime question is about the same as the one to the principal offense question, it is advisable to conduct a more complete guilt complex test by devising several detailed questions about the fictitious crime and asking them on another test as questions *3, 5* and *9*, while relegating the principal offense question to the number *8* position. If on such a test the subject continues to give responses to the fictitious crime questions which are similar to the principal offense responses, this fact is strongly indicative of truthtelling regarding the principal offense.

If the foregoing criteria are lacking—as when the first test record is rather devoid of responses, or when the responses are just generally erratic—the previously described card test, administered as a second test, becomes extremely helpful in rendering the next regular test much more significant than the first one. The psychological effect of the card test and the examiner's selection of the chosen card will usually produce the following results on the subject's next "control question" test:

(a) An unresponsive guilty subject, realizing that the test is effective, becomes responsive when later asked about the offense under investigation. (This will now place his record in the foregoing classifications *2* or *4*.)

(b) An unresponsive innocent subject, also satisfied of the technique's accuracy, will become responsive when he next lies about the control question. (This will now place his record in classifications *1* or *3*.)

(c) A generally disturbed guilty person (the one whose first record contains generally erratic responses) will realize that since his efforts to control his reactions on the card test were of no avail, his guilt responses are likewise uncontrollable. (This will now place his next record in classifications *2* or *4*.)

(d) A nervous, innocent subject, whose first record is a generally disturbed one, will feel more secure on the next regular test; there will then be a subsidence of the general disturbance in favor of a specific response to the control question only. (This will place his record in classifications *1* or *3*.)

In the event the third test record continues to be either a generally unresponsive one or one with generally erratic responses, the following procedure should then be followed:

(a) Interrogate the unresponsive subject regarding the control question and seek an admission of previous lying. This is usually accomplished without much difficulty because of the very fact that the question was originally selected on the basis of a reasonable assumption that the subject would make a denial and that his denial would represent a lie. Consequently, in our hypothetical case, where the control question was "Did you ever steal anything?", the subject should be asked to tell what it was he stole. The effect of this discussion and any admission of lying (e.g., "I once took a pencil [or a book, knife, etc.] that didn't belong to me") will frequently render the subject responsive on the next test, either to the principal offense question or to the control question.

(b) Interrogate the generally disturbed subject rather cautiously regarding the control question and discuss the main offense with him, but without definitely accusing him of lying to either question.

Following the procedure outlined in *a* or *b* above, a fourth test should be administered in much the same manner as the third test. However, if the subject has made any admission respecting the control question (*6*), that question, on his fourth test, will become: "Besides what you told me about, did you ever [steal anything else]"? If the fourth test record remains a generally unresponsive one or one with generally erratic responses, it is very probable that regardless of what tests the examiner conducts thereafter he will be unable to arrive at a definite diagnosis.[29] In a few instances of this type, however, the examiner should, if circumstances permit, conduct an interrogation of the subject in a manner as though he were actually considered guilty; or as an alternative, the examiner may arrange to conduct a re-examination within the next few days. There have been occasions when an interrogation at this point has produced confessions from guilty subjects, and in other instances, a re-examination at a later date produced records of such a nature as to permit a definite diagnosis of guilt or innocence.[30]

ILLUSTRATIONS OF "CONTROL QUESTION" TEST CRITERIA

A separate restatement will now be made of the various "control question" test criteria and after each one there will appear several photographic reproductions of actual criminal case records illustrating the particular criterion. This method was considered preferable to one whereby the illustrations would be used before fully setting forth all the various criteria themselves.

(The reader's attention is again called to the fact that only the blood pressure-pulse and respiration tracings are shown in the following group of illustrations. The G.S.R. and muscular activity tracings were omitted from the reproductions and will be reserved for separate treatment on later pages.)

[29] We are assuming in this statement that the circumstances of the case do not permit the administration of a "peak of tension" test.

[30] Of the subjects whose third and fourth records remain indefinite—in other words, of the subjects who have not been affected by the previously described stimulation procedure, most are in the lying rather than the truthtelling classification. This fact has been demonstrated by the confessions gained when interrogations were conducted despite the indefiniteness of the third and fourth records.

Control Question Test
Criterion # 1

If the control question (6) response is greater than the responses to the questions about the principal offense under investigation, the subject may be considered as telling the truth, particularly where there is positive evidence that his answer to the control question was a lie, or where the subject makes an admission to that effect during the interrogation following the test (see Figs. 11 to 19).

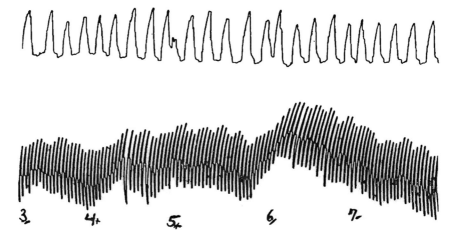

FIG. 11. Questions *3* and *5* pertained to an arson for which the motive was destruction of the employer's books and records. *4* and *7* are irrelevant. *6* is the control question: "Did you ever steal anything"?

The only significant response appears at control question *6*, a known lie reaction since shortly after the test the subject admitted having stolen money at various times and places. In view of the reaction to the known lie at *6*, and the lack of any response at arson questions *3* and *5*, the proper interpretation is one of truthtelling regarding the arson. This conclusion was later verified by the apprehension and confession of the actual perpetrator of the offense.

FIG. 12. Questions *3* and *5* pertained to the embezzlement of a large sum of money. *4* and *7* are irrelevant questions. At *6* the subject was asked "Did you ever steal anything?", the answer to which was a lie according to the subject's later admission.

In this case the subject's card test record contained no response at his chosen card question, and were reliance placed upon the card test for control purposes the subject would have been classified as "unresponsive". But upon the basis of the above control question test record the examiner was able to definitely report the the subject as innocent of the embezzlement of the missing money, a conclusion later verified as accurate by another suspect's confession.

FIG. 13. Questions *3* and *5* pertained to an embezzlement. *2, 4,* and *7* are irrelevant. *6* is the control question "Have you ever stolen anything"? Observe the suppression in respiration and the increase in blood pressure at *6*. Also note the cyclical changes in blood pressure from *2* to *6* and again after *7*, in contrast to the relative absence of such cyclical changes between *6* and *7*.

In view of the responses at control question *6*, to which the subject admitted he lied, and the absence of any significant response at *3* and *5*, the examiner's conclusion was one of truthtelling and innocence. Another suspect later confessed the theft of the missing money.

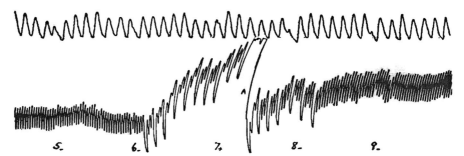

FIG. 14. Questions *5, 8,* and *9* pertained to a burglary. *6* is the control question "Besides when you were a child, have you ever stolen anything else"? (The question was phrased this way because in the preliminary interview the subject stated he had taken money as a child.) His answer of "no" to *6* was later admitted to be a lie.

The response at *6*, which was so great as to require, at *A*, an adjustment of the recording pen, and the lack of a significant response at *5, 8,* and *9*, indicated quite clearly the subject's innocence of the burglary, a conclusion subsequently verified as accurate by another suspect's confession.

This unusual pulse-blood pressure type of reaction also occurred on the subject's card test record, previously illustrated in Figure 8-B.

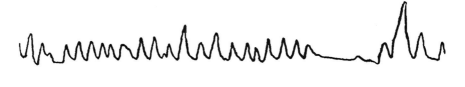

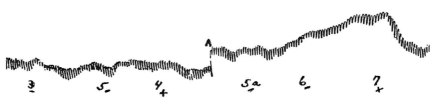

FIG. 15. Record of small town tax collector who had already confessed the embezzlement of $4500 from tax funds but who was now being tested primarily for the purpose of ascertaining whether any other officials had been in collusion with him. The questions regarding the involvement of other officials were asked at *3, 5,* and *5a*. *4* and *7* are irrelevant. (*A* between *4* and *5a* represents an adjustment of the blood pressure-pulse pen.) At *6* he was asked, "Have you stolen more than $4500 from the tax funds"? After this test he admitted taking an additional $1000.

Because of the relative lack of response at *3, 5,* and *5a*, the conclusion was reached that no other persons were involved with him in his acts of embezzlement.

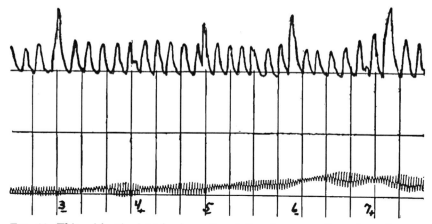

Fig. 16. This subject's girl friend was the victim of a sex motivated murder. On *3* and *5* he was questioned regarding the murder. *4* and *7* are irrelevant. On *6* he was asked "Did you ever have sexual intercourse with [the victim]?", to which he answered "no". The response at *6*, and the lack of significant responses to *3* and *5*, indicated his innocence of the murder, a conclusion which was later verified as accurate by the actual murderer's confession. (The respiration response at *6* is another example of "staircase suppression".)

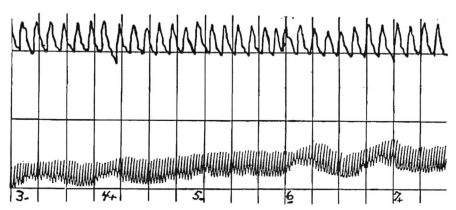

Fig. 17. Questions *3* and *5* pertained to a sex murder of a child. *4* and *7* are irrelevant. Control question *6* pertained to an indecent liberties case involving another child, which latter offense led to the subject's arrest and subsequent police suspicion regarding the sex murder. At *6* observe the blood pressure response and the slight suppression in respiration. Following this test the subject admitted his guilt regarding the indecent liberties charge.

In view of the lack of response regarding the murder and the clear cut deception response at control question *6*, dealing with the indecent liberties incident, the examiner reported the subject to be telling the truth and innocent of the sex murder, a conclusion later verified as accurate by the actual murderer's confession.

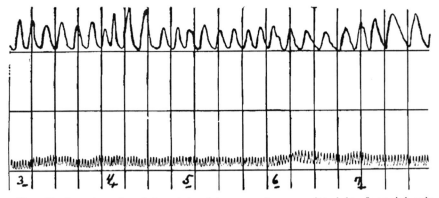

Fɪɢ. 18. Questions *3* and *5* pertained to a murder committed for financial gain. *4* and *7* are irrelevant. Control question *6* was: "Did you ever commit a robbery?", which was considered appropriate in view of the subject's known criminal activities.

The significant response at *6*, in both blood pressure and respiration, in contrast to the lack of significant responses on *3* and *5*, indicated truthtelling and innocence regarding the murder, a conclusion later verified as accurate by another's confession.

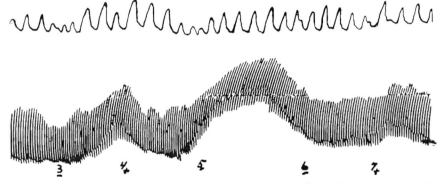

Fɪɢ. 19. Questions *3* and *5* pertained to a burglary. *4* and *7* are irreleveant. *6* is the control question: "Have you ever stolen anything?", to which the subject's answer of "no" was a known lie.

The lying and guilt regarding the burglary were of paramount concern to this subject (verified as guilty), whereas his general stealing was of no consequence. This is the reverse of the situation as regards an innocent person whose main concern on the test is the control question lie.

Control Question Test Criterion #2

If the responses on the principal test questions are greater than on the control question, that fact is suggestive of deception, provided, of course, that the subject's later admission or other independent evidence establishes the fact that the subject's answer to the control question was a lie (see Figs. 19 to 24).

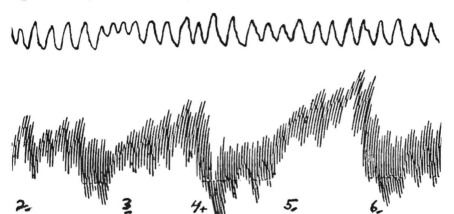

FIG. 20. Questions *3* and *5* pertained to the taking of a missing sum of money. *2* and *4* are irrelevant. *6* is the control question: "Have you ever stolen anything"?

Even though the answer to *6* was a known lie there is no appreciable response, whereas considerable responses occurred when the subject denied taking the missing money. Notice particularly the response in both blood pressure and respiration at *3*.

The taking of the missing sum and his lying about it were the only concern of this subject. His general stealing and his lying about it on *6* were relatively unimportant to him, just as when irrelevant question *4* was asked. After his tests the subject admitted taking the missing money.

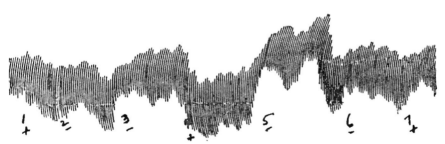

FIG. 21. Questions *3* and *5* pertained to an embezzlement. *1*, *2*, *4* and *7* are irrelevant. *6* is the control question: "Besides what you told about, did you ever steal anything else"?

The specific responses at *3* and *5* and the much lesser response to *6* were indicative of lying and guilt respecting the embezzlement, a conclusion later verified by the subject's confession.

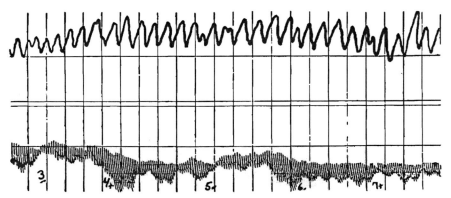

FIG. 22. Questions *3* and *5* pertain to the theft of $65,000. *4* and *7* are irrelevant. *6* is the control question: "Besides what you told about, did you ever steal anything else"?

Observe the changes in blood pressure at *3* and *5*, and also the change in base line of the respiratory tracing at *3*, which does not return to normal until after irrelevant question *7*. Following his test the subject admitted his guilt and led investigators to the place where he had concealed the entire sum.

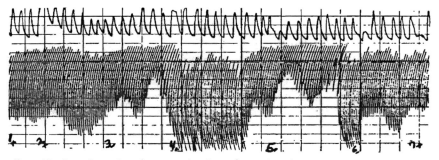

FIG. 23. Questions *3* and *5* pertained to the embezzlement of some money in a gas station. (The subject whose test record appears above was an attendant who had previously served a sentence for burglary.) *1*, *2*, and *4* are irrelevant. *6* is a control question, "Besides the burglary, have you ever stolen anthing else"?

Observe the relatively greater response at *3* and *5*, in comparison with the known lie response at *6*. The interpretation of lying and guilt was verified by the subject's confession.

Control Question Test Criterion *#3*

Where there is no appreciable difference between the control question response and the principal offense question response, a specific response on the guilt complex question is suggestive of truthtelling (see Figs. 24 and 25).

FIG. 24. Questions *3, 5,* and *9* pertain to a burglary. *4* and *7* are irrelevant. *6* is the control question: "Besides what you told me about did you ever steal anything else"? *8* is the guilt complex question pertaining to a fictitious burglary.

Observe the far greater response to the fictitious burglary question than when the subject was questioned at *3* and *5* regarding the actual burglary under investigation. A conclusion of truthtelling and innocence was later verified as accurate by another person's confession.

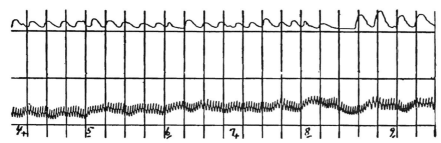

FIG. 25. Questions *5* and *9* pertained to a sex murder of a child. *4* and *7* are irrelevant. Control question *6* pertained to an indecent liberties case involving another child, which latter offense led to the subject's arrest and subsequent police suspicion regarding the sex murder. *8* is the guilt complex question regarding the fictitious killing of a woman in a locality with which the subject was familiar.

The lack of response at *5* and *9*, in contrast to the fictitious crime question response at *8*, was considered indicative of truthtelling and innocence, a conclusion later verified as accurate by another person's confession.

As to the possible reasons for the response to the fictitious crime question *8*, particularly as regards the respiratory block, see the article by Harney cited in footnote 27. Harney conducted experiments which showed that pseudo-deception respiratory responses might be produced by non-deception test situations, such as when the subject is given a relatively simple problem to solve. Harney also suggests the possibility that pseudo-deception responses might also appear in an actual case as a result of a mental conflict due to a misunderstanding or uncertainty in the instructions previously given the subject. In the above illustrated case the subject's pseudo-deception response at *8* may have been due to some other factor than one of the type suggested by Harney, but whatever the cause may have been, the fact remains that the response at *8* is an excellent control for evaluating the lack of response to the child murder questions.

Control Question Test Criterion #4

Where there is a specific response to the principal offense question, and no response to either the control question or the guilt complex question, that fact is strongly indicative of deception (see Figs. 26 and 27).

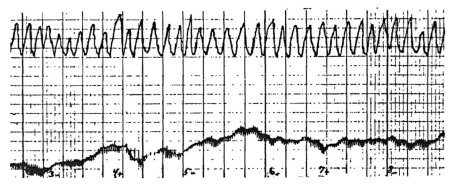

Fig. 26. Questions *3* and *5* pertain to an assault and attempted rape. *4* and *7* are irrelevant. *6* is the control question "Did you ever have sexual intercourse with a girl under sixteen years old"? *8* is a guilt complex question regarding a fictitious rape. The responses at *3* and *5* and the lack of any response at *6* and *8* indicated the subject's guilt regarding the principal offense, a conclusion later verified by the subject's confession.

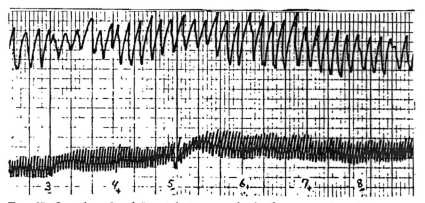

Fig. 27. Questions *3* and *5* pertain to a murder in the course of a robbery. *4* and *7* are irrelevant. *6* is a control question regarding general stealing. *8* pertains to the fictitious killing of a merchant in the course of a robbery. The response in blood pressure and the raised baseline in the respiration at *3* and *5*, and the absence of responses at *6* and *8* indicated the subject's guilt of the principal offense, a conclusion later verified by the subject's confession.

As previously stated, in many instances the control question criteria will frequently permit an accurate diagnosis on the basis of the first test record alone. In other words, to be significant the various responses which we have described and illustrated need not be duplicated on two, three, or more test records. Furthermore, experience with the control question technique indicates the fallaciousness of the theory, held by some examiners using the conventional technique, that the more a guilty subject is tested the more responsive he becomes to pertinent questions, or that he will maintain a consistency in his responses. In fact, in many instances the responses diminish considerably or disappear altogether on subsequent tests (see Fig. 28). It is also a fallacy to assume that the more tests an innocent sub-

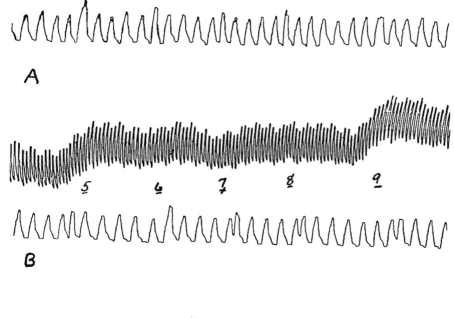

FIG. 28. The above records are illustrations of the fact that a guilty person's relevant question responses may diminish or disappear altogether on repeat tests. On A a pickpocket suspect responded to pertinent questions 5, and 9. B, a repeat test run immediately after A, is devoid of any significant responses, yet the subject's guilt was later established by his confession.

ject is given the less responsive he becomes to the pertinent questions. Oftentimes the more an innocent subject is tested the greater are his disturbances. These disturbances may result from his anger at being detained, his disgust with the test procedure generally, or from his apprehensiveness regarding the possibility of his being falsely accused or punished.

CARD TEST SIGNIFICANCE AND CRITERIA

The previously described card test, when used to stimulate an unresponsive subject or to alleviate the apprehension of the nervous subject, is of much greater assistance than when employed for control purposes. In fact, for control test purposes it can be very misleading if the examiner acts upon the assumption that a subject who gives a specific response to his chosen card will, if guilty, respond specifically to the principal offense question (see Figs. 29 and 30). During a card test the subject may cooperate by concentrating on the chosen card and letting his reactions take a normal course; on a test concerning the offense he committed he will be resisting a reaction to the pertinent question and by various psychological and physiological means he may succeed in avoiding the type of specific response that appears on the card test. As a general rule, the card test for control purposes is reasonably dependable only as indicative of an overall reaction pattern (see Figs. 31 and 32).

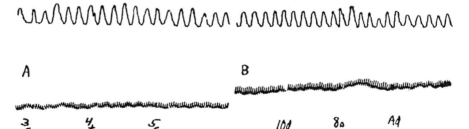

FIG. 29. An illustration of the risk involved in relying upon a card test for control purposes. In *A* a sex murder suspect, William Heirens, was questioned at *3* and *5* about the killing and dismemberment of six year old Suzanne Degnan. *4* is an irrelevant question. *B* is a portion of his card test record which contains a specific and significant response at the *8* of spades (8s), his chosen card. On the basis of the conventional testing theory his response on the card test clearly establishes his regular test record *A* as that of an innocent person, yet the subject's guilt was later established with absolute certainty.

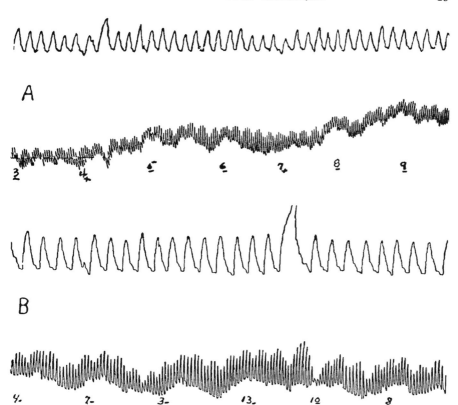

FIG. 30. Record *A* is of the same innocent burglary suspect whose record was previously shown in Figure 24. Questions *3, 5,* and *9* pertain to the burglary; *4* and *7* are irrelevant; and *8* is a guilt complex question—and the interpretation thus warranted is that of innocence. *B* is the same subject's card test in which *3* is his chosen card lie. If the card test record had been used for control purposes this subject's responses on *A* may have been erroneously considered indicative of deception. By the use of the guilt complex procedure (question 8) the correct diagnosis of innocence was clearly indicated.

In addition to its main value for stimulation purposes, the card test is a practical aid in several other respects. In many instances a subject will try to "beat the machine" during a card test and thereby disclose his guilt which might otherwise have remained undetected. This effort to "beat the machine" may be in the form of deliberate muscular movements, muscular pressures, or distortions in breathing at the time the question is asked regarding the chosen card. The subject who resorts to this practice usually does so on the supposition that by creating a definite and pronounced response to the chosen card question he will mislead the examiner in his interpretation of the lesser but natural response to the pertinent questions on the main test. Fortunately for the examiner, the subject's efforts and

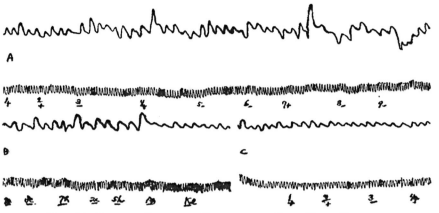

FIG. 31. OVERALL REACTION PATTERN ON CARD TEST HELPFUL
FOR CONTROL PURPOSES

On *A*, a conventional relevant-irrelevant test, questions *3, 5, 6, 8,* and *9* are pertinent; *1, 2, 4,* and *7,* irrelevant. The examiner experienced considerable difficulty in his interpretation, until he used card test *B*. Observe, on *B*, the difference in the respiration recording from the 9 of spades until after the 5 of hearts, the subject's chosen card, as compared with the recording from that point on to the end of the test. The card test thus indicated the possibility that as to this particular individual the general respiration irregularities in *A* were of some significance and not merely the result of nervousness or possible emotional instability. After *B* the subject admitted embezzling small sums of money. On test *C* the subject was questioned as to whether or not she had told the entire truth. Observe on the last test the absence of respiration irregularity as compared with *A*.

Fig. 32. RESPIRATION PATTERN ON CARD TEST HELPFUL FOR
CONTROL PURPOSES

On this larceny suspect's card test *A* his respiration cycle was 14 a minute, whereas on the regular test *B* it was 6½ a minute. Such variations are often helpful for diagnostic purposes. As with this subject, who confessed his guilt after the tests and admitted he tried to "beat the machine" by controlled breathing on the regular test, a comparison should be made between the respiration cycle on the card test with that on the regular test. It is also advisable to compare the respiration tracing on the main portion of the test record with the tracing which was made while the blood pressure cuff was being inflated and the other instrumental adjustments were in progress, at which time the subject ordinarily will not yet have begun his efforts at controlled breathing.

purpose become readily apparent, and in addition to revealing the subject's probable guilt the examiner is supplied with a strong psychological advantage in the ensuing interrogation directed toward a confession (Fig. 33).

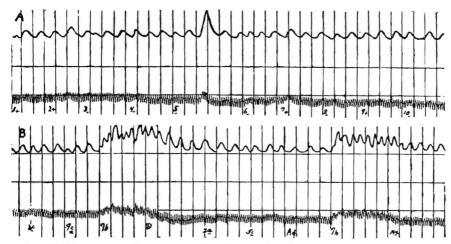

FIG. 33. RECORD OF EMBEZZLER WHO TRIED "TO BEAT" THE LIE-DETECTOR

The subject in this case, a bank teller, was examined concerning the disappearance of $1525. The conventional "relevant-irrelevant" test procedure had been employed, and his first two tests were devoid of any deception responses when questioned about the $1525. On his card test, however, he gave a reliable indication of his guilt by attempting "to beat" the machine.

In the above illustration observe the distortion in the respiration and blood pressure-pulse recording whenever the subject was questioned concerning his chosen card, the 7 of hearts (7h). Although the examiner observed what appeared to be a deliberate effort to breath abnormally and flex the biceps muscle the first time the question about the 7 of hearts was asked, the question regarding the 7 of hearts was again asked, in order to eliminate the possibility of mere coincidence. The result was the same when the subject again denied having chosen the 7 of hearts.

Upon completion of the card test the examiner accused the subject of attempting to "beat the machine", and requested an explanation. In the course of the explanation the subject confessed to embezzling $1525 and admitted that on the card test he attempted to accentuate the response when he lied about the 7 of hearts so as to render insignificant, by comparison, any responses in his records when questioned regarding the more serious matter, the missing money. He did not realize, of course, that his previous records contained no indications of deception.

After his confession the subject stated that whenever he was questioned about the $1525 he would "concentrate on something else".

The card test may be of practical assistance in another way. After a card test, when a guilty subject realizes the lie-detector technique is effective, he may then, for the first time, resort to an effort to distort the record on his subsequent regular tests. Here again his efforts along that line should be easily detected by the examiner and put to the same interrogation advantage as in the case of an attempt to "beat the machine" on the card test itself.

Occasionally on a card test the subject will say "yes" when asked about his chosen card—even though he has been carefully instructed to answer "no" to each card question, including the one about the selected card. This failure to follow the examiner's instruction is often a deliberate device on the part of a guilty subject who thinks he has thereby deprived the examiner of a valuable part of his test procedure.[31] It is well, therefore, for the examiner to again repeat the card test.

The most desirable position for the card test is between the first and third regular tests. Under some circumstances, however, it is advisable to use it before the first regular test. Whenever the subject exhibits a fear of being physically harmed by the test it is well to ask him at the outset to submit to a card test in order to satisfy himself that the test procedure is physically harmless. This experience and the results of the card test will relieve the fears of the innocent not only as to physical harm but also as to the feared inaccuracy of the technique.

In cases of re-examination of subjects whose first test records were indefinite in their indication, the examiner should begin with a card test. It will serve to alleviate the apprehensiveness of an innocent subject; and as regards the guilty it will further convince him of the efficacy of the technique.

With the "wise guy" type of subject it is also advisable to begin the examination with a card test. We refer to the subject who, upon entering the examination room, remarks: "So this is the lie-detector! But the courts don't accept its results". The examiner's reply should be "That's the latest instrument, and with the accuracy we're now getting its admissibility as evidence isn't far off." The card test should then be given and even though the record shows and the examiner knows which card was selected the subject should be told: "I can't pick out your card. You're pretty good, so I'll adjust the sensitivity of the instrument and then give you another test." After the second card test the examiner identifies the chosen card and where feasible points out the deception response on the card. This will usually change the subject's attitude, instill in him a respect for the test procedure, and thereby better condition him for the regular tests to follow.

Another type of case in which it is advisable to use the card test first is

---

[31] The examiner should also view with strong suspicion the remarks of a subject who declines to submit to a card test on the ground that it is against his principles to lie. Very rarely does such a statement come from an innocent person.

where the subject is angry and resentful over the necessity of taking the test. In such a case the examiner should first spend some time with the subject discussing the reasons why the lie-detector is being so widely used (e.g., because it helps to eliminate the innocent person as much as it permits the identification of the guilty). A leisurely discussion along this line, with an opportunity afforded the subject to express his feeling about the whole matter, will do much to condition him for an accurate diagnosis of his guilt or innocence. Then the giving of a card test and an identification of the chosen card will further pacify the angry, innocent subject and at the same time assure him that the test is a simple, effective means of removing him from further suspicion. On the other hand, the angry, resentful subject who is guilty will sometimes refuse to submit to any more tests after the running of the card test. In either event, however, the preliminary discussion and the card test constitute the most effective procedure to meet the situation of anger and resentment. For the protection of the innocent this procedure is imperative, for otherwise the anger and resentment may produce a recording which could be misinterpreted as containing guilty reactions.

PEAK OF TENSION TEST CRITERIA

A "peak of tension" on a lie-detector record may appear in any one of the following forms:

1. "Peak of tension" in blood pressure
  (a) *Gradual rise up to the critical question and either a gradual or a sharp decline thereafter* (diagrammatic sketch, Fig. 34-A).

FIG. 34 A

  (b) *Gradual rise up to the critical question and a continuation of the tracing at that high level* (diagrammatic sketch, Fig. 34-B).

FIG. 34 B

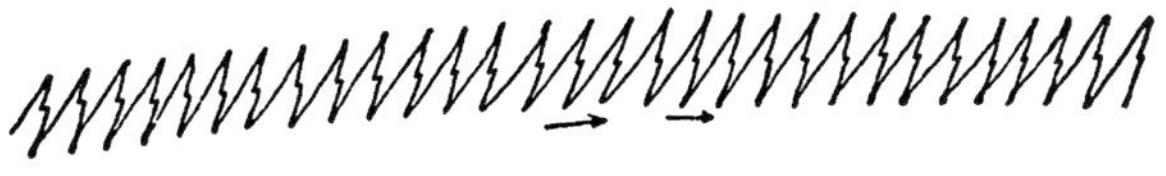

  (c) *Normal baseline up to the critical question and a gradual or sharp decline to a lower level thereafter* (diagrammatic sketch, Fig. 34-C).

FIG. 34 C

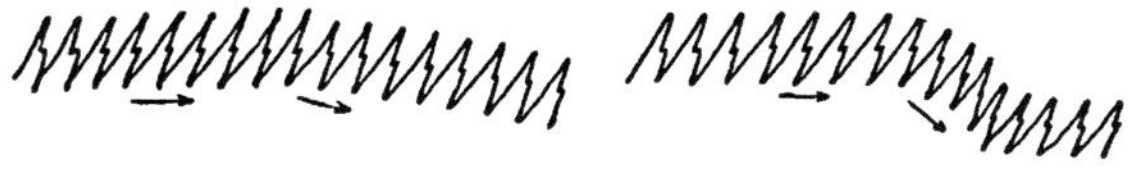

In some "peak of tension" tracings the high blood pressure level reached at the critical question (as in *a*) will continue on until the next question is asked and then the decline will follow. Likewise, the decline from a normal baseline may not occur until the asking of the question which follows the critical one. In such instances the examiner should repeat the "peak of tension" test with the critical question followed by a different question than the one used on the first test. This rearrangement will permit the examiner to ascertain whether the change in the tracings on the later question is a delayed reaction to the critical question or one that was of no significance at all.

2. "Peak of tension" in pulse

(a) *Change in pulse frequency, pulse amplitude, or general irregularity in pulse beat at the critical question* (diagrammatic sketch, Fig. 35-A, B, C).

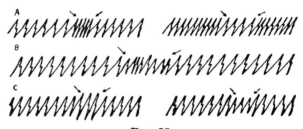

FIG. 35

3. "Peak of tension" in respiration

(a) *Suppression at the critical question* (diagrammatic sketch, Fig. 36-A).

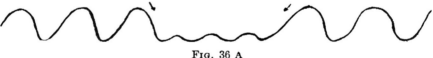

FIG. 36 A

(b) *General suppression up to the critical question, followed by normal breathing thereafter* (diagrammatic sketch, Fig. 36-B).

FIG. 36 B

(c) *Gradual rise in baseline up to and including the critical question, followed by a return to normal thereafter* (diagrammatic sketch, Fig. 36-C).

FIG. 36 C

(*d*) *Gradual decline in baseline to the critical question and a return to normal or a rise thereafter* (diagrammatic sketch, Fig. 36-D).

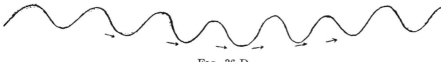

FIG. 36 D

(*e*) *Specific rise in baseline at critical question* (diagrammatic sketch, Fig. 36-E).

FIG. 36 E

(*f*) *General irregularity up to the critical question, followed by general regularity thereafter* (diagrammatic sketch, Fig. 36-F).

FIG. 36 F

In listing and illustrating the foregoing forms and types of peaks of tension, the writers do not intend to imply that there are no others. These, however, appear to be the most prevalent.

CASE ILLUSTRATIONS OF PEAK OF TENSION CRITERIA

1. "Peak of tension" in blood pressure

(*a*) *General rise up to the critical question and either a gradual or sharp decline thereafter* (see Figs. 37, 38, 39, and 40).

(*b*) *Gradual rise up to the critical question and a continuation of the tracing at that high level* (see Fig. 41).

(*c*) *Normal baseline up to the critical question and a gradual or sharp decline to a lower level thereafter* (see Fig. 42).

FIG. 37. In this case a woman had been assaulted and robbed of her purse containing $47.00. The suspect whose record is shown here had not been told of the amount of money which the purse contained. On this peak of tension test he was asked whether the purse contained $10, $20, etc., as shown on the above record. Observe the peak of tension in his blood pressure just before the $50.00. (It might even be suggested that the exact amount, $47.00 is the peak!)

After the test the examiner showed the record to the subject and asked him to point out the highest point ("peak of tension") in the blood pressure tracing. The subject looked the record over, then pointed to the peak in the blood pressure tracing and said "Holy smoke, right at $47.00! What a machine!" He then promptly admitted his guilt.

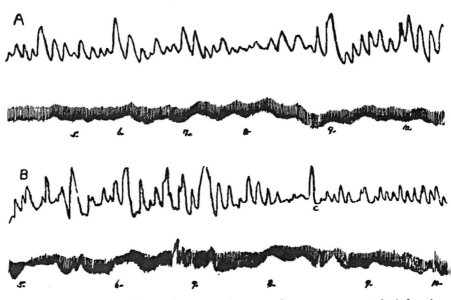

FIG. 38. The two subject's whose records appear here were suspected of shooting a sheriff. Their previous tests indicated deception and guilt. Peak of tension tests A and B above were conducted for the purpose of ascertaining who among ten possible persons drove the automobile from which the shooting occurred. On each test

the names of persons, including the two principal suspects, were included in the questions "Did ——— drive the automobile"? Observe on *A* how suspect Tony G. reached his peak at *8*, at which point he was asked "Did you, Tony G., drive the automobile"? Then observe on *B* how suspect Cecil L. reached his peak at the same question, "Did Tony G. drive the automobile"?

Subsequent to the conviction of Tony G. and Cecil L. one of them wrote a letter to the trial judge admitting their guilt and verifying this particular detail of the offense—that Tony G. drove the automobile.

700   710   725   750   765   775   780   800

FIG. 39. The history of the case in which this record was obtained is briefly as follows. The manager of an exclusive men's club in Chicago, who was accustomed to carry on his person several hundred dollars for the purpose of accommodating members who wished to cash checks or otherwise obtain ready cash, on one occasion neglected to remove the money from his trousers when he gave them to the club valet to clean and press. Upon discovering the absence of his money the following day he requested the valet to search for it. Much to the surprise of the manager the valet reported that instead of attending to the trousers himself as was his custom, he had, on this occasion, sent them to a nearby cleaning and pressing establishment. Failure to locate the money from the pressing shop resulted in suspicion being directed toward the valet, despite his many years of faithful service. When tested on the lie-detector, however, his records contained no significant responses. The examiner then suggested an examination for the errand boy who carried the trousers from the club to the shop. His records were also free from deception responses. Finally an examination was arranged for the owner of the pressing shop. His records indicated a very fast pulse and contained some response when asked if he had found and kept the money which had been in the club manager's trousers. Since the subject had not been informed by anyone as to the amount of money in question the examiner decided to give him an "amount test". Although the loser of the money did not know exactly how much money was in the trousers he estimated the amount to be between $700 and $800. On the first peak of tension test the suspect reached his peak betwen $700 and $800. He was then given a test with the amounts narrowed down from $650 to $850, and covering varying amounts in between. On that record, part of which is shown above, observe the peak at $765. (Notice also the cough at *c* right after the $765 question was asked.)

Following these tests the subject admitted his guilt and admitted that the amount was exactly $765, which he promptly returned.

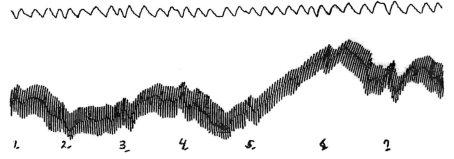

1.   2.   3.   4.   5.   6   7

FIG. 40. The subject whose record appears above was suspected of having received $10,000 from a maid who stole the money from her employer. Up to the time of his test no investigator had disclosed to him the amount of money that was involved. When confronted with the prospects of a lie detector test he admitted having received $4000 but claimed that was the full amount. On the peak of tension test record shown above the subject was asked whether the amount was $4500 (#1), $5000 (#2), $6000 (#3), $7000 (#4), $8000 (#5), $10,000 (#6), and $15,000 (#7). Observe the peak of tension at the $10,000 amount (question #6). Following the test he agreed to and did pay the victim the full $10,000.

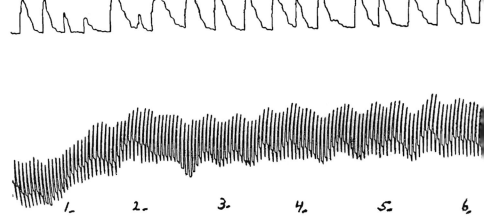

1.   2.   3.   4.   5.   6.

FIG. 41. This subject was suspected of embezzling a sum of money over a period of several years. The above test record was obtained before a complete audit had been made. Observe the gradual rise in blood pressure up to 2 and the continuation of the tracing at that same level throughout the remainder of the record. The amounts asked on the tests were as follows: $4650 (#1), $5500 (#2), $7500 (#3), $8500 (#4), $10,000 (#5). The subject confessed to the taking of $5500. (Another one of the subject's peak of tension test records is shown in Figure 42.)

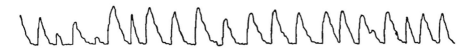

FIG. 42. This test record was obtained from the same subject whose record is shown previously in Figure 41. His peak of tension appears here in a different form at the same amount of money from the other record, at the missing amount of money ($5500), represented as #2 on the record.

2. "Peak of tension" in pulse

(a) *Change in pulse frequency, pulse amplitude, or general irregularity in pulse beat, at the critical question* (see Figs. 43 and 44).

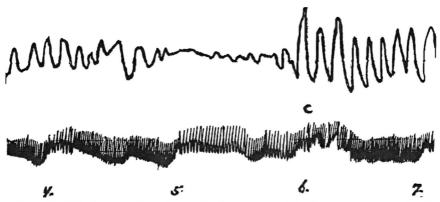

FIG. 43. This is a portion of a peak of tension test in the same case previously illustrated and described in Figure 38. On this test the names of ten persons, including this subject and his alleged accomplice, were included in the question "Did ——— shoot the sheriff"? Observe the change in pulse frequency at *5*, along with the suppression in respiration, when the subject was asked "Did you, Cecil L., shoot the sheriff"? (The *c* represents a cough at *6*.)

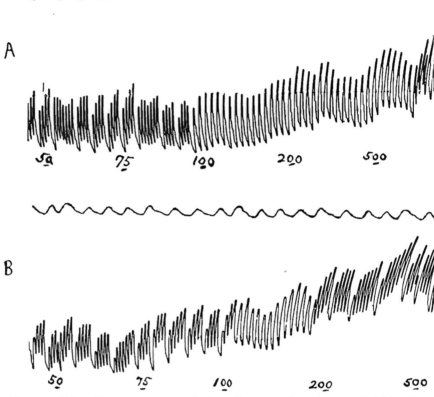

FIG. 44. This subject was suspected of stealing a number of cases of whiskey from his employer's liquor store. Observe on his two peak of tension tests *A* and *B* the change in pulse frequency and pulse pattern at 100, the number of cases which the subject later admitted stealing.

3. "Peak of tension" in respiration

(a) *Suppression at the critical question* (see Fig. 45).

(b) *General suppression up to the critical question, followed by normal breathing thereafter* (see Fig. 46).

(c) *Gradual rise in baseline up to and including the critical question, followed by a return to normal thereafter* (see Fig. 47).

(d) *Gradual decline in baseline to the critical question and a return to normal thereafter* (see Fig. 48).

(e) *Specific rise in baseline at critical question* (see Fig. 49).

(f) *General irregularity up to the critical question, followed by general regularity thereafter* (see Fig. 50).

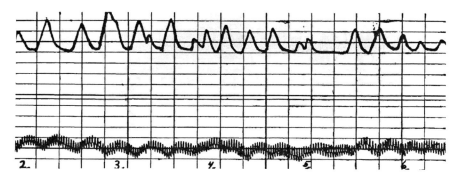

FIG. 45. The subject in this case admitted embezzling $4.00 prior to the above test in which the true amount of her thefts was sought to be ascertained. At *2* she was asked whether the amount she had taken was $15; at *3*, $25; at *4*, $100; at *5*, $300; and at *6*, $400. After the test the subject admitted embezzling $300.

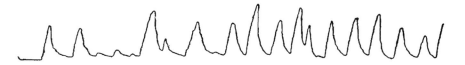

FIG. 46. On this embezzler's record he was asked whether the following varying amounts constituted the extent of his embezzlements: $5500 (*1*); $6000 (*2*); $6500 (*3*); $7000 (*4*); $7500 (*5*); $8000 (*6*). Observe the general respiratory suppression up to and including question *3* ($6500), the correct amount, which he admitted.

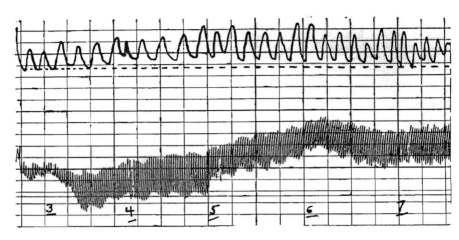

Fig. 47. The subject in this case was an employee of a large meat packing firm. He was suspected of disposing of the company's meat products for his own gain. On the above test an effort was made to ascertain the cumulative amount of his thefts. On *3* he was asked whether the amount was $100, on *4*, $500, on *5*, $1000, on *6*, $5000, on *7* $10,000. Observe the rise in the base level of his respiration up to and including *6*, the $5000 amount. Subsequent to his test he admitted that his thefts totalled $5000. (The dotted line underneath the respiration tracing has been inserted in this illustration to indicate the normal respiration baseline.)

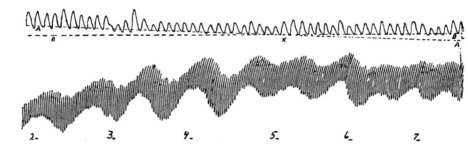

Fig. 48. In this peak of tension (amounts) test record, observe the gradual decline in respiration baseline to *x* at question *5* and a return to normal thereafter. Dotted line *A* was inserted to indicate the baseline of the respiration up to question *5*, and dotted line *B* to indicate the baseline from that point on. The amount at *5* was later admitted by the subject to be the amount of materials stolen from his employer.

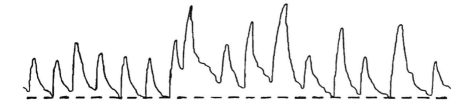

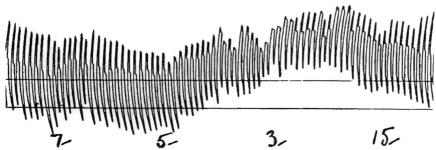

FIG. 49. Part of a card test on a suspected embezzler who subsequently admitted his guilt. Observe the specific rise in the baseline in his respiration at *5*, his chosen card. (The dotted line has been inserted in the above illustration to show the normal respiration baseline.)

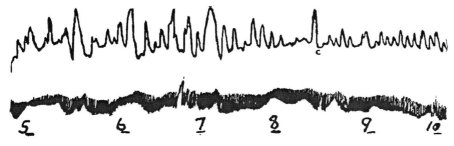

FIG. 50. Observe the general irregularity in respiration up to and including *8* and the general regularity thereafter. Each question contained the name of a person suspected of being the driver of a car used in a robbery and shooting. A subsequent confession verified the fact that the person whose name was mentioned in question *8* did drive the car.

This same record was previously shown in Figure 38–B as an illustration also of a blood pressure peak of tension.

Factors Affecting Test Results

Fear of detection appears to be the principal factor accounting for the physiological changes which are recorded and interpreted as symptoms of deception (see Fig. 51). Consciousness of wrongdoing, or remorsefulness, may serve as contributing factors, but their effect upon these physiological changes seems to be of minor importance when compared with the fear of detection.[32]

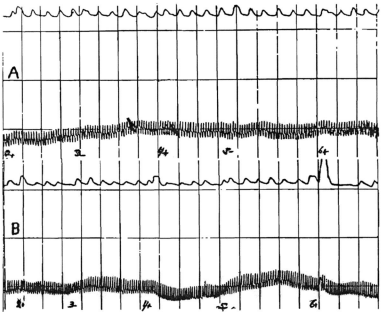

FIG. 51. An illustration of what appears to be the effect of the absence, and then the presence, of fear of detection. This subject was suspected of having dynamited certain property. His first test record, A, contained no indication of deception. Two days later he was again tested (on B), after his accomplice had been examined and confessed his guilt. Although the subject did not know of the admission of his accomplice he was aware that the latter had been examined and was kept in custody. This knowledge seemed to have aroused the subject's fear that now his own guilt would be detected, which fact apparently accounts for the deception responses at 3 and 5 on test B when he was questioned regarding his implication in the offense.

(This case arose before the use of the control questioning technique.)

---

[32] But see Floch, "Limitations of the Lie Detector", J. Criminal L. & Criminology, **40** (5): 651, p. 652, in which he expresses the view that "conscience" should be put in the same class as "fear of detection", and further states: "after all, psychologically conscience is also fear of detection. Only the fear is of the superego or moral principles which, in the final analysis, represent the father or authority in general. In brief, conscience is fear of detection and retribution and not an abstract concept".

The factors which occasion the chief difficulties in the diagnosis of deception by the lie-detector technique may be enumerated as follows:

1. Nervousness or extreme emotional tension experienced by a subject who is telling the truth regarding the offense in question but who is nevertheless affected by:
   (a) Apprehension induced by the mere fact that suspicion or accusation has been directed against him;
   (b) Apprehension over the possibility of an inaccurate lie-detector test result;
   (c) Over-anxiety to cooperate, in order to assure an accurate test result;
   (d) Apprehension concerning possible physical hurt from the instrument;
   (e) Anger and resentment over having to take a lie-detector test;
   (f) Over-anxiety regarding serious personal problems unrelated to the offense under investigation;
   (g) Previous extensive interrogation, especially when accompanied by physical abuse;
   (h) A guilt complex or fear of detection regarding some other offense which he had committed.

2. Physiological abnormalities, such as:
   (a) Excessively high or excessively low blood pressure;
   (b) Diseases of the heart;
   (c) Respiratory disorders.

3. Mental abnormalities, such as:
   (a) Feeblemindedness, as in idiots, imbeciles, and morons;
   (b) Psychoses or insanities, as in manic depressives, paranoids, schizophrenics, paretics, etc.;
   (c) Psychoneuroses, and psychopathia, as among so-called "peculiar" or "emotionally unstable" persons—those who are neither psychotic or normal, and who form the borderline between these two groups.

4. Unresponsiveness in a lying or guilty subject, because of:
   (a) No fear of detection;
   (b) Apparent ability to consciously control responses by means of certain mental sets or attitudes;
   (c) A condition of "sub-shock" or "adrenal exhaustion" at the time of the test;
   (d) Rationalization of the crime in advance of the test to such an extent

that lying about the offense arouses little or no emotional disturbances;

(e) Extensive interrogation prior to the test.

5. Attempts to "beat the machine" by controlled breathing or by muscular
flexing.

6. Unobserved application of muscular pressures which produce ambiguities or misleading indications in the blood pressure tracings.

NERVOUSNESS OF THE INNOCENT

The possible effects of a truthful or innocent person's "nervousness"
must be given serious consideration in diagnosing deception by the lie-
detector technique. Various physiological changes or disturbances may be
produced as the result of (a) apprehension induced by the mere fact that
suspicion or accusation has been directed against him; (b) apprehension
over the possibility of an inaccurate lie-detector test result; (c) over-anxiety
to cooperate, in order to assure an accurate test result; (d) apprehension
concerning possible physical hurt from the instrument; (e) anger and resentment over having to take a lie-detector test; (f) over-anxiety regarding
serious personal problems unrelated to the offense under investigation; (g)
previous extensive interrogation, especially when accompanied by physical
abuse; and (h) a guilt complex or fear of detection regarding some other
offense which he committed. It becomes necessary, therefore, to distinguish
between the changes or disturbances due to nervousness and those which
result from deception. Obviously, unless the technique provides for such a
distinction, the test is of no practical value.

Nervousness in a lie-detector subject usually is discernible—and its
recorded reactions distinguishable from deception criteria—by either the
generally erratic character of the blood pressure-pulse or respiration tracings
or else by the uniformly irregular nature of the tracings, in which there is
an absence of any consistently specific responses to pertinent questions
(see Fig. 52 and contrast it with Fig. 53). In other words, the physiological
changes or disturbances induced by nervousness usually appear on the lie-
detector record without relationship to any particular question or questions. They are usually of no greater magnitude—or in any event not
consistently so—when pertinent questions are asked than when irrelevant
or control questions are used. Moreover, the previously described test procedure, involving a proper pre-test interview and a card test demonstration
on either the first or second test, will minimize the number of instances
where nervousness will persist as a factor in the testing of innocent
persons.

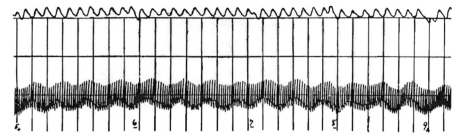

FIG. 52. RECORD OF A NERVOUS INNOCENT SUSPECT

Observe the uniformly irregular nature of the blood pressure-pulse tracing in which there is an absence of any specific responses. Questions *5* and *9* are irrelevant; the others are pertinent to the crime.

This subject had been arrested and accused of the crime principally because blood-hounds had led investigators from the scene of the burglary to the subject's home. When questioned by the police the suspect was unable to furnish a satisfactory explanation of his whereabouts at the time of the burglary. In an effort to ascertain the truthfulness of his statements the prosecuting attorney requested a lie-detector examination of the subject. The tests were made on November 9, 1935. Although the records, as illustrated by the one above, indicated general nervous tension they contained no significantly specific responses. The examiner reported that in his opinion the subject was innocent of the crime charged. Shortly thereafter he was released from custody. Nothing further developed until February 18, 1936, when the same prosecuting attorney requested assistance in another burglary case. He had in custody two young men whom he wished to have examined. (Neither one of them knew the previous suspect or had ever visited his residence.) Their records indicated deception, and during the course of the examination both men confessed to a series of burglaries—one of the crimes being the very one for which the subject examined in 1935 had been arrested on the basis of the bloodhound evidence. Sufficient evidence has been obtained to confirm the confessions, so there can be no doubt that the bloodhounds were in error.

It appears that the original suspect—the one of November 9th—had upon several occasions petted the bloodhounds, who belonged to a resident in the subject's neighborhood. Moreover, upon one occasion the subject had visited the home of the owner of the bloodhounds. These facts may possibly explain the reason for leading the police authorities to the innocent man's home, even though this person had not recently passed near the burglarized premises.

Once an innocent subject knows how the test is conducted and he becomes satisfied of the technique's accuracy and the examiner's integrity, his general apprehensiveness will disappear or greatly diminish. A reduction of emotional tension in an innocent person is also effected by the very conditions and surroundings (e.g., quietness and privacy) under which the test is conducted. The asking of all test questions in a moderate and uniform tone of voice is also helpful, in that there will be no variation in the stimulus that may be produced by the mere sound of the voice itself when the questions are asked. A desirable effect may be derived from the assurance to an inquiring subject that his mere nervousness will not produce the type of reactions that are indicative of deception.

A subject's over-anxiety to cooperate in order to be sure the test results will be accurate may become evident not only in his behavior and from what he says to that effect, but the recording itself may indicate that fact by reason of an increase in blood pressure as each question is being asked. Such a subject will many times "hang on" to each and every question, listening carefully and being anxious to answer promptly and accurately. In instances of this sort, a test should be conducted in which long, drawn out irrelevant questions are asked. The fact of innocent over-anxiety will become apparent from the nature of the responses on such a test, since the effect of "hanging on" to the questions will manifest itself with respect to irrelevant as well as relevant questions.

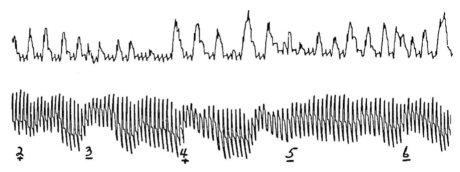

FIG. 53. RECORD OF VERY NERVOUS GUILTY SUSPECT

Observe the tremor in respiration in this embezzler's record, but at the same time note the suppression at questions *3* and *5* pertaining to the embezzlement. However, even without the suppression criteria, a record containing evidence of nervous tremor in the respiration tracing should be viewed as suggestive of deception. Tremors of this sort in respiration occur much more often in guilty records than in innocent ones.

Persons who may be apprehensive over possible physical hurt from the instrument can be put at ease quite readily by an examiner's assurance that the only physical sensation will be a temporary discomfort in the arm as the result of pressure from the blood pressure cuff. Occasionally, where it appears to the examiner that a rather timid-appearing subject is still apprehensive about physical hurt, it is well to inflate the blood pressure cuff and let him experience the slight discomfort before proceeding with the test. At times it is also helpful to run the card test first in order to completely satisfy a timid subject as to the absence of hurtful physical effects.

Any anger or resentment, which a subject may harbor at the time he enters the interrogation room, will usually subside considerably after he has been given an opportunity during the pre-test interview to express himself frankly regarding his attitude about being subjected to the test. Of comparable value is the explanation offered by an understanding, tolerant examiner that the lie-detector technique is as helpful to falsely suspected persons as it is to investigators in search of the guilty.

A subject's over-anxiety regarding serious personal problems unrelated to the offense under investigation will usually not become known to the examiner until after the first one or two generally erratic tests, when the examiner invites the subject to tell what it is that has been disturbing him on the test. Affording such a subject the opportunity of explanation, and his discussion of it with an understanding, sympathetic examiner, will contribute greatly to a more satisfactory recording on the next test. In one actual case an innocent subject's erratic recording was accounted for by the fact that on the very day of his test he and his family were being evicted from their living quarters for non-payment of rent. The same disturbing effect may stem from such factors as a suspected embezzler's worry over the newly discovered pregnant condition of a fellow employee with whom the suspect had been intimate. Only by a proper interview and solicitation of an explanation can the disturbing factor be ascertained and the way thereby paved for a satisfactory recording on the next test.[33]

An ordinary, routine interrogation by an investigator prior to the examiner's interview and test does not seriously impair the effectiveness of the lie-detector technique. However, an extensive interrogation based upon frequent and constant accusations of guilt may adversely affect the accuracy of the test, and especially so if the test follows soon thereafter. This is particularly true if the prolonged interrogation is accompanied by physical abuse, or threats of physical harm, administered in an effort to obtain a confession. For a lie-detector test, in which so much reliance is placed upon the presence or absence of delicately detected physiological changes, a person who has encountered such an experience is no longer a proper subject for deception diagnosis[34] (see Fig. 54). He is as unsatisfactory a subject for deception diagnosis as would be a medical patient who appears in a doctor's office for a metabolism test or heart examination soon after being chased up ten flights of stairs. Moreover, the positive suggestions of guilt constitut-

[33] In instances where the subject reveals information about his personal problems it should be treated as a confidential disclosure and withheld from the report made by the examiner regarding the offense under investigation. It should only be disclosed when the personal matter is directly associated with the principal offense.

[34] See in this connection the interesting illustrated article, Trovillo, P. V., "What the Lie-Detector Can't Do", J. Crim. L. & Criminology 23 (1). 121 (1941)

ing part of the "third degree" procedure may produce test reactions which will simulate true deception criteria. The writers are familiar with at least one case in which this actually happened.[35]

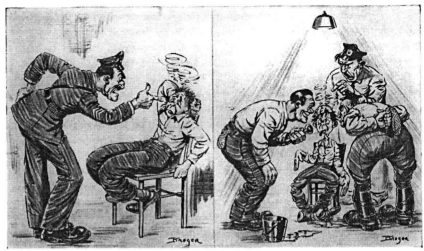

FIG. 54. IMPROPER PRELIMINARIES FOR A LIE DETECTOR TEST
Neither one of the above suspects will be a fit subject for a lie-detector test after undergoing extensive interrogations based upon frequent and constant accusations of guilt—and particularly when such interrogations are accompanied by physical abuse or threats of physical harm administered in an effort to obtain a confession.

An innocent subject's nervousness due to his involvement in another offense is a factor which can create a very serious problem and result in a mistaken diagnosis unless a proper testing procedure is employed. For example, a suspected burglar, upon being examined regarding a particular offense which he did not commit, may exhibit considerable emotional tension because of his fear of being detected as the perpetrator of another burglary, or because of his guilt complex regarding it. Likewise, a bank employee, guilty of some petty peculation of the bank's money, may be greatly concerned over the minor offense and exhibit considerable emotional tension because of this offense. In fact, there may be a sufficient mental association between the offense under investigation and the unrelated offense that a subject may give a seemingly guilty response to the principal offense itself.

Cases involving an innocent subject's guilt complex or fear of detection regarding some other offense are the ones in which an inexperienced or incompetent examiner is likely to make a mistake. In instances of this

[35] Extensive interrogation or physical abuse and threats may also produce an unresponsive condition in a guilty subject. See *infra* p. 83.

type the lie-detector responses occasioned by a lie regarding some other offense may be very easily misinterpreted by an unqualified examiner as indicative of deception regarding the principal offense. This is also the kind of case where the control questioning technique renders itself of much greater value than the original "relevant-irrelevant" test procedure. According to the latter procedure the subject is informed that the test questions will be confined to the principal offense under investigation— the theory being that this instruction will eliminate the disturbing effect of other possible offenses. But even though an innocent subject may be told that the test questions will be confined to the single offense under investigation, he nevertheless may be considerably disturbed over the other unrelated offense or offenses he did commit. However, with the control questioning technique, the subject is specifically told that he will be asked about other offenses in addition to the one under investigation (e.g., "Have you ever stolen anything?", "Did you burglarize a home at First and Main?" [referring to a fictitious burglary]). Instead of accentuating the already disturbing factor of guilt respecting the other possible offense not under investigation, the disclosure of the questions before the test in the control questioning technique has the effect of localizing the response to the proper question. Thus, the innocent subject knows before the test that he will be asked about other offenses, and for this very reason his concern about the latter will not be reflected as a specific reaction to the main offense questions, but will localize itself where it belongs—as a response to the control question or questions.

PHYSIOLOGICAL AND MENTAL ABNORMALITIES

As to the influence of physiological and mental abnormalities, it may be stated *as a general rule* that if the abnormalities are sufficiently serious *to materially affect the results of the test*, they are usually recognizable as such, either in the type of recording they produce or else in the appearance and demeanor of the person being tested.

Regardless of the limitations of the lie-detector technique, even when conducted under the best conditions and circumstances, practical experience has indicated that comprehensive medical and mental examinations prior to the tests are as a rule unnecessary. Perhaps further research in the field of detecting deception will disclose additional criteria, which will depend for their proper interpretation upon a careful consideration of many more physiological and mental characteristics than those deemed essential at the present time.

The principal disadvantage of the lie-detector technique is the inability to detect deception in certain persons because of their non-responsive nature. It is this type of subject who accounts for practically all the inconclusive or indefinite determinations made by competent examiners. In these cases, however, the examiner can determine the unresponsiveness of the subject from his records alone and without resorting to a medical or mental examination.

As subsequently discussed, the effects of the presence of physiological and mental abnormalities are not such that they produce criteria likely to be mistaken by a trained and experienced examiner as indications of deception. For although the examiner may not be qualified to ascertain or identify the particular physiological or mental abnormality accounting for irregularities in a lie-detector record, it is sufficient for all practical purposes that he is able to recognize such irregularities as not representing deception criteria. The ability to do so can be acquired by means of instruction from more experienced examiners or from his own carefully studied case experiences and experimentation.

Physiological Factors

High or low blood pressure conditions ordinarily do not prevent accurate deception diagnoses. In the first place, the respiration recording remains available for consideration. Secondly, despite conditions of high or low blood pressure (within reasonable limits) deception responses may still make their appearance in the blood pressure tracing. Moreover, an abnormal blood pressure condition does not, of itself, produce responses which simulate true deception criteria.

The type of case in which an abnormal blood pressure condition is most likely to affect the test results is exemplified by one occurring in a small town in the Middle West several years ago. A woman about forty-eight years old was suspected of murdering the wife of her paramour; she was questioned almost incessantly for two days by the various law enforcement agencies of the community (the agencies having refused to cooperate with each other because of a regrettable political situation), and at the end of this period the police department requested a lie-detector examination of the suspect. Her systolic blood pressure was definitely over two hundred millimeters of mercury, and needless to say she was in a fatigued condition generally. Because of these facts the examiner refused to conduct a deception test and cautioned the investigators as to the inadvisability of persisting in their own interrogation of this person. They continued to do so, however, and about two hours later the woman drifted into a state of unconsciousness. Medical attention thus became necessary, and before the arrival of a physician the investigators were considerably concerned over their own possible predicament should their suspect expire while in their custody. Fortunately for them, she responded to treatment, although the physician ordered several days' complete and undisturbed rest for the patient.

Under the circumstances of this case it was inadvisable to conduct a lie-detector test. In the first place, even if the suspect were guilty, in view of her physical condition at the time it was very probable that any potential emotional disturbances resulting from deception would have been masked or overshadowed by the emotional strain or tension already present. Secondly, her condition was such that from a medical standpoint she should not have been subjected to a lie-detector test, or, as events actually disclosed, to even the effects of an ordinary interrogation.

No set rules can be promulgated as to the exact blood pressure conditions under which deception tests may or should be conducted. Considerably more research and experimentation will be necessary before such information is available. At the present time, therefore, an examiner must use his own discretion with regard to the particular facts of each case. In cases of a doubtful nature the examiner either should decline to conduct the test or else proceed without recording blood pressure-pulse changes, and base his interpretation on the other tracings (respiration, etc.) alone. If these remaining tracings fail to show the proper indices, the examiner should make an inconclusive report.

The foregoing comments with regard to blood pressure also apply to some extent to abnormal heart conditions. Moreover, in many cases where a heart condition is sufficiently serious to affect the results of the test, the subject probably will be aware of the existence of such a condition because of prior medical diagnosis or treatment, and information to this effect is usually forthcoming from the subject about to be tested.

In this discussion of the effects of abnormal heart conditions, and of other physiological abnormalities as well, the point which the writers wish to emphasize and clarify is as follows: It is true, of course, that the polygraph is inadequate for medical diagnosis of abnormal heart conditions (i.e., for identifying or determining the exact nature of cardiac disorders). It is also true that the lie-detector examiner may not possess the necessary qualifications for a medical diagnosis. Nevertheless, the instrument is an adequate one for indicating to the examiner the presence of (though not the particular nature of) heart conditions which are sufficiently serious to affect the results of a lie-detector test. In other words, although the examiner is not able to determine just what particular heart disorder is present, he can ascertain whether or not there is present an abnormal condition which will prevent or seriously affect a deception diagnosis. For example, Figure 55 is an illustration of a lie-detector record which indicates, by virtue of the peculiar pulse tracing, the presence of an abnormal heart condition of some sort. The particular defect is not identifiable from the tracing, but the examiner at least will know from the peculiar nature of the pulse tracing that the subject is afflicted with some kind of abnormal heart condition.

Indications of a relatively minor cardiac disorder characterized by "extra systoles" or "double heart beats" are present on an occasional lie-detector record. This condition appears reflected on the tracing as a lost pulse—that is, a beat so rapid or of such short duration that a more sensitive medical apparatus would be required to record its occurrence as an actual heart pulsation. On the lie-detector record it appears more or less as a lag in the diastole tracing, and it usually is followed immediately by an increase in

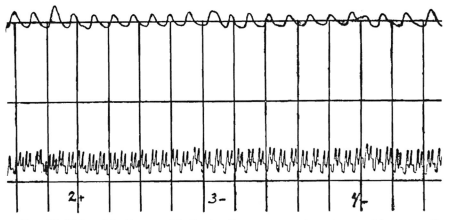

FIG. 55. This subject's record indicates the presence of an abnormal heart condition sufficiently serious to materially affect the results of a lie-detector test. The peculiar pulse beat may be due to a condition known as aortic regurgitation (defective cardiac valve), or to a condition characterized by the heart skipping a systolic beat, or to other possible cardiac disorders. Regardless of the cause, however, the examiner immediately realizes, from the nature of the record, that some abnormality is present.

blood pressure. An examiner with a reasonable degree of experience is not apt to confuse a blood pressure increase following an "extra systole" as an indication of deception. Where such systoles occur at infrequent intervals during the test they usually do not prevent a deception diagnosis, for very often the test questions can be spaced at intervals which are unlikely to coincide with the "extra systoles"; or if they do happen to coincide the response at that point may be discarded for purposes of deception diagnosis. In certain cases where this or any other similar abnormality appears at very frequent intervals on the record, as in Figure 55, the blood pressure-pulse recording may be rendered valueless as a basis for deception diagnosis. (Figure 44, however, is an illustration of a case record in which the presence of extra systoles did not interfere with a deception diagnosis. And, as illustrated in Figure 8-B, the timely occurrence of extra systoles may even constitute a deception response.)

Another physiological abnormality occasionally encountered by an examiner is "hyperthyroidism"—a condition which may account for a very fast pulse persisting throughout the tests. Since a consistently rapid pulse is not by itself considered as an indication of deception, the hyperthyroid factor is of no particular consequence, except to the extent that a lying subject so afflicted may have the benefit of an inconclusive opinion made necessary by the existence of this abnormality.

In addition to the foregoing, there are other physiological conditions of a temporary or relatively minor nature which impair the test results or else render the making of such tests inadvisable. For instance, a person with a severe cold, who has coughing spells during the test, is not a fit subject; nor is one who is experiencing a hay fever or asthmatic attack. The same is true of a person who is under the influence of alcohol or who is experiencing hiccoughs or other similar disturbances. Precautions must be taken, however, against the possibility that disorders of this type are not feigned for the purpose of evading detection. Moreover, the fact that a subject's actual physiological condition is such that a dependable test cannot be conducted is no reason for eliminating that person from consideration as a guilty party. The writers know of some cases where persons considered as unfit subjects were in fact responsible for the offense in question. This possibility seems rather obvious, but there is a tendency toward according such unfit subjects the benefit of doubt in their favor.

The use of drugs, stimulants or sedatives, is sometimes resorted to by guilty persons attempting to avoid detection. Experience has indicated, however, that if a drug or its effect is sufficiently potent to materially reduce a subject's responsiveness, his physical appearance or behavior will clearly indicate the fact of an artificially induced abnormal condition. In such a situation the examiner should interrogate the subject with a view to ascertaining the causative factor. In any event, the lie-detector test should be postponed, and if possible the subject should be placed under observation and examined at a later date.

Mental Factors

Feeblemindedness, as in idiots, imbeciles, and morons, is a factor of some importance in deception tests. We here speak of idiots as individuals whose intelligence does not exceed that of the normal child of three years of age; of imbeciles as those whose intelligence is that of the normal child between three and seven; and of morons whose intelligence is equivalent to that of a normal child between seven and ten.[36]

The lie-detector technique is predicated upon the theory that deception criteria appear in a record because of the emotional disturbances resulting from the subject's consciousness of lying and his fear of detection. It is obvious, therefore, that a person of inferior intelligence (who may be unable to distinguish properly between truths and falsehoods, or to understand the moral obligation for truthtelling and lawful behavior, or to have any fear of detection) is not a fit subject for a test of this nature. For this reason, therefore, the first two groups of feebleminded persons—the idiots and the imbeciles—are usually beyond the reach of an examiner who seeks to detect deception by means of this technique. However, since they are quite easily recognizable as mentally deficient, they do not constitute much of a problem for the lie-detector expert. On the other hand, the moron group cannot be disposed of so lightly.

Because of his proximity to the so-called normal group of persons, a moron occasionally may be overlooked as such by a lie-detector examiner who has not resorted to the use of an intelligence test. But even in such an eventuality no harm will result to the subject and no serious loss to the investigator. In the first place the subject's mental inferiority does not give rise to lie-detector responses which may be mistaken for deception criteria, and this fact, of course, operates as an adequate safeguard to the innocent and truthful. Secondly, the control questioning technique itself will indicate a mentally deficient guilty person's possible unresponsiveness and place the examiner on his guard against an erroneous conclusion of innocence—for in dealing with any person who is unresponsive a deception diagnosis should be indefinite or qualified.[37]

Although the lie-detector test results on mentally deficient persons may not permit a deception diagnosis, the tests themselves may be of considerable value for their psychological effect in inducing a confession from a person actually guilty of the offense in question. In other words, even though a subject of limited mental qualifications may not experience emotional disturbances when lying during the test, he may be influenced subsequently by the examiner's accusations allegedly based upon the results of the test. For instance, such an effect is known to have accounted for a

[36] See Fisher, V. E., *An Introduction to Abnormal Psychology* (1937), 470. The word "moron" is here used in its correct sense and not in the erroneous though popular reference to "sex pervert" or "sex maniac".

[37] It is sometimes assumed that colored persons as a group are unresponsive because of intelligence or social factors. Although this is true as regards the unintelligent, uneducated Negro—as well as of the unintelligent, uneducated white person—it is certainly not true of the intelligent, reasonably educated Negro.

confession obtained from a Chicago rapist-murderer of sub-normal intelligence. In this case, although the records did not contain reliable indications of deception, there were suspicious circumstances which prompted the examiner to interrogate the subject on the assumption that he was guilty. Soon thereafter the subject confessed his guilt. He drew a detailed diagram of the crime scene and gave such a detailed version of his activities at the time that there remained absolutely no doubt at all as to the validity of his confession. (Previous questioning of this subject by police officers had failed to such an extent that until the confession they were inclined to accord him the benefit of doubt in favor of his innocence. Yet within a few minutes of his lie-detector test the subject made a confession which served as the basis for his subsequent conviction.)

As regards the effects of mental deficiency, mention should also be made of the use of lie-detector tests on children. The very young are not fit subjects for several reasons. In the first place, the discomfort of the inflated blood pressure cuff may be more than a child can tolerate without moving his arm for the period of time required to conduct the test. Secondly, due to their mental immaturity, children may not fully recognize the difference between truth and falsehood, or they may not have much of a conception of the moral obligation for truthtelling. Consequently, if to them a lie is meaningless and constitutes no wrong, they will experience little or no fear regarding detection. As a general rule, however, adolescents over thirteen or fourteen years of age are suitable subjects, but this will depend, of course, upon the stage of the mental development of the particular person under consideration.

Psychoses or insanities, as found in paranoids, manic depressives, schizophrenics, paretics, etc., present another factor which must be considered in diagnosing deception. This factor, however, does not occasion much difficulty for the lie-detector examiner. First of all, only on rare occasions will such persons be presented to him for examination—because of the fact that their abnormal mental condition (e.g., delusions of grandeur, persecution complex, etc.) is usually recognized by previous investigators in the case who realize that their mental condition may preclude the possibility of a deception diagnosis. Nevertheless, even when subjects of this type come to the attention of the lie-detector expert—and, incidentally, it seems that they are encountered more often as complainants or alleged victims of crimes than as offenders and suspects—their abnormal condition usually will become apparent during the course of the examination. The generally irregular and erratic lie-detector records of such persons will usually furnish an indication of the possible existence of a mental abnormality.

Although there is always the possibility that a guilty subject may evade detection because of the fact that his mental abnormality precludes the possibility of a reliable deception test, the writers are not aware of any case where an innocent person was diagnosed as a liar because of misleading indications produced by an unrecognized psychotic condition.

Of the three classes of mentally abnormal subjects previously mentioned, the psychoneurotics and psychopaths occasion the most difficulty. They are the persons who in the layman's terminology are "peculiar", "cracked", or "unstable"—though ordinarily not to the extent that they must be incarcerated in a mental institution, as is generally true with the previously discussed group, the psychotics.[38]

The mere fact that a criminal suspect is psychoneurotic or psychopathic does not necessarily mean that it is impossible to detect his deception or to determine the fact of his innocence. Nevertheless, the group does include some types of persons upon whom it is impossible to make a reliable deception test. An outstanding example of such a type is the so-called pathological liar, a term used to characterize a person who lies for no profit or gain, and whose lying is compulsive or uncontrollable—one who would lie regardless of his position or situation in life and who eventually reaches a stage where he himself is no longer certain of what is true and what is not.[39] For these reasons his "deception" is undetectable by this technique, or indeed, by any other method short of the interrogator's independent discovery or possession of the actual facts about which the subject is lying.[40] On the other hand, the sexual deviants, as a group, have been found to be no more difficult as lie-detector subjects than the average normal suspect.

The emotional instability which characterizes many psychoneurotics and psychopaths frequently produces such an irregular and erratic recording of physiological changes (particularly with regard to the respiration) that it is practically impossible to arrive at a diagnosis of deception. Fortunately, however, an experienced examiner is not apt to misinterpret a record of

[38] The classification of psychotics, psychoneurotics, and psychopaths as stated in Fisher's "An Introduction to Abnormal Psychology", *supra* note 36.

[39] See Fisher, *op. cit. supra* note 36 at p. 265. Also see Hulbert, H., "Constitutional Psychopathic Inferiority in Relation to Delinquency", J. Crim. L. & Criminology **30** (1): 3, 15 (1939).

[40] So few instances of lie-detector tests on known pathological liars have come to the writers' attention that they hesitate to recommend any procedure to be used either to determine the presence or absence of this mental trait. As a matter of fact, psychiatrists and psychologists themselves encounter considerable difficulty in their own attempted diagnosis of this abnormality. Indeed, a well-known psychiatrist and author of a book upon the subject states that "appreciation of the nature of the phenomena can only be obtained through acquaintance with an entire career", and "any of us may be confronted by fabrications so consistent as to leave at one or several interviews the impression of truth". Healy, W., and M., *Pathological Lying, Accusation, and Swindling* (1915) 3. The lie-detector expert should realize, however, that such a group of persons does exist.

this kind as one indicative of deception. The chief source of difficulty, when it does occur, is more likely to result from the fact that a normal guilty person's responses may be so unspecific and generally disturbed that they may be accredited to "emotional instability".

The examiner's most effective safeguard against the possibility of an error due to a subject's abnormal physical or mental condition is the card test, which constitutes a routine phase of the examination procedure. If a subject does actually have a physical or mental abnormality, which has affected his regular test recordings, his card test record should also contain evidence of that fact. On the other hand, if what appears to be an indication of abnormality is actually feigned, or otherwise false, the card test record will usually be free of such an indication.

UNRESPONSIVENESS OF THE GUILTY

With fear of detection ordinarily operating as the principal factor accounting for significant physiological changes, a subject's lack of fear will result in an absence of any deception criteria on the lie-detector record. Although persons of inferior intelligence and some of abnormal mentality are more apt to be devoid of this fear of detection (for reasons previously discussed), there are persons of normal intelligence and mentality who may be sufficiently lacking in this fear element that their deception cannot be detected by the lie-detector technique. This is particularly true of the subject who really believes that the test technique has no validity and is only used "to bluff" guilty persons into confession. It is important therefore that the pre-test interview be conducted in such a way as to "build up" the subject's respect for the technique and the examiner. Toward this end it is sometimes advisable to run a card test first in order to demonstrate to the subject the efficacy of the instrument and technique.

Occasionally this element of no fear of detection appears in the form of a guilty subject's more or less "fatalistic" attitude regarding his predicament as a suspect or accused person. He may express this attitude by telling the examiner, "I don't care what happens to me; they can send me to the penitentiary or do whatever they want". Having no fear of the consequences of detection or conviction, he will probably be devoid of any specific deception responses during a lie-detector test. In such instances where a subject possesses this attitude the examiner should proceed to interrogate him on the assumption of his being guilty. Rarely, if ever, will an innocent person display this type of attitude.

Another factor, which may account for the absence of deception criteria in the record of a person who is actually lying, is the ability seemingly possessed by some individuals to control their responses by certain mental sets or attitudes. A person who appeared to possess a fair measure of such qualifications was Jerry Thompson, the perpetrator of the Mildred Hallmark rape-murder. His lie-detector records, obtained before the use of the control questioning technique, were rather indefinite in their indications, but because of various circumstances pointing to Thompson's possible guilt, the examiner began interrogating him on the assumption that he was actually guilty, and a complete confession resulted. Several days before Thompson's execution the examiner interviewed him in the death cell primarily for the purpose of learning from Thompson what his attitude was during the lie-detector test. He stated that whenever he was asked during the test whether he raped and killed "Mildred", he would concentrate upon and re-enact in his own mind various abnormal sexual experiences he had had with another girl—of the same name (Mildred). He stated that by doing this each time the question was asked, he was able to dismiss temporarily from his mind the rape and murder of Mildred Hallmark.

In another case involving an attempt to control responses by certain mental sets and attitudes, an embezzler admitted after his confession that whenever the examiner asked a test question about the embezzlement he would think about a certain sex affair, whereas when an irrelevant or control question was asked he would think about the act of embezzlement. His records contained no specific indications of deception, and the only reason for the detection of his guilt and the obtaining of his confession was the suspicion he aroused by his delayed answers to the irrelevant test questions and his unexplained delay in keeping the appointment for his test. (For an illustration, however, of a case where the same type of evasion attempt was revealed on the test record, see Fig. 56.)

Fortunately, there are relatively few persons who possess the ability to avoid detection by utilization of mental sets and attitudes. Moreover, the present "control questioning" technique—employing known lie questions for control purposes—minimizes the extent to which a person can now resort to this evasive process. Then, too, as a general rule the more a subject tries to "beat the machine" by this or any other method, the easier it is to detect his guilt.

A condition of "subshock" or "adrenal exhaustion" is another factor that may account for a guilty person's unresponsiveness at the time of his test. This condition is most apt to be encountered in cases where a guilty subject is examined within a few hours after the commission of the offense for which he is suspected. The following case history is an example of such an occurrence. A bank teller, who had reported that he had been compelled to relinquish ten thousand dollars in cash to a man who threatened to "blow up" the bank if his demands were not met, was examined on the lie-detector within several hours after the alleged robbery. His records were absolutely devoid of any indications of deception when questioned as to whether or not the robbery was a genuine one or as to whether or not he was implicated in it in any way. It developed later, however, that the man to whom the subject had given the money was a friend of his, with whom he had conspired to steal ten thousand dollars. Following his arrest and confession the subject was questioned by the lie-detector examiner in an effort to ascertain the explanation for his unresponsiveness on the test. The subject quite willingly supplied the following information. Immediately after reporting the robbery he began to "shake like a leaf", and continued to do so from then on until about five minutes before he was brought into the examination room in which his test was to be conducted. Then, all of a sudden, his shaking disappeared and he felt quite calm and collected, although he still maintained a fear of having his deception detected on the lie-detector. He reported that during the test he thought that his deception would be indicated on the record and was surprised after the test was over that he was not then accused and interrogated further. He volunteered the explanation that apparently he had shaken and trembled so much prior to the test that "it was all out of my system during the period of the test". He added, however, that the shakes recurred several hours later and that he was considerably upset and worried from then on until the time of his arrest and confession. He commented that if he had been called back for a re-examination on the lie-detector at any time after the initial test, he felt sure that his deception would have been detectable. He even went so far as to state that he probably would have confessed before undergoing a re-examination. (This case occurred before the use of the control questioning technique, which would have revealed the unresponsiveness of the subject.)

We do not know definitely what accounted for this bank teller's "all in" feeling and unresponsiveness at the time of his test, but there is reason to presume that he was in a state of sub-shock or adrenal exhaustion. In such a condition it would not be reasonable to expect him to experience the physiological disturbances which otherwise might have produced deception criteria in the lie-detector records. For the very principle of the lie-detector technique is based upon the theory or fact that internal emotional strain draws forth a temporary excess of adrenalin into the blood from the adrenal glands and produces a moment of adrenalin flutters (or "internal jitters"), which demonstrably affect the heart and lungs. Unlike the thyroid gland, however, the adrenals have no ready supply; they produce adrenalin from moment to moment according to the body needs. From acute and continued fear, or other emotional stress, the adrenal cells may become so fatigued as to be unable to continue to meet the full demands of the situation. Hence the condition of sub-shock or adrenal exhaustion.[41]

[41] In view of some recent medical experiments by Dr. Daniel J. Condon of Phoenix, Arizona, and Dr. Richard Ford of Boston, Massachusetts, the question as to the

An examiner who is called upon to conduct a lie-detector test on a subject soon after the commission of the offense in question may take certain precautionary measures to guard against an error in deception diagnosis. First of all, he may conduct a rather crude but yet, for his purposes, satisfactory test for determining whether or not the subject is in a condition of adrenal exhaustion—by stroking his thumb nail across the inner area of the subject's knee or upper arm and observing the reaction of the capillaries to the pressure of the stroke. If the stroke produces a red mark it is considered normal; a red mark with white borders, however, is an indication of partial adrenal exhaustion; and a white line with no red in it indicates a condition of total adrenal exhaustion. Whenever there is any such evidence of a condition of adrenal exhaustion, or where the existence of such a condition is even considered a possibility because of the proximity of the lie-detector test to the time of the occurrence of the offense, it would be well to conduct a re-examination a day or two after the initial examination. Until then the examiner should refrain from making any definite report as to the results of the lie-detector test.

There is some indication to support the view that it is possible for a person to rationalize his criminal behavior so that he may minimize his lie responses during a lie-detector examination. If the subject can accomplish this feat it matters little whether he is a first offender or an habitual criminal.

An example of effective rationalization or self-deceit is to be found in a criminal sentenced to death. So engrossed does he become in his present predicament that his crime memories are rendered somewhat obscure; and he so vehemently protests his innocence in an effort to avoid execution that eventually he goes to the electric chair almost convinced himself that he is innocent. Were a person in such a state of mind given a lie-detector examination, he might give no specific deception responses but would probably display general nervousness throughout his records. His fear of approaching execution would be a far more dominating factor than fear of having his guilt detected. And the same general nervousness and fear of execution would probably also render unreliable any such test results on an innocent person.

---

involvement or the extent of involvement of adrenal activity with deception criteria has become a very challenging one. Dr. Condon and Dr. Ford ran polygraph deception tests of an experimental nature on two patients who had undergone complete bilateral adrenalectomy for malignant hypertension. Both subjects gave pronounced deception responses. In a communication to the authors, in response to an inquiry addressed to him, Dr. Condon stated: "From a scientific standpoint we have not explored this type of thing enough to draw any conclusions, but I have no doubt that other workers will, and we shall have to re-evaluate our concepts of the physiology involved in attempts at deception."

Effective rationalization and self-deceit may also be found in the case of a convict who has been proclaiming his innocence over a period of years and attempting to convince the authorities that he should be given his freedom. He may have so rationalized his offense that his deception might not be detected on a lie-detector test.[42]

For somewhat similar reasons, it may be possible that a confession made to a clergyman by a guilty individual, prior to his lie-detector test, would relieve him of his mental conflicts to such an extent that his deception might not be detectable. The writers are familiar with an actual case in which there was considerable evidence to support the view that a confession made to a priest two days before the lie-detector examination probably accounted for the subject's unresponsiveness during his lie-detector test.

As previously stated, the positive suggestions of guilt constituting part of a "third degree" procedure may produce reactions during a subsequently administered lie-detector test of an innocent person which will simulate true deception criteria, thereby giving rise to the possibility of an erroneous conclusion of guilt. Moreover, the same pre-test experience may so condition a guilty subject that his enmity toward the investigators, rather than the offense itself, becomes the center of his thinking. The ordeal may actually relieve him of whatever mental conflicts are present because of his criminal act, in which event it is highly probable that a "third degree" victim's deception may not be detected by the lie-detector technique.

ATTEMPTS TO "BEAT THE MACHINE" BY CONTROLLED BREATHING OR BY MUSCULAR FLEXING AND MOVEMENTS

Occasionally a lying subject will attempt to "beat the machine" by distorting his breathing pattern or by flexing various muscles, particularly the biceps muscle of the blood pressure cuff arm. Indications on a record, therefore, of an abnormal breathing pattern, or of muscular flexing—evidenced by sharp deflections of the blood pressure pen—is ordinarily indicative of deception (see Figs. 56, 57, 58, 59 and 60).

Controlled Breathing

Whenever the examiner observes an abnormal breathing pattern on a test record it is advisable, at the beginning of the next test, to obtain a

[42] Maurice Floch presents the following psychological explanation for this condition of "circumscribed amnesia" which he describes in his article "Limitations of the Lie-Detector" in J. Crim. L. & Criminology 40 (5): 651, at p. 653 (1950): the prisoner's crime becomes so thoroughly unacceptable and reprehensible to his conscience or superego that he goes through an unconscious process of repression which leaves him with a complete forgetfulness or amnesia of the events of the crime. A person like this may take a lie-detector test and deny his guilt without showing any physiological changes inasmuch as the instrument does not tap the unconscious itself.

recording of the respiration before the blood pressure cuff is inflated and before any questions are asked. At such a time the subject will usually be off guard and display his normal respiration pattern, just as he did when the control breathing was registered prior to his first test (see, again, Fig. 32). A card test, in its usual number two position, will also ordinarily reveal a subject's normal respiration.[43] In addition to these two methods for determining whether an unusual breathing pattern is the subject's norm or whether it is due to controlled breathing, it is helpful for the examiner

Fig. 56. This subject was examined regarding a sex offense involving a child. The pertinent questions are 3 and 5; 1, 2 and 4 are irrelevant. The slower, blocked respiratory pattern on the irrelevant questions, suggested the probability of an attempt to "beat the machine" either by a physical respiratory effort or by mental sets and attitudes. Following an interrogation based upon an assumption of guilt the subject confessed and also admitted that when he was asked irrelevant questions 1, 2, and 4 he concentrated on the crime but that when asked relevant questions he thought about the irrelevant ones.

In addition to confessing this one crime the subject confessed to seventeen other sex offenses against children.

to observe the subject's breathing at a time when no instrument recording of any sort is being made.

A distorted respiratory pattern on the regular test, unaccompanied by a similar distortion during the card test or on a sample respiratory tracing (i.e., when the blood pressure cuff is not inflated and when no questions are being asked) is indicative of deception. If, however, the respiration distortion persists on the card test and in the sample respiratory tracing, that fact suggests the possibility that the distortion may be due to some physio-

[43] The normal respiration of a person undergoing a test is between 12 and 20 cycles a minute. A respiration rate outside these limits should be viewed as possible deliberate efforts at distortion.

logical defect or to the subject's general nervousness. This is particularly
true in those instances where breathing irregularity is noted when the

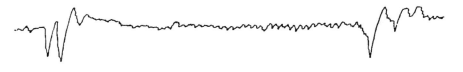

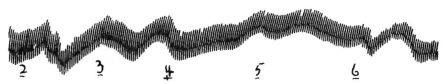

FIG. 57. This is the record of a subject who was examined regarding the disappearance of several payroll checks. *2* and *4* are irrelevant questions; *3* and *5* pertain
to the disappearance of the checks; and *6* is a general control question ("Did you ever
steal anything"?). Observe the distorted respiratory tracing throughout the test.
(Following his test the subject confessed taking and cashing the missing checks.)

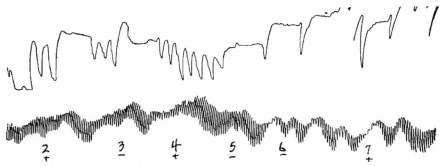

FIG. 58. Record of a subject suspected of a burglary and forgery of checks belonging to a manufacturing company where he worked. *2*, *4*, and *7* are irrelevant; *3* and *5*
pertain to the burglary and forgery; and *6* is a general control question. Observe the
respiration distortion throughout the test, following which the subject confessed his
guilt.

subject is not undergoing a test. On the other hand, if a subject's breathing
appears normal during such free periods then the distorted breathing during
a test should be viewed with suspicion.

Muscular Flexing

Muscular flexing, or a shifting or lifting of the cuff arm, during the early part of the test questioning, which is ordinarily accompanied by the subject's complaint that the cuff is hurting his arm, is usually indicative of deception. The innocent subject will almost always reserve any such movement or complaint until the latter part or end of the test.

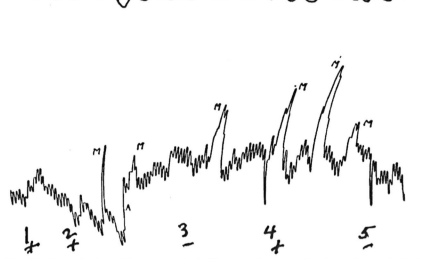

FIG. 59. Record of a subject suspected of larceny from a safe where she worked. As soon as the blood pressure was applied she began to wince and complain of cuff discomforture and started to move her arm. Observe the obvious evidence of muscular movements at *M* throughout the test. (The *A* between *2* and *3* indicates an adjustment of the blood pressure pen.) Following her test the suspect confessed her guilt.

In instances where there is muscular flexing or movement during all or part of a regular test, the examiner should proceed with the usual card test. If the card test is devoid of flexing distortions the assumption is warranted that the muscular activity on the first test was deliberate and for the purpose of preventing a detection of deception. It is well, however, in such cases to then repeat the regular test. A resumption of flexing will render more certain the assumption of deliberate distortion.

If muscular activity continues during a card test and on the following regular test, the examiner should thereafter inform the subject that the regular test will again be repeated and that on this next test the subject should give his full cooperation. This admonition will either result in an innocent person's normal recording on the third regular test or render significant of deception a continuation of such muscular activity.

Sometimes controlled breathing or muscular flexing occurs only on the chosen card question during the card test. The purpose of this is to make certain that a pronounced "lie reaction" appears on the chosen card in the

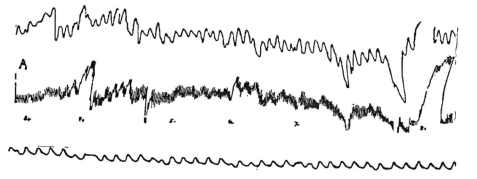

FIG. 60. During the examination of this subject, who was being questioned concerning the death of his wife, the examiner observed a flexing of the biceps muscle and some abnormally heavy breathing at various times through the test. A repetition of the test was accompanied by the same behavior on the part of the subject. The records themselves (see A) showed a very erratic respiratory and blood pressure tracings. There appeared very little doubt that this represented a deliberate effort to defeat the test. Subsequently, the subject confessed to killing his wife and admitted that he attempted to distort his record in order to confuse the examiner. B is the record obtained after the confession, when the subject was asked incriminating questions which he answered truthfully.

expectation that any responses to relevant questions on the regular test will thereby be rendered insignificant by comparison (see Fig. 33). On other occasions controlled breathing or muscular flexing occurs on another card or cards but not on the chosen card. The purpose of this is to mislead the examiner into believing that the lie-detector failed to properly indicate the chosen card and, thereby, render the test invalid regarding the crime under investigation. If a subject indulges in either of these two practices, it is strongly suggestive of his guilt.

UNOBSERVED APPLICATION OF MUSCULAR PRESSURES

In addition to muscular flexing and movements, which usually are rather easily detectable either by visual observation or by the sharp deflections of the blood pressure recording pen, another form of muscular activity is

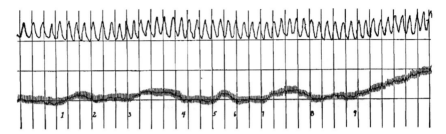

FIG. 61. EXPERIMENTAL RECORD ILLUSTRATING VARIOUS SIMULATED BLOOD
PRESSURE RESPONSES BY MUSCULAR PRESSURE AND BY MUSCULAR
CONTRACTION
At 1, slight contraction of the thigh muscles; at 2, thigh muscles relaxed; at 3, sustained contraction of the thigh muscles; at 4, thigh muscles relaxed; at 5, slight pressure exerted on the right forearm; at 6, pressure released; at 7, gross pressure exerted on the right forearm; at 8, pressure released; at 9, gradual and sustained pressure exerted on the right forearm without relaxation.

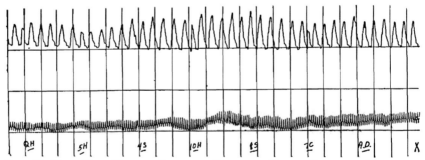

FIG. 62. CARD TEST RECORD SHOWING FALSIFIED BLOOD PRESSURE RESPONSE
The card chosen before the test was the four of spades, but, by means of pressure on the muscles of the right forearm at the ten of hearts, the "deception" response appears at the ten of hearts.

possible which can prove to be very troublesome and even produce misleading indications. It is muscular pressure exerted either in the arms or legs which produces a restriction in the normal flow of blood and a consequent increase in blood pressure. It may be applied in such a way that evidence of its occurrence cannot be observed visually, nor can it be readily distinguished from the usual type of uninduced blood pressure changes.

It is also a form of muscular activity that may result from either a deliberate or an unintentional effort on the part of the subject.

An examiner's unawareness of the possible effects of unobserved muscular pressures may cause him to occasionally make an erroneous diagnosis of

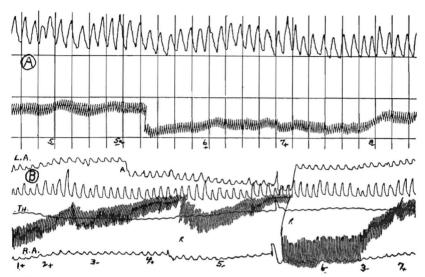

FIG. 63. ILLUSTRATIONS OF THE POSSIBILITY OF MUSCULAR PRESSURE MASKING OUT
DECEPTION RESPONSES

On *A*, the record of a confessed guilty subject, note the rather slight blood pressure response at *5*, a question pertaining to the sex offense under investigation, in contrast to the much greater specific response at *8*, a repeat of question *5*. The difference in responses may have resulted from a release in muscular pressure after irrelevant question *5a*, as seems to be indicated by the sharp drop in baseline at that point. Also note on *B*, the record of another confessed sex offender, the much greater response on the repeat of question *3*, than on the original *3* and on *5* before the release in muscular pressure between *5* and *6*, at the point marked *R* where the subject was instructed to relax and actually did relax. Since a muscular activity recorder was used at the time test *B* was run, here we know definitely that a change in muscular pressure occurred between *5* and *6*. Note the changes in the left arm pressure tracing L.A., the thigh pressure tracing TH., and the right arm pressure tracing R.A.—particularly at *R* between *5* and *6*.

truthtelling or else to sometimes assume that certain irregularities or ambiguities in the blood pressure tracing are the result of physiological abnormalities. As a result of certain experiments and research conducted by one of the authors (Reid) several years ago, these consequences may be avoided to a considerable extent.[44] On the basis of this experimentation and research

[44] The 1945 report of this study appeared in The Journal of Criminal Law and Criminology, **36** (1): 201–215.

it may be reported: (1) that in many instances where a blood pressure tracing rises more or less in a straight, gradual path to the upper portion of the chart, the causative factor is unobserved muscular pressure applied either deliberately or unintentionally; (2) that in many instances where a blood pressure tracing takes a rather straight, gradual decline toward the bottom of the chart it is due to the unobserved gradual release of pressure which was being applied, either deliberately or unintentionally, at the outset of

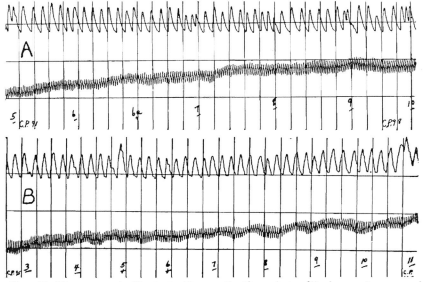

FIG. 64. These records illustrate the application of steadily increasing muscular pressure. A is the record of a sex offender. Note the gradual blood pressure rise from question 5 to question 10, an increase of 7 mm. of Hg. Compare A with B, wherein the experimenter simulated the A tracing by exerting steadily increasing pressure on his forearm which bore the blood pressure cuff. (The c.p. notations on the records indicate cuff pressure.)

the test;[45] (3) that all the typical blood pressure responses of deception can be produced artificially by unobserved muscular pressure, and that by this means an unwary examiner may be deceived by the resulting test record; (4) that simulated responses due to unobserved muscular pressure usually can only be differentiated from true deception responses through the use of an auxiliary unit for recording the indication of such muscular activity; and (5) that the recorded evidence of muscular pressure may also occasionally serve as deception criteria.

An adequate explanation of the muscular pressure phenomenon, as a

[45] This decline may also be due, of course, to a leak in the system.

factor in the lie-detector technique, may be facilitated by the presentation here of an account of the experiments and research from which the foregoing conclusions were drawn.

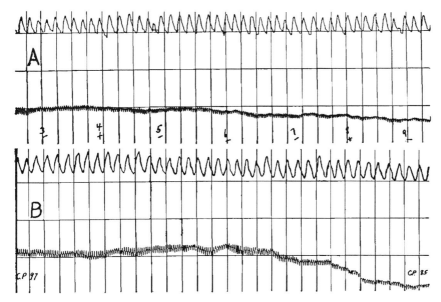

FIG. 65. On A, the record of a sex offender suspect who subsequently confessed his guilt, observe the downhill path of the blood pressure as well as the gradual reduction in pulse amplitude. Compare A with experimental record B in which there is a similar downhill trend in blood pressure and a reduction in pulse amplitude as the experimenter exerted pressure on the right forearm at the outset of the test and then midway through the test he began to gradually release the pressure.

For some time it has been known that blood pressure changes could be artificially induced by muscular contraction and relaxation.[46] Apparently unrecognized, however, even within the medical profession, was the possi-

[46] See Mulliner, M R. and McKinzie, R. T., *Elementary Anatomy and Physiology* (3rd ed., 1931), at p. 328, in which the following statement is made: "As the blood goes into the 'arterial tree', there is more resistance to its onward flow, due to the narrowing of the tube. This is *peripheral resistance*, which is increased or lessened by muscular contraction or relaxation. The greater the resistance, the harder the heart has to pump to send the blood to its destination, with consequent increase in arterial tension. Arterial tension or *blood pressure* represents the pressure against the sides of the blood vessels exerted by the moving blood."

Also see Howell, W. H., *Textbook of Physiology* (10th ed., 1928) 494; Crandall, L. A., *An Introduction to Human Physiology* (3rd ed., 1943) 134; Abramson, D. E., *Vascular Responses in the Extremities of Man in Health and Disease* (1944) 142; and Jacobson, E.. *Progressive Relaxation* (1938).

bility that the mere exertion of unobserved muscular pressure would produce a similar effect.[47]

Muscular pressure as well as muscular contractions can produce a recording of blood pressure changes, which to all appearances is similar to recordings of normal, uninduced changes. (This is clearly illustrated in Figure 61.) It is possible for some persons to deceive an examiner using only the conven-

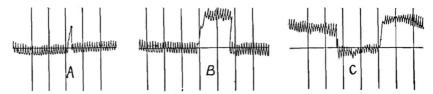

FIG. 66. ILLUSTRATIONS OF DIFFERENCES BETWEEN ORDINARY ARM MOVEMENTS
AND THOSE PRODUCED BY SUDDEN MUSCULAR PRESSURES

At *A*, right arm to which blood pressure cuff is attached, is moved momentarily and then returned to its former position. Note deflection in the recording which returns to approximately the same baseline. At *B*, great and immediate pressure is exerted on the right forearm. Note the change in the blood pressure baseline which is maintained for several seconds until the pressure is released. At *C*, pressure is exerted on the right forearm at the outset of the recording and then released (indicated by downward deflection). A new baseline is established until the pressure is reapplied.

tional lie-detector by artificially inducing blood pressure changes (see Fig 62). There is also the possibility that a subject may steadily apply muscular pressure and thereby raise his blood pressure to a level that may mask out whatever deception responses might otherwise have appeared in a normal tracing (see Fig. 63). A subject might even simulate one or the other of the two principal types of blood pressure tracings which have always been

[47] Up to the time of the original report on this study in 1945, a reasonable search of the medical literatures revealed no direct comment regarding blood pressure changes due to muscular *pressure* of the type with which we are presently concerned. Indirectly it was reported by Barker, L. F. and Cole, N. B., in *Blood Pressure, Cause, Effect and Remedy* (1924) at p. 37, that veins near the surface of the body are subject to muscular pressure during bodily movements and that "such pressure from without is easily exerted, since the veins have thin muscular and elastic coats and are easily collapsible in contradistinction to the arteries which always maintain their tubular shape". Also see *Blood Pressure Simplified*, a manual published by the Taylor Instrument Company, in which the Katzenstein method of testing the function of the heart is reported, and is based on the observation that when both femoral arteries are digitally compressed, the blood pressure will rise from 10 to 20 mm. of Hg. Likewise see Jansen, W. H., Tams, W., and Achelis, H., "Blutdruckstudien, I. Zur Dynamick des Blutdrucks", Deutsches Arch. f. Klin. Med., **144** (1), 1924 (cited by Abrahamson, *op. cit. supra* note 47 at p. 235), which states "that binding the extremities of normal persons with elastic bandages caused only an insignificant increase in blood pressure".

rather confusing to examiners: (1) a tracing which steadily and gradually climbs toward the top of the chart, and (2) a tracing which makes a steady decline to the bottom of the chart. The first one can be produced by gradually increased muscular pressure; the second by a gradual release of muscular pressure which had been applied at the outset of the test (see Figs. 64 and 65). In all experiments of this sort, or whenever an attempt is made in this way to deceive an examiner, the muscular pressure must be exerted in the arms, hands, thighs or feet, because if the torso muscles are utilized for this purpose, distorted recordings in the respiration will reveal the efforts at falsification.[48]

The reader must be mindful of the fact that in these various experiments the subject used his full power of concentration to simulate guilt reactions without being burdened with the guilt complexes of an actual criminal suspect. It is believed that the task of successfully simulating such blood pressure responses would be practically impossible for an untrained subject. It is believed, however, that an untrained subject can consciously or unconsciously influence his blood pressure reactions to such a degree as to at least introduce ambiguous responses which may confuse the examiner. In other words, in actual cases ambiguous blood pressure responses, which are misplaced in relation to deception indices, but which are somewhat similar in pattern to the simulated illustrations, may or may not be consciously accomplished. Heretofore the reasons for these unexplained blood pressure responses have usually been ascribed to a faulty apparatus or an abnormal physical or mental condition in the subject. There is now ample evidence available that many such ambiguous records were the result of muscular pressures, and that in many instances the pressure had been applied deliberately in an effort "to beat the machine".[49]

[48] Experiments were conducted to determine whether simulated blood pressure responses such as are obtainable from pressures in a subject's forearm are the result of compression of the muscles of the forearm itself or the result of the contraction of various other muscles used to produce the compression. The experimenter's forearm was placed in a relaxed position upon a table and while a recording of the blood pressure was made an assistant forced a wooden compress against surface of the forearm. This resulted in a blood pressure variation comparable to that obtained when the pressure is self-exerted, thereby establishing the fact that at least the major portion of such changes is due primarily to muscular pressure and not to muscular contraction.

[49] On one occasion a young man, who after his test confessed to an automobile larceny, said that he "held one arm rather stiff during the tests". The blood pressure recordings of this subject were so irregular that a definite blood pressure interpretation was precluded, although the respiratory responses were sufficiently indicative of deception to report him guilty of the theft. In another case, a confessed rapist informed the examiners that he had read a publication on lie detection and learned that lying "slacks up your breathing", and therefore he decided that during the test he

FIG. 67. PORTABLE CHAIR AND EQUIPMENT FOR RECORDING MUSCULAR MOVEMENTS WITH REID POLYGRAPH

Forearm board rests are attached to the tops of bellows A and B. The base of the bellows is connected to six-inch long hollow rods C and D, which slip through clamps E and F and can be adjusted up or down to accommodate the subject's arms. The rubber tubing which is attached to each of the tapered rods C and D passes under the chair seat and is joined to two ends of a hollow tee fitting, G. Another length of rubber tubing is connected to the third outlet of the tee fitting, G, and it leads (see top arrow) to the sensitive bellows within the lie-detector itself. By this method pressure exerted on one or both arm rests forces the air in the bellows through the rubber tubing and into the instrument bellows, thereby increasing its air pressure and actuating the arm recording pen (Fig. 3-D). (Cont. bottom of p. 95).

---

would breathe "fast". He also learned that blood pressure "slows up and goes fast" during the telling of a lie, so he "pressed his hand down hard to beat it". In still another case a guilty subject admitted that during the test he clamped his fingers around the end of the chair upon which his hand rested. (These case experiences were encountered before the subsequently described instrument was available for use during the tests.)

Where the deliberate attempt to distort the blood pressure tracing consists of a movement of the cuff-bearing arm, the resulting tracing is entirely different in nature from the result of a distortion induced by the sudden application or release of pressure. In the former instance a gross movement of the cuff-bearing arm produces a sharp upward deflection of the tracing which immediately returns to the original baseline (see Fig. 66-A). However, when a deflection is produced by the prompt application of pressure, the tracing thus deflected will not return to the original baseline until the pressure is released (see Fig. 66-B), and if the deflection is produced by an immediate release of pressure maintained at the outset of the test, the tracing thus deflected will not return to its former baseline until the pressure is reapplied (see Fig. 66-C).

As a result of these various experiments, and of actual case observations of what appeared to be the effects of the application of muscular pressure, an auxiliary lie-detector unit was constructed for the purpose of recording such muscular activity. This unit, as shown in Figure 67, consists essentially of a chair equipped with a set of metal bellows for picking up movements and pressures in the muscles of the arms and legs. Hollow rubber tubing leading to a more sensitive bellows arrangement within the lie-detector itself and a set of recording pens complete the instrumentation for this

---

H is a movable and adjustable thigh board which is cut out of the chair seat itself. The under portion of this board is screwed to dual bellows, J and K. The base of these bellows is fastened securely to a metal bar, below the seat, which is part of the raising and lowering mechanism. This horizontal metal bar, to which the bellows are fastened, is attached to the wide prongs of the "wishbone" brace under the seat. The top open ends of the "wishbone" brace are hinged to the front of the chair and protrudes back to the rear underside of the chair, forming the "wishbone" handle. By this handle, the "wishbone" brace can be raised upward or downward from the rear of the chair, thereby raising or lowering the seat bellows. When the desired height of the bellows has been reached the single strand metal handle of the "wishbone" brace can be slipped into a perforated narrow flat piece of metal (L) which stabilizes the position of the seat bellows throughout the test.

The air in the dual seat bellows communicates from one to the other by means of two short lengths of rubber tubing, the ends of which are attached to tee connection M under the seat. The third outlet of the tee connection is attached to a length of rubber tubing leading (see lower arrow) to the bellows within the instrument itself. As with the arm bellows, pressure exerted on the thigh bellows forces the air through the rubber tubing into the instrument bellows and thereby actuates the recording pen (Fig. 3-H).

The air communication between the chair bellows and the instrument bellows operates as a closed pneumatic system. The air displacement is caused by pressures exerted by the forearms or thighs.

The same type of open bellows is used for the muscular movement recording as was described in Figure 4-A, B.

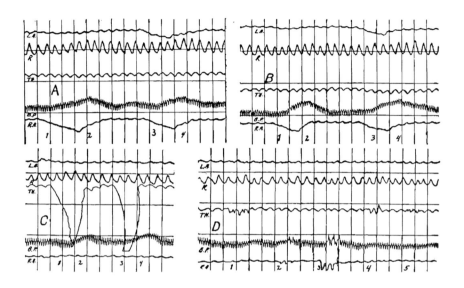

Fig. 68. Patterns of Muscular Movements in Experimental Records

The letter symbols, L.A., R.A., TH., R. and B.P., below each tracing signifies the recordings of the left forearm muscles, the right forearm muscles, the thigh muscles, the respiration and the blood pressure.

A. At 1, gradual pressure exerted on the right forearm; at 2, pressure released; at 3, gradual pressure exerted simultaneously on both forearms; at 4, pressure released. Note deflection of the R.A. recording at 1; and at 3, both L.A. and R.A. recordings deflected. Each exertion is accompanied by a blood pressure increase.

B. At 1, contraction or tension of the muscles of the right forearm and hand; at 2, muscles relaxed; at 3, muscles of both forearms and hands contracted simultaneously; at 4, muscles relaxed. Blood pressure increase at 1 and 3; also at 1 a downward reflection of R.A. recording; at 3, both L.A. and R.A. tracings are deflected.

C. At 1, pressure exerted on both feet by pushing down against the floor; at 2, release of pressure; at 3, muscles in both thighs contracted; at 4, thigh muscles relaxed. Blood pressure increases indicated at 1 and 3, along with downward deflection of the thigh recording.

D. At 1, knees moved together slightly (in and out); at 2, fingers of right hand moved; at 3, right hand moved; at 4, right foot moved by pivoting on the heel; at 5, toes moved. Note distortion in thigh tracing at 1, 4 and 5, as well as distortion of the R.A. recording at 2 and 3.

(Since the above records were made, a change has been made in the instrument by means of which one pen will record muscular activity in either or both arms, so that only two instead of three tracings are made of muscular activity.)

purpose.[50] The type of muscular activity tracings obtainable from the unit is illustrated in the experimental records shown in Figure 68.

In addition to recording muscular movements and unobserved muscular pressures for the purpose of distinguishing induced blood pressure changes from deception stimulated responses, the muscular activity tracings also occasionally furnish independent deception criteria. In fact, there are occasions when evidence of muscular pressures during a test furnishes the only indication of deception. (See for illustrations of muscular activity criteria, Figs. 69 to 75.)

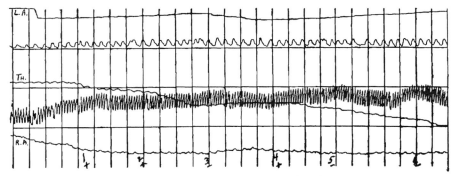

FIG. 69. Although this record of a lying subject produced no significant responses in blood pressure or respiration when he was questioned about a burglary, the application of muscular pressure in the arms and particularly in the thigh (TH.) suggested the probability of deception. A subsequent interrogation based upon an assumption of guilt resulted in the subject's confession.

[50] Various types of body movements have been recorded by both physiologists and psychologists, although neither the mechanism nor the method described herein had been previously employed. See Jacobson, E., *op. cit. supra* note 46, and Gaskill, H. V., "The Objective Measurement of Emotional Reactions", Gen. Psych. Monog., **14**: 177–280 (1933); Cason, H., and Cason, E. B., "Affectivity in Relation to Breathing and Gross Bodily Movements", J. Gen. Psychol., **9**: 130–156 (1933); and Burtt, A., "Motor Concomitants in Word Association", J. of Exp. Psych., **19**: 51–64 (1936). A few psychologists have recorded motor reactions, especially tremor as related to deception. See Luria, A. V., *The Nature of Human Conflicts* (translated from the Russian and edited by Horsley Gantt, 1932), and Runkel, J. E., "Luria's Motor Method and Word Association in the Study of Deception", J. Gen. Psych., **15**: 23–27 (1936).

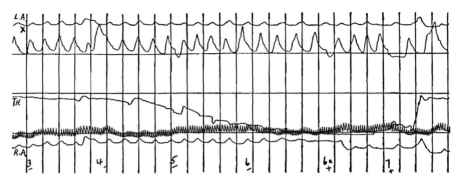

FIG. 70. As in the preceding illustration, the only clue as to this subject's deception and guilt regarding a robbery was furnished by the tracings which revealed the application of muscular pressure, particularly in the thigh (TH.). He confessed after the examiner's subsequent interrogation.

Observe in this case that the subject's blood pressure was unaffected by the exertion of muscular pressure. Although muscular pressure usually effects a blood pressure change there are some cases, such as this one, where there is no accompanying blood pressure change.

The greatest thigh (TH.) activity occurred just before, during, and after the asking of question 5, which pertained to his participation in the robbery. This muscular activity did not subside until after irrelevant question 7 was asked.

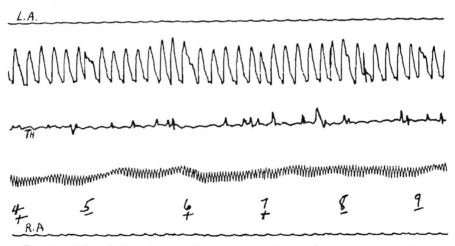

FIG. 71. Although there is a significant response in blood pressure and respiration at 5, when this subject was asked whether he committed the murder under investigation, the evidence of toe movements in the thigh muscular activity tracing TH. was an additional indication of deception. Following the test the subject confessed his guilt.

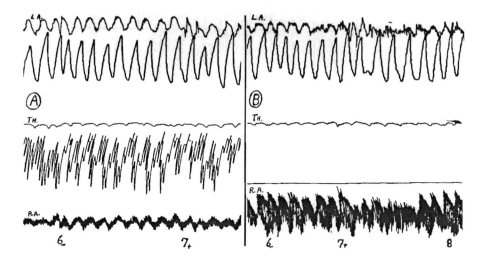

FIG. 72. The subject in this case had been previously examined in a police laboratory as a suspect in a sex offense (indecent liberties with a child) investigation. After having there confessed his guilt, he was formally charged with the offense. At the preliminary hearing his attorney asked the presiding judge for permission to have another test made in a private laboratory so that the lawyers as well as the judge might have the benefit of an "impartial" test report.

The judge acceded to counsel's request and in the subsequent tests it was apparent that the subject—now better informed of the nature of the test and presumably also as to possible ways to "beat it"—was resorting to arm muscular pressure in an effort to distort his test record. Observe in A, a portion of one of his records, the evidence of muscular pressure in the right arm tracing, R.A. Notice also the evidence of some such activity in the erratic blood pressure tracing. On test B the examiner left the blood pressure cuff uninflated, to be sure that the muscular activity on A was not produced by cuff discomfiture. Here, on B, however, the subject increased his efforts to deceive by applying greater muscular pressure. A consideration of all these various factors left no doubt as to the validity of the subject's police laboratory confession.

The Psychogalvanic Skin Reflex or Electrodermal Response

In addition to blood pressure, pulse, respiration, and muscular activity, tracings, a recording may be made of another physiological phenomenon— the psychogalvanic skin reflex, usually referred to as the G.S.R. and otherwise known also as the electrodermal response.

The instrumentation for this purpose consists of an electrical device for recording changes or variations in the conductance of external current between the palmar and dorsal surfaces of the subject's hand (or of the fingers, etc.) to which are attached electrodes charged with an imperceptible

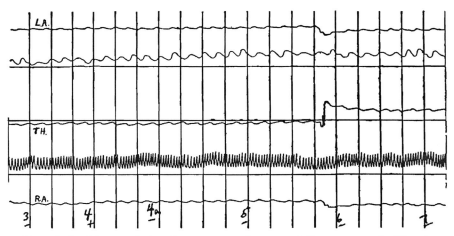

FIG. 73. In this record of an innocent murder suspect there was no significant response in blood pressure or respiration to the known lie at control question *6*, but observe the evidence of muscular pressure changes at that question. At *6* pressure was exerted by the left arm (L.A.), and the right arm (R.A.), while at the same time there was a release in thigh pressure (TH). This evidence of muscular activity at control question *6* (as well as the rise in respiration baseline up to *6*) indicated deception at that point. The absence of any such changes when questions were asked concerning the murder indicated that subject's innocence, a conclusion later verified as accurate by another person's confession.

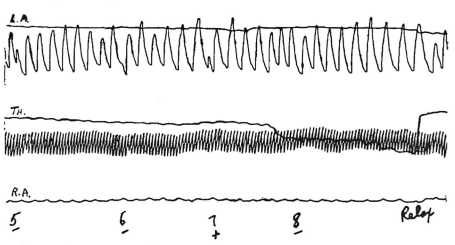

FIG. 74. The evidence of thigh muscular pressure (TH.) at guilt complex question *8* was helpful in reaching a correct diagnosis regarding this subject's innocence of a murder about which he was questioned at *5*. Observe the evidence of the release in pressure at the point where the subject was told to "relax". The muscular activity at *8* seems to indicate the subject's greater concern over the fictitious offense than over the actual one at *5*, a circumstance indicative of truthtelling at *5*. (This subject's innocence was later verified by the actual murderer's confession.)

100

current of electricity. (For a diagrammatic sketch of the galvanometer system see Figure 75.) With the Reid Polygraph, as well as with other polygraphs containing such a unit, a recording of the G.S.R. is made simultaneously with the blood pressure-pulse and respiration changes.

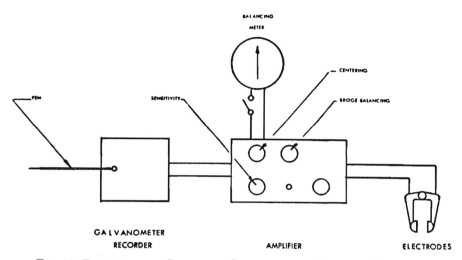

FIG. 75. DIAGRAMMATIC SKETCH OF GALVANOMETER UNIT FOR RECORDING THE PSYCHOGALVANIC SKIN REFLEX (G. S. R.)

The electrodes, cushioned by sponges dipped in a salt solution, are attached to the palmar and dorsal surfaces of the subject's hand. The bridge is balanced by adjusting the bridge balancing knob until the arrow points to zero (as indicated) on the balancing meter. The sensitivity is adjusted by slowly turning the sensitivity knob clockwise until a slight deflection from center is recorded by the pen. The pen may then be adjusted to the center of the chart by the centering knob. This unit should be operated at the lowest sensitivity possible so that minor and insignificant responses will not register.

A unique advantage to the unit illustrated is that it is equippped with an automatic centering device. Due to the centering action of the amplifier circuit the pen will return to the center of the chart in five to seven seconds after the full excursion of the pen. This action obviates the necessity of manually centering the pen during the test. With this unit, however, the examiner must refrain from asking a test question until the automatic centering device has completed its cycle. (Sketch by courtesy of Robert Koller of the C. H. Stoelting Company of Chicago.)

The exact nature of the G.S.R. is not definitely known. Authorities differ considerably even as to theoretical explanations. Some believe it is due to a change in polarization of the body tissues. Others consider it to be the result of changes in the activity of the sweat pores (i.e., in quantitative changes of perspiration on the surface of the skin). Still others express the opinion that the G.S.R. is a matter of skin constriction and circulatory changes.[51] For present purposes, however, our interest is not so much with the scientific explanation of this phenomenon but rather with its possible value in deception diagnosis.

In experimental cases (i.e., card tests, etc.) a subject's G.S.R. offers a very reliable criteria of deception, permitting an accurate deception diagnosis in about nine cases out of ten.[52] (For typical G.S.R. criteria of deception in experimental cases see Figures 76 and 77.) Unfortunately, however, in actual case tests with either the control question or relevant-irrelevant question technique, a comparable degree of accuracy is unobtainable (see Fig. 78). Only occasionally in such cases is the G.S.R. helpful for deception diagnosis. In peak of tension tests in actual case situations the G.S.R. is of value more often, but even then the results are in no way comparable to those obtainable in experimental case situations. (For illustrations of helpful criteria in actual case peak of tension tests see Figures 79 and 80.)

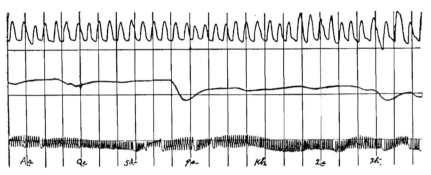

FIG. 76. In the above experimental card test record, observe on the center tracing the deviation in the G.S.R. psychogalvanic skin reflex tracing at 9s, the subject's chosen card. This response at 9s represents an increase in conductance of external current between the palmar and dorsal surfaces of the subject's hand to which the electrodes are attached.

[51] For more detailed information and references to publications regarding the psychogalvanic skin reflex, see Trovillo, P. V., "A History of Lie Detection", J. Crim. L. & Criminology, 30 (1): 104–111 (1939). Also see Trovillo, P. V., "Deception Test Criteria", J. Crim. L. & Criminology 33 (4): 338, 340 (1942).

[52] This is quite the reverse of the situation with regard to blood pressure-pulse and respiration recordings, which are much more dependable in their indications in actual cases than in cases of an experimental nature.

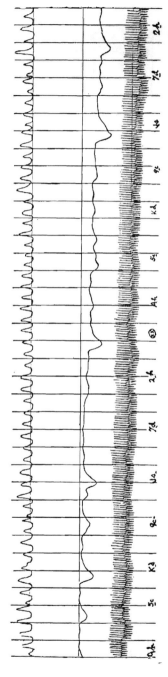

FIG. 77. Where the G.S.R. tracing contains a number of responses throughout the record, as in the above illustration, it has been found that significance may be attached to the last sizable deflection on the record or to the greatest curve deflection.

In the above illustration the tracing reaches its lowest point on the record (in both the first and the repeat test) at Js, the chosen card "lie"; on the first test (from Ah to the ringed xx) the Js response was also the last, but in the repeat test (from the ringed xx to the end of the record) it is the largest rather than the last response.

It is of interest to observe the G.S.R. response at the ringed xx, when the subject was told that the questions would be repeated. His aroused alertness or mental adjustment in an effort to successfully lie on the ensuing test occasioned a response at this point which simulates a criterion of deception.

Neither the respiration nor the blood pressure-pulse tracing disclosed the chosen card "lie" (Js), although the G.S.R. tracing indicated it quite plainly, as it usually does in experimental cases.

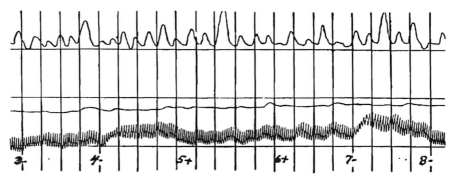

FIG. 78. Record of embezzler whose deception was indicated in the blood pressure-pulse and respiration tracings, but not in the psychogalvanic skin response. The subject in this case had been suspected of embezzling $900 from his employer. He and two other employees were given a deception test by an examiner who relied solely upon a galvanometer. The examiner reported to the employer that the results of the tests indicated the innocence of all three employees. Several months later the subject whose records appear above was arrested by the police as he attempted to dispose of a quantity of stamps stolen from the same employer. Because of his established responsibility for this offense the subject was again considered as a likely suspect in the disappearance of the $900, and the arresting officer arranged for another lie-detector test, this time with a polygraph and not just with a galvanometer.

In the above record observe the responses in blood pressure and respiration at 4 and 7, which questions pertained to his guilt regarding the $900. The G.S.R., however, contained no such criteria, as apparently was the case in the previous examination with a galvanograph alone.

Shortly after this test the subject confessed to the theft of the $900. (At the time when the above record was obtained the polarity of the external exciting potential of the galvanometer was reversed from what it was in Figures 76 and 77, so that in the above illustration, and also in the next two, a rise or upward trend in the electro-dermal response tracing represents an increase in conductance. In the two previous illustrations the conductance increase appears as drops or declines in the tracing.)

On the basis of what limited knowledge is available at the present time with regard to the G.S.R., we can only offer a conjecture as to the reasons for the differences in results obtainable in experimental cases, regular test cases, and peak of tension test cases. It does seem, however, that significant G.S.R. responses result from the rather superficial factor of a subject's alertness or attention respecting some matter about which he is lying. In an experimental card test, for instance, the primary if not the only factor involved is the alertness and attention required for lying about the one chosen card. The subject views it as a game. He does not have the fears which affect a person trying to lie about a crime or other serious incident. Nothing else is involved other than his alertness and attention. With regard to a criminal offense or other matters of serious import,

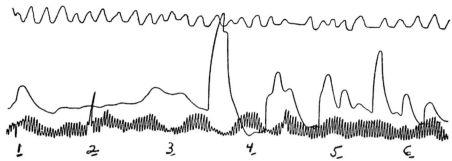

Fig. 79. This is the record of a subject who was caught stealing merchandise in the store where she was employed. Upon being interrogated by the store's investigator she admitted stealing approximately $2000 in money and merchandise. Later, after a consultation with her brother who was a court bailiff, she agreed to pay the store $1000, claiming then that the amount of $2000 which she previously admitted was an overstatement. To determine the total amount of her thefts all parties agreed to be guided by the results of a lie-detector test. In the above test the subject was asked at the various numbered questions: "Did you steal more than ——— from the store?", with the amount at *1* being $1000; at *2*, $2,000; at *3*, $3,000; at *4*, $5,000; at *5*, $7500; and at *6*, $10,000. Observe the definite change in the pattern of the G.S.R. tracing after *3* but before *4*. Following this test and without being told of its indications other than that the amount stolen was more than she admitted, the subject stated that the actual amount was $4000.

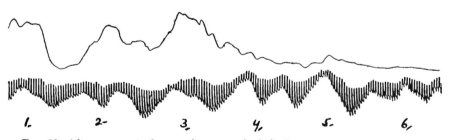

Fig. 80. After a control question test had indicated this suspected embezzler's guilt, he confessed taking $500. He was then given the above peak of tension (amounts) test, with the following questions asked at each of the various numbers *1* to *6*: "Did you steal more than ———?" The amount at *1* was $500; at *2*, $700; at *3*, $900; at *4*, $1100; at *5*, $1500; at *6*, $2000. Compare the electrodermal response tracing from *1* to *4* with the tracing from *4* on through *6*. Question *3* seemed to be the focus of the subject's attention. Following this test, and without being told what the test indicated, the subject admitted emblezzing $1000.

however, much more is involved than alertness and attention. Here the subject harbors a deep rooted, instinctual fear of detection and of the consequences of being caught. The resulting emotional disturbances seem to completely subordinate and render insignificant the minor factors of alertness and attention. Only in actual cases involving peak of tension test situations is the factor of alertness or attention of any consequence, and, as previously stated, this occurs far less frequently than it does in experimental tests.[53]

Behavior Symptoms of Lie-Detector Subjects

Every experienced lie-detector examiner must have observed instances where a subject's general conduct and unsolicited statements before, during, and after a test seem to indicate his guilt or innocence regarding the matter under investigation. In order to make an evaluation of such conduct and statements, a five-year study, of a large number of subjects in a variety of case situations, was undertaken at the laboratory of John E. Reid and Associates.[54] During this time the behavior reactions and statements of 4280 subjects were closely observed and immediately written into the case file. The final evaluation of the study had to be confined, of course, to the subjects whose guilt or innocence had been verified by trustworthy con-

[53] In contrast to this evaluation of the G.S.R. in actual case situations, Summers and MacNitt have considered the G.S.R. of greater value than blood pressure and respiration. However, their reports are based upon experiences with a small number of actual cases.

Sumners claimed 98–100 per cent accuracy for his "pathometer", and stated that it was "quite impossible for anyone so to control his emotions as to deceive the experienced interpreter of the records". From his testimony in the *Kenny* case (*infra* p. 123), it will be noted that Sumners had only examined forty-nine actual case suspects, as against six thousand experimental subjects. Having learned of no subsequent contradictory evidence in his actual case tests, Sumners concluded that the instrument was operating with an accuracy of 100 per cent. The fallacy in this line of reasoning is obvious, of course. For information regarding Sumners' contention, see his article entitled "Science Can Get the Confession" in Fordham L. Rev. 8: 334 (1939).

MacNitt's report was based upon fifty-nine embezzlement cases in which he used a modified Esterline-Angus Model A W Ammeter, which circuit he considered more satisfactory than the usual Wheatstone Bridge arrangement. See MacNitt, R. D., "In Defense of the Electrodermal Response and Cardiac Amplitude as Measures of Deception", J. Crim. L. & Criminology 33 (3): 266 (1942). Along with the electrodermal response, MacNitt records, by means of an electrical stethoscope placed over the heart, the "cardiac rate and amplitude".

[54] The analysis of the data in this study was made by Richard O. Arther of John E. Reid and Associates. The discussion as here presented of behavior symptoms originally appeared in an article by John E. Reid and Richard O. Arther in the Journal of Criminal Law, Criminology, and Police Science for July-August, 1953.

fessions. In its ultimate analysis the study was based upon observations and data regarding 486 verified guilty and 323 verified innocent subjects who were suspected of various criminal offenses.[55]

The behavior symptoms of the guilty and the innocent were found to differ widely in some respects, while in others they were quite similar. Naturally, no specific type of behavior—even though it is highly typical of one or the other group—should ever be considered proof of guilt or innocence, because there are or may be some exceptions to each general rule. Nevertheless, an examiner will find it helpful at times to consider the probable significance of a subject's behavior pattern.

Behavior Symptoms of the Guilty

As might be assumed, a guilty subject is usually far from anxious to take a lie-detector test. None of the 486 verified guilty subjects examined during the five-year study period had requested the lie-detector test. In a few instances, however, an effort was made to deceive the examiner into believing that the subject himself was the one who originally suggested the test. Guilty subjects will frequently attempt to postpone the date for their examination to a later one than that suggested by the investigators. Guilty subjects who are not in custody, as in personnel investigations, also have a characteristic tendency to be late for their test appointment. They also have a tendency to fail to appear at all on the date of their original appointment.

Once in the examining room the guilty person often looks very worried and is highly nervous. This nervousness is manifested in a variety of ways, e.g., acting aggressive, having a bitter attitude, appearing to be in a shocked condition, experiencing mental blocks, being evasive, having an extremely dry mouth, continually sighing or yawning, refusing to look the examiner in the eye, and moving about. Sometimes he is too friendly or too polite.

Guilty subjects repeatedly feel it necessary to explain before the examination why their responses might mislead the examiner into believing that they are lying. Hence, they complain of being nervous, and if that doesn't seem to impress the examiner, they further emphasize their "nervous condition" or mention a physical defect which they may or may not actually have. Also, they frequently feel it necessary to assure the examiner that

[55] The entire group of 4280 subjects does not include personnel subjects tested as applicants for employment, nor does it include employees who are examined periodically as a check on their honesty in handling the affairs of their employers. In other words, any personnel subject included in this study was examined as a suspected criminal offender.

they are very religious, hoping that the examiner will dismiss them as innocent because of their alleged righteousness.

Guilty subjects sometimes claim that the apparatus is causing them physical pain. They do this for at least one of several reasons. First, they hope that the examiner will turn off the instrument, remove the apparatus, apologize for the pain that was caused, and report to the investigators that this subject cannot be examined because of his great pain sensitivity. Second, it provides them with an excuse for not sitting still and thereby preventing the examiner from obtaining a satisfactory recording. Third, they are hoping that the examiner, when interpreting the record, will wrongly decide that their guilt responses are pain responses and report them innocent.

During this five-year research period, it was found that approximately one out of five guilty subjects purposely attempted to distort his lie-detector records so that the examiner could not tell if he were innocent or guilty. Wiggling the toes, applying muscular pressure, moving the arms, coughing, sniffing, yawning, changing the breathing rate, and talking are some of the methods that are used by guilty subjects for this purpose.

Since the entire lie-detector situation is unpleasant to most guilty subjects, they usually want to leave the examining room as soon as possible. Therefore, they inquire after the first test as to how they came out, ask if the examination isn't over yet, complain that the examination is taking much too long, seek a speedy release by alleging that they have another appointment, or refuse to continue with the examination. When leaving they often quickly shake the examiner's hand and hurry out of the laboratory.

Behavior Symptoms of the Innocent

Because everyone given a lie-detector examination is suspected of some wrong-doing, innocent subjects are usually very glad to be given an opportunity to prove their innocence. Often they have requested it so that no suspicion will be directed toward them. This belief that the innocent have in the accuracy of the lie-detector, and that they will be exonerated, is usually shown by their attitude. This attitude is one of genuine confidence in both the machine and the examiner. Because of this confidence they regard the examination as an experience they will want to relate to their family and friends.

Innocent subjects may refer to their nervousness, but after the assurance of the examiner that nervousness makes no difference, they are usually convinced and make no further reference to it. Innocent subjects are often at ease, light-hearted, and talkative. However, they are very sincere and their straight-forwardness is displayed when they discuss the case during the interview.

Their attitude is later manifested by their giving complete cooperation during the test. Of the 323 verified innocent subjects, not one of them purposefully attempted to distort his lie-detector records. However, while being cooperative and sincere, innocent subjects are not overly polite or solicitous.

Behavior Symptoms Common to Both Guilty and Innocent

Some behavior symptoms are exhibited almost equally by both guilty and innocent subjects. Anger is one of these symptoms. So, as regards the angry subject, the value of the test should be explained at the beginning of the interview and then demonstrated by a card test. As a rule, the innocent-angry subject becomes much more relaxed and jovial, while the guilty-angry subject often becomes more abusive and argumentative, sometimes to such an extent that he refuses to continue any further with the tests.

Impertinence is similarly shown by both types of subjects, but it is usually confined to the "teen-age" group. They display this symptom because of resentment against authority and as an effort at bravado. Consequently, little significance can be placed upon this as to guilt or innocence. A guilty woman may be impertinent, as part of her defense mechanism, but this trait is also occasionally observable in an innocent woman who is resentful toward the examiner because of his non-belief in her oral plea of innocence. The guilty man may be impertinent because he knows he is caught and feels he must show defiance and lack of fear.

Quietness, another behavior symptom common to both, can be generally categorized as to whether it is quietness of the guilty or that of the innocent. The guilty-quiet try to blend in with the surroundings and become as inoffensive as possible. Often they are afraid to speak for fear of trapping themselves. The innocent-quiet are seemingly only quiet because they are either afraid or awed by the situation and are waiting for the interview to begin. When they are relieved, they usually become more responsive and begin to talk quite freely. However, the guilty-quiet subject rarely, if ever, changes from his non-talkative state.

Frequently both types of subjects display interest in the lie-detector. They inquire as to the types of recording, whether they will receive an electric shock, what the various attachments are for, and whether the examiner can tell them if their blood pressure is high. Also, both occasionally ask if the lie-detector really works. When told it does, the innocent are usually satisfied, while the guilty often make a caustic comment, such as, "But the courts don't think so".

Both the guilty and the innocent alike often make some half-humorous comment when entering the examining room, e.g., "Boy, the electric chair", or, "Now I'll know how the hot seat feels".

A definite advantage can be gained from observing and classifying a subject's behavior symptoms. As was mentioned previously, the advantage is not in determining whether he is guilty or innocent, since practically all behavior symptoms are subject to general rule exceptions. The real value of studying and classifying a subject's behavior symptoms is for the purpose of determining the particular subject's attitude towards the entire lie-detector situation. Thus, the examiner will know whether the card test should be given at the beginning of the interview or at its regular time, what the subject should be told about the lie-detector and its workings, how the interview should be conducted and, generally, how this subject should be handled. When a subject, regardless of guilt or innocence, is of a certain behavior pattern, he is treated in a certain, specific manner.

If he is a highly nervous person, he must be quieted. If he is angry, he must be appeased. If he is quiet, he must be reassured. When these and similar procedures are followed with the guilty, he will receive no emotional relief when the lie-detector test is conducted. However, if he is innocent, he will usually be sufficiently relieved by these procedures. In both cases, more easily interpreted lie-detector records will result.

The lie-detector examiner should be able to recognize each subject's various behavior symptoms and then be able to determine the suitable procedure to be followed. If this is properly done, the writers are confident that fewer errors will result and that a substantial reduction in indefinite reports will follow.

Practical Utility and Accuracy of Lie-Detector Tests

Lie-detector tests—with instruments recording such physiological phenomena as changes in blood pressure, pulse, respiration, psychogalvanic skin reflex, and muscular activity—are of great practical utility in both criminal and personnel investigations, provided the examinations are conducted by competent and experienced examiners. In the first place, with the aid of the lie-detector technique, it is possible to detect deception with much greater accuracy than is otherwise attainable. Secondly, the instrument, the tests, and the accompanying procedures have a decided psychological effect in inducing confessions from guilty individuals. Thirdly, by means of the technique innocent persons are readily eliminated as suspects, thus sparing them any further fear, embarrassment, or inconvenience, and at the same time expediting the search for the guilty offender. Fourthly, the use and availability of the lie-detector technique will reduce the extent of "third degree" practices, especially upon innocent suspects.

Since confirmatory or contradictory evidence is not always forthcoming after a deception diagnosis has been made in an actual case, exact figures are unavailable as to the accuracy of lie-detector test results. There is a sound basis, however, for making an estimate. The following estimate is based upon the experience of the examiners on the staff of John E. Reid and Associates during the last five year period. This estimate accords to the lie-detector technique, *when applied under the most favorable conditions*, an accuracy of 95 per cent, with a 4 per cent margin of indefinite determinations and a 1 per cent margin of possible error. In other words, in the examination of 100 subjects the examiner may make a definite and accurate diagnosis as to the guilt or innocence of 95 subjects. As to 4 of the subjects the examiner may be unable to arrive at a definite opinion as to guilt or innocence. With the 1 remaining subject the examiner may make an erroneous diagnosis of guilt or innocence.

The foregoing estimate involved a study of 4280 subjects who were suspected of criminal offenses.[56] Of these 4280 subjects, 64.5 per cent were reported innocent, 31.1 per cent as guilty, and 4.4 per cent were reported as indefinite in their indications. The percentage of known error was .0007 per cent—in other words 3 known errors out of 4093 subjects. (This figure of 4093 subjects represents the total number less the group of indefinites.) On the basis of known figures, therefore, the percentage of error is considerably lower than the estimated one per cent. There is no assurance, of course, that all errors were discovered. It does appear, however, that the one per cent estimate will cover whatever errors may be present. Following is a complete statistical tabulation of numbers and percentages, as well as of pertinent verification data:

Total number of criminal offense subjects. 4280

	no.		per cent
Reported innocent.	2759		64.5
Reported guilty	1334		31.1
Reported indefinite.	187		4.4
Total	4280		100.0
Number of subjects reported guilty who were interrogated with the aim of obtaining a confession . . .	791	or 59.2	per cent
Number of confessions obtained from above group of subjects. . . .	486	or 61.4	per cent
Number of subjects reported innocent who were verified innocent by another's confession	323	or 11.7	per cent
Number of verified errors. .	3	or .0007	per cent

[56] See *supra* note 55.

The difference between our present estimate of 95 per cent accuracy and that stated in the 1948 edition of this book reflects essentially the effects of the improved procedures and practices in reducing the percentage of cases in which indefinite opinions were necessary. By the earlier "relevant-irrelevant" technique the percentage of indefinite reports was between 15 and 20 per cent. It is now reducible to 5 per cent by the use of the currently available "control questioning" technique and the examination procedures and practices previously described.

In order to thus reduce the percentage of indefinite reports and achieve an accuracy approximating 95 per cent, a number of factors must prevail, and they did prevail in the examinations involved in the five-year study from which we derived this percentage of accuracy. First of all, and for reasons to be subsequently discussed in more detail, the subject must be in a satisfactory physical and mental condition; he must not have been extensively interrogated or physically abused. In this respect, of course, the private consultant has an advantage over the examiner in a police department whose subjects sometimes have been interrogated rather extensively before their scheduled lie-detector test.

In addition to the prerequisite of a subject's satisfactory condition, the attainment of an accuracy approaching 95 per cent will depend to a considerable extent upon the basic qualifications, training, experience, and general competency of the examiner. An examiner lacking in the essential qualifications, which are later outlined in the ensuing discussion of "The Qualifications of an Examiner", will meet with great difficulty in attaining the efficiency herein suggested. And at this point mention should be made of the fact that in considering the foregoing estimate of the technique's accuracy, it must be understood that the percentage of actual error to be found in any examiner's results will depend to a large extent upon his own cautiousness in resorting to indefinite diagnoses. The more he is inclined to render positive opinions in all his cases—as the novice and inexperienced examiner is so apt to do—the greater are his chances of actual error. Even as regards the experienced, competent examiner, the chief source of error with the lie-detector technique is in its failure to detect deception in a guilty individual rather than in the misinterpretation of an innocent subject's records. But here again we speak with reference to the type of examiner who is quite willing to accept the technique in the light of its undeniable limitations, and who will not hesitate to render an indefinite report whenever there is a reasonable doubt in his own mind.

This lie-detector technique's limitation of indefinite reporting should be viewed in the same light as the indefinite reports which must occasionally be made by the fingerprint expert, the document examiner, the firearms identification technician, etc. For instance, if a finger mark at a crime scene is only a smudge, we do not consider this a discredit to the science of fingerprint identification. If the significant markings on a bullet have been destroyed by the bone it shattered, and no helpful comparison can be made between it and a test bullet, we still maintain confidence in the science of firearms identification. There is no reason, therefore, why any derogatory implication should be attached to the lie-detector technique because of the occasional unfitness of the person upon whom a deception diagnosis has been attempted.

The instrument used is of importance, not as to make or model, but only to the extent that it must furnish a satisfactory recording of at least blood pressure-pulse and respiration and not just one of the physiological phenomena considered helpful for deception diagnosis.

Apart from the value of the lie-detector technique in determining the guilt or innocence of a subject, it possesses another quality of much merit, and that is the psychological effect it has in inducing admissions or confessions from guilty individuals.

There have been innumerable instances of confessions made as a result of a mere proposal to have a suspect submit to a lie-detector test. On occasion suspects have confessed their guilt while waiting in the laboratory to be tested. There are also instances when suspects have confessed immediately after the examiner has adjusted the instrument preparatory to making the test. (At this point mention should be made of the fact that the writers know of no case where a false confession has resulted because of the psychological effect of the instrument and its attending technique.)

Once a test has been administered to a guilty individual it is extremely effective to display the records to him and point out the deception criteria —at the same time reminding the subject that the recordings represent his own heart beats, his own blood pressure changes, etc., and not those picked up by the machine out of thin air or placed there by the examiner. At times it is amazing to observe the shocking effect such a display of lie-detector records will have upon a person, who up until then has maintained considerable poise and outward composure. It is also helpful, on appropriate occasions, to show a subject the response at his chosen card question and have him compare it with the lie responses on his regular test records.

SOME ADVOIDABLE PITFALLS

Experience on the part of competent examiners, who restrict their practice largely to personnel investigations, indicates that their percentage of accuracy far exceeds that of examiners in police cases. The difference may be attributed in large part to the fact that the personnel investigator's subjects are in much better condition for their tests. They have not been physically abused and usually not extensively interrogated.

What can the police-employed lie-detector examiner do to remedy the present situation? Three things:

1. Establish a practice of refusing to test a subject who has been physically abused.

2. Where the circumstances are in the extreme, refuse to examine a subject who has been extensively interrogated, even though no direct physical abuse has been administered.

3. Try to develop a procedure within the particular police department whereby lie-detector tests will ordinarily be conducted during the early stages of an investigation or interrogation rather than as a last resort when all else has failed.

To some persons these suggestions may appear to be naïvely conceived. They will say that only a very unrealistic individual will expect a lie-detector examiner who is working in or for a police department to adopt such an attitude and survive the consequences. In the writers' opinion, however, a person who does not have the necessary courage or the ability to meet the situation is unfit for the role of lie-detector examiner.

The Qualifications Of An Examiner

In assessing the qualifications of a lie-detector examiner, it must be remembered that his task is not simply the manipulation of an instrument; in fact, the actual operation of the instrument itself requires very little ability or training. The examiner's most important task and responsibility consists of properly conducting the examination and making an accurate diagnosis. Along with this skill he must be able to perform the next most important task—the skillful interrogation of a guilty subject for the purpose of obtaining a confession.

To qualify for this two-fold assignment, an examiner need not be a physician or a psychologist, but he must be an intelligent person with a reasonably good educational background, preferably college training. He should have an intense interest in the work itself, a good practical understanding of human nature, and suitable personality traits which may be evident from his otherwise general ability to "get along" with people and to be well liked by his friends and associates. No amount of training or experience will overcome the lack of these necessary qualifications.

Many persons now functioning as lie-detector examiners do not possess these basic qualifications. They should never have been encouraged to embark upon such a career. Unfortunately, however, a number of established examiners have conducted schools for trainees and have followed a practice of accepting as students practically anyone who applied with the necessary tuition fee or who had been selected by his own police department or governmental agency to attend the school at his employer's expense.

A person without a better-than-average intelligence, a fair educational background, and a good practical understanding of human nature, will inevitably make more mistakes than a trained individual with the necessary basic qualifications. The basically unqualified examiner is the one who, in view of his own personal shortcomings, will feel impelled to make a definite diagnosis in practically every case, and for that reason is more likely to make outright mistakes. To him an indefinite report is an admission of personal failure. He is also less likely to succeed in private practice as a lie-detector examiner if he makes such an attempt, and with a realization of impending failure he will be more receptive to rendering opinions favorable to that side in a controversy or investigation which is prepared to pay the higher price for a suitable opinion.

No experienced examiner who values the status of the lie-detector technique or his own reputation should accept for training, at any price, individuals who are basically unqualified.

Training

Although it is possible for a person with proper basic qualifications to ultimately develop into a competent examiner after a few months of intensive study, instruction, experimentation, and actual case observations, the desirable minimum period of training is about six months. During that time his course of study should include readings and instruction in the pertinent phases of physiology and psychology; frequent observations of an experienced examiner working on actual cases; personal experience in experimental case testing and actual case testing under an instructor's supervision; and the examination and interpretation of a considerable number of records in solved cases. His course of training should also include instruction, as well as observational and personal experience, in the application of psychological tactics and techniques for obtaining confessions or admissions from untruthful subjects.

Regardless of the time element, however, adequate training cannot be given by an instructor to more than about six persons at a time. The student in larger groups cannot acquire the necessary practical experience or receive the individual attention required from the experienced examiner. Here again, therefore, is a prevailing practice that should be modified in the interest of better examiners and fewer mistakes.

During his course of instruction the student should be made to realize fully that the technique is subject to limitations and that he should not represent it to any client as possessing any infallibility in its indications.

Specialization

Mastering the lie-detector technique is no simple matter. It requires much time and effort. In fact it requires all of one's working time and energy. An examiner cannot do justice either to the technique or to himself if one day he is a chemist, or a firearms expert, and the next day, or hour, he functions as a lie-detector examiner. Moreover, the personality requirements for a lie-detector examiner are vastly different from those of laboratory technicians generally. As a rule the man who is good with the microscope or chemicals either does not have the required interest in testing and interrogating people or else he lacks the essential personality characteristics. By this suggestion no reflection is intended, of course, upon the laboratory technicians; in fact, the situation is no better when reversed. The capable lie-detector examiner is usually a misfit when he tries to work in these other fields.

It is a mistake, therefore, for any police department to assume that laboratory personnel can be readily shifted from a chemistry section or a firearms section into the laboratory's lie-detector unit. It is also unwise for an individual to attempt to shift back and forth from the one type of work to the other. He should realize quite early in his career that the lie-detector technique is a "jealous mistress". It will demand and require his undivided attention.

Apropos of this discussion of examiner qualifications, mention should be made of the fact that since we are dealing with nothing more than *a technique*, it is not ordinarily feasible for an experienced, qualified examiner to make a diagnosis from another examiner's test records without being at the scene of the examination itself. In making a diagnosis, an examiner must not only have before him records obtained during a carefully and properly conducted test; he must have a complete account of the subject's behavior indications and the general circumstances and conditions under which the examination was conducted; and, most important of all, the diagnosing examiner must be in a position to direct some additional test variations. If the person who actually conducted the test is unable to make a diagnosis from the records, after having had before him all the essential facts as well as the subject himself, the occasion will indeed be rare when anyone else can do it from the records alone.

Future Research Possibilities in Scientific Lie Detection

Although the previously discussed psycho-physiological phenomena are the only ones which thus far have been employed extensively or considered of practical value as part of any lie-detector technique, there undoubtedly are others which could be used to good advantage.[57] As a matter of fact,

[57] Indicative of the many unexplored possibilities are the interesting "eye movement" experiments conducted by Berrien. His research was suggested by the hypothesis that deceitful persons have "shifty eyes". He photographed a spot of light

the entire field of lie detection remains a very fertile one for further research and experimentation.

There are some definite research possibilities even with the presently recorded phenomena. For instance, as regards respiration criteria, at least two challenging explorations are suggested:

1. Should two respiration recordings be made simultaneously—one from a chest pneumograph, the other from an abdominal pneumograph?

In Figure 81, two respiration recordings were made during the test of a rape suspect. Although the chest-pneumograph recording (the top tracing) revealed deception responses, better deception indications appeared in the

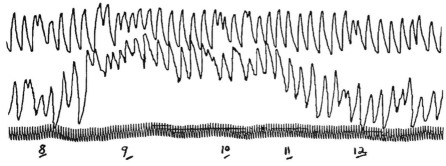

Fig. 81. In this record the top tracing was obtained from the chest pneumograph and the middle tracing from the abdominal pneumograph. Observe particularly the dramatic baseline changes in the abdominal respiration tracing, which change is only partially revealed by the chest pneumograph. The lower recording above the numbers is the blood pressure-pulse tracing. After this subject's test he confessed the rape under investigation.

abdominal-pneumograph recording (the center tracing). The latter recording shows a very significant baseline change which is only partially indicated in the chest-pneumograph recording. (After this test the subject confessed.)

---

reflected from the cornea of the eye in forty subjects, half of whom were guilty of a "laboratory crime" and half innocent. The subjects were required to look straight ahead and hold their eyes as steady as possible throughout a series of relevant and irrelevant questions. No significant differences appeared to distinguish falsehoods from truthful responses during the question period, but after a short rest the subjects again attempted to hold their eyes steady during a no-question period. "The guilty subjects improved the steadiness of their gaze while the innocent in most cases became less steady as the period progressed". The consensus of the judges gave an accuracy of 80 per cent. According to Berrien, "subsequent studies with a few criminal cases show sometimes a very noticeable increase in eye tremor after falsehoods". See Berrien, F. K., "Ocular Stability in Deception", Jr. App. Psy. 26 (1): 55–63 (1942); also same author's book, Practical Psychology (1945) 449–450.

2. The possibilities indicated in Figure 81 suggest the next question: Is any advantage to be gained from obtaining on one tracing a combined recording of the chest and abdominal respiration patterns? This is mechanically feasible, of course, by simply joining the two pneumograph tubes together by a T-connection.

In the case record shown in Figure 82, the T-connection arrangement was used to obtain a single tracing of the combined chest and abdominal respiration patterns. It contains excellent respiration deception responses

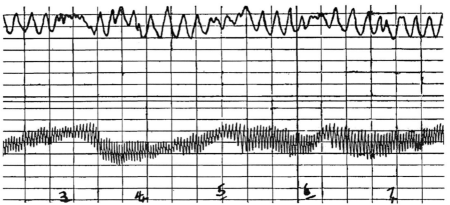

FIG. 82. The respiratory tracing in this record is a combination of both the chest and abdominal respiration recordings. It was obtained by utilizing a T-connection which joined together both the chest and abdominal pneumograph tubes. The lower recording above the numbers is the blood pressure-pulse tracing.

Notice the suppressions and specific rises in basline in the respiration at questions *3, 5* and *6*. Questions *3* and *5* pertain to the offense; *6* is the general-sex control question; *4* and *7* are irrelevant. Since a lesser change occurred in the respiration at *6* when compared to *3* and *5*, the subject was interrogated. He then confessed his guilt regarding the indecent exposure charge under investigation (see Fig. 83).

from an indecent-exposure case suspect who subsequently admitted his guilt.

The effect obtained from joining the two respiration patterns is indicated in Figure 83, in which *A* is the chest-pneumograph tracing, *B* the abdominal-pneumograph tracing, and *C* the combination tracing of both the chest and abdominal respiration patterns. *A*, *B*, and *C* in Figure 83 were from the same subject whose record appears in Figure 82. In this case it is possible that if either the chest or abdominal respiration had been recorded alone, the deception responses would not be so dramatically clear-cut.

The G.S.R. (Psychogalvanic Skin Reflex) phenomenon also offers some future research possibilities. Although its utility in actual case examinations

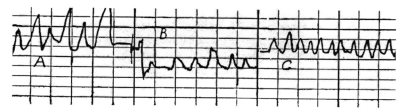

FIG. 83. The above tracings were made by the same subject whose test record is shown in Figure 82. *A* is the chest-pneumograph tracing and *B* the abdomen-pneumograph tracing, each of which was made separately and alone. *C* is the combination tracing of both the chest and the abdominal respiration.

Tracing *A* was obtained by placing a pneumograph tube around the subject's chest and recording his respiration for approximately 25 seconds. Notice the erratic nature of the recording.

A second pneumograph tube was then placed around the subject's abdomen and connected to the instrument without adjusting the centering knob on the panel. This resulted in recording *B*. Notice in *B* the lower level of the tracing on the chart, and also its small amplitude and irregular nature.

In obtaining *C*, both pneumograph tubes were left in place on the subject's chest and abdomen, but the tubes were joined together by a T-connection, and the tracing was recorded without adjusting the instrument's centering knob. This resulted in a smoother and much more regular recording of the respiration, as is also demonstrated by the same subject's actual case record (Fig. 82).

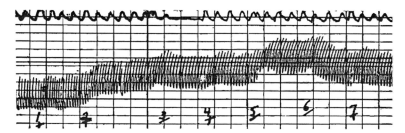

Fig. 84. This record illustrates the use of short-term answers to direct, unambiguous test questions. These answers require the usual "yes" or "no" reply, followed by a very short sentence. Examples of this type answer are, "Yes, I do", or, "No, I did not". To all questions in the above shown case record the subject replied with this "short-term answer" response ("Yes, I did", "No, I don't", etc.). Notice the complete lack of respiration distortion to all questions but *3*, a pertinent crime question, at which a suppression of approximately 9 seconds occurs. Question *5* is the other pertinent question on this test, *6* is the general control question, and *1*, *2*, *4*, and *7* are irrelevant. Because of this subject's respiration response at *3* and his significant blood pressure rise at *5* he was reported guilty. Later the subject was implicated by another's confession in the assault and battery and attempted rape, the offense under investigation. Question *3* in the above record pertains to the attempted rape, while question *5* pertains to the assault and battery.

has been rather negligible, the fact that it is very effective in experimental case situations, and occasionally helpful in actual peak of tension tests, warrants further exploration of its possibilities. It does seem, however, that

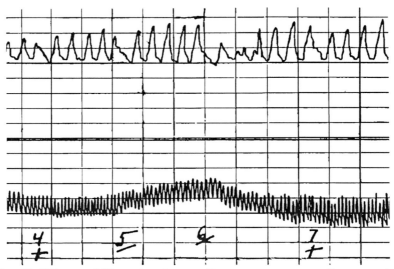

FIG. 85. This record illustrates the use of long-term answers to direct, ambiguous test questions. The answers also require the usual "yes" or "no" reply, but then a statement follows which repeats the essential points of the test questions. For example, if the question was, "Did you shoot John Jones last Saturday night?", the answer would be, "No, I did not shoot John Jones last Saturday night".

Every single-word answer ("yes" or "no") to a test question comes during the expiration cycle, which answer is often recorded on the moving chart as a small bump or notch on the down-stroke of the respiration recording pen. With all one-sentence answers, as here illustrated, the same was found to be true, except that several bumps or notches occurred during the one expiration cycle.

In the above illustration all questions were answered by the subject with this long-term answer response. (Question 4 answer is, "Yes, I did go to school", while the answer to 5 is, "No, I did not help beat up Lillian's father".) Notice the slight drawing-out and "saw tooth" pattern of the expiration cycles when each question was answered. Questions 4 and 7 are irrelevant; 5 pertinent; and 6 the general control question. Note the significant suppression in respiration at 6, which the subject later admitted to be a lie.

This record is a clear illustration of the fact that a one-sentence answer does not destroy significant deception criteria in the respiration pattern, as is generally assumed to be the case.

any such research should be directed toward ascertaining to what extent the G.S.R. may be of value as a general indication of a subject's mental cooperation or lack of mental cooperation during a test. For reasons suggested in the previous general discussion of the G.S.R., it seems that there are more latent possibilities regarding the mental cooperation factor in the G.S.R. than in determining specific deception responses.

The problem presented by a guilty person's resort to previously described "mental sets and attitudes" in an effort to avoid detection is another area for some promising research possibilities. In other words, when examining a guilty person who is attempting to "get his mind off" his offense and present predicament by "concentrating on something else", is there anything the examiner can do to render such evasion efforts unsuccessful?

It seems reasonable to suppose that if a subject had to give a full answer, instead of just a "yes" or "no" answer, in response to the examiner's questions, this requirement would prevent or at least render more difficult a subject's "concentration on something else". But it has been generally assumed that the subject's talking to that extent would materially distort the respiration tracing and render it valueless for deception criteria purposes. However, some recent preliminary study and experimentation at the laboratory of John E. Reid and Associates has indicated the fallacy of this latter notion and at the same time suggested some encouraging possibilities for coping with this troublesome type of subject (see Figs. 84 and 85).

INTERROGATION TACTICS AND TECHNIQUES

Although the psychological effect of the mere presence or use of a lie-detector is sometimes sufficient to induce a confession from a guilty subject, a period of skillful interrogation after the completion of the tests is usually required before a confession is forthcoming. The examiner's task in this respect is by no means a simple one. It usually requires considerable patience and effort, despite the assistance he derives from the psychological effect of the instrument itself.

The interrogation tactics and techniques subsequently discussed under the title of *Criminal Interrogation*, although designed primarily for use by an interrogator who does not have the assistance of a lie-detector, are nevertheless well suited for interrogations conducted by a lie-detector examiner. As a matter of fact, these various tactics and techniques were formulated as a result of case experiences in interrogating subjects immediately after they had been tested on a lie-detector.

LEGAL STATUS OF LIE-DETECTOR TEST RESULTS

Although perfection in test results is not a prerequisite to the admissibility of evidence obtainable by the use of scientific instruments or techniques, the practice has been to grant judicial recognition only after the proponents of the unprecedented evidence have shown that the instrument or technique has a reasonable measure of precision in its indications, and that it is an accepted one in the particular profession or field of science to which it belongs.[58] According to this standard of admissibility, what is —and what should be—the legal status of lie-detector test results?

PRESENT STATUS

The first appellate court decision upon the admissibility of lie-detector evidence was rendered in 1923 by a federal court in *Frye v. United States*,[59] in which the accused (on trial for murder) offered as evidence the results of a Marston "systolic blood pressure" test. The trial court refused to permit Marston to testify concerning his results, and upon appeal this ruling was affirmed. The reasons which impelled the court to arrive at the conclusion of inadmissibility are very clearly stated in the following excerpt from its reported opinion:

"Just when a scientific principle or discovery crosses the line between the experimental and demonstrable stages is difficult to define. Somewhere in this twilight zone the evidential force of the principle must be recognized, and while courts will go a long way in admitting expert testimony deduced from a well-recognized scientific principle or discovery, the thing from which the deduction is made must be sufficiently established to have gained general acceptance in the particular field in which it belongs.

"We think the systolic blood pressure deception test has not yet gained such standing and scientific recognition among physiological and psychological authorities as would justify the courts in admitting expert testimony deduced from the discovery, development, and experiments thus far made."

Ten years later the Supreme Court of Wisconsin, in *State v. Bohner*,[60] had occasion to pass upon the admissibility of lie-detector evidence. In this case defense counsel offered to prove by means of a lie-detector test the truthfulness of the defendant's alibi to a robbery charge, which offer the trial court refused. Upon appeal the Supreme Court sustained the trial court's ruling and held that although the instrument (a Keeler Polygraph) "may have some utility at present, or may ultimately be of great value in the administration of justice . . . a too hasty acceptance of it during this

[58] Wigmore, Evidence (3d ed., 1940) §990.
[59] 293 Fed. 1013 (D.C. 1923).
[60] 210 Wis. 651, 246 N.W. 314 (1933).

stage of its development may bring complications and abuses that will overbalance whatever utility it may be assumed to have".

Two cases regarding the admissibility of lie-detector evidence were decided by the New York courts in 1938. One of the cases, *People v. Kenny*,[61] was a trial court decision; the other, *People v. Forte*,[62] a decision of the New York Court of Appeals. In the *Kenny* case the defendant (on trial for robbery) offered in evidence the testimony of the late Father Summers regarding the results of a test conducted with a psychogalvanometer. Over the objection of the prosecuting attorney, the trial court admitted the evidence and permitted the jury to consider the witness' opinion as to the defendant's innocence or guilt. The court in the Kenny case apparently was impressed with Summers' assertion to the effect that his "pathometer" was "effectively 100 per cent efficient". It must be remembered, however, that this is only a trial court decision; and were it not for the New York practice of reporting decisions of its lower courts, the case would carry with it no more significance than several other similar but unreported decisions in other states. Moreover, the effect of the *Kenny* case must be viewed in the light of the later and more authoritative decision of the New York Court of Appeals in the *Forte* case.

In the *Forte* case the defendant (on trial for murder) requested the court's permission to be tested on the same instrument and by the same examiner (Summers) as in the *Kenny* case. This request was denied on the ground that despite the view taken by the court in the *Kenny* case, the validity of such a test had not been sufficiently well established to warrant its judicial acceptance. Upon appeal the trial court's ruling was affirmed by the New York Court of Appeals. The latter court decided that since the trial court record was "devoid of evidence tending to show a general scientific recognition that the pathometer possesses efficacy", the appellate court could not hold "as a matter of law that error was committed in refusing to allow the defendant to experiment with it".[63]

In a 1942 Michigan case, *People v. Becker*,[64] the defendant (on trial for manslaughter) offered in evidence the results of lie-detector tests in support of his contention that he killed the deceased in self-defense. The trial judge refused to admit the test results, and his ruling was sustained by the Michigan Supreme Court on the ground that there was no testimony in the

[61] 167 Misc. 51, 3 N.Y. Supp. (2d) 348 (1938).

[62] 167 Misc. 868, 4 N.Y. Supp. (2d) 913; 279 N.Y. 204, 18 N.E. (2d) 31 (1938).

[63] The Court of Appeals made no mention of the Kenny case, and therefore that case cannot be considered technically as overruled. Nevertheless, the significance of the Kenny case is considerably diminished by the Court of Appeals decision in the Forte case.

[64] 300 Mich. 562, 2 N.W. (2d) 503 (1942).

case to show that there exists at the present time "a general scientific recognition of such tests". The Michigan court said that "until it is established that reasonable certainty follows from such tests, it would be error to admit in evidence the result thereof".

A unique offer regarding the use of the lie-detector was made in a 1945 Missouri case, *State v. Cole.*[65] The defendant, on trial for the murder of a seven-year old child, made a motion at the beginning of the trial for a court order requiring all witnesses in the case to be given lie-detector tests. The defendant also requested that he be given a similar test. The trial court denied the motion and also refused to grant the defendant's request for a test upon himself. The Missouri Supreme Court, in addition to holding that the lie-detector technique had not gained sufficient recognition of its efficacy to warrant judicial acceptance, stated:

"In our opinion the day has not come when all the witnesses in a case can be subjected to such inquisitorial and deceptive tests (or to drugs like scopolamine, or to hypnotism) without their consent. Furthermore, such dramatics before the jury would distract them and impede the trial—this latter also because it is necessary for the inquisitor to ask both harmless, irrelevant and 'hot' questions in order to bring out the contrast in the witness' emotional responses. No doubt the lie detector is useful in the investigation of crime, and may point to evidence which is competent; but it has no place in the court room."[66]

The Supreme Court of Kansas, in the 1947 case of *State v. Lowry,*[67] reversed a trial court conviction because the prosecution had been permitted to introduce in evidence the results of lie-detector tests upon a complaining witness and a defendant accused of felonious assault. The Kansas Supreme Court held that the lie-detector technique had not yet gained sufficient scientific recognition to warrant the acceptance of test results as competent legal evidence. At the same time, however, the court pointed out that its holding should not be interpreted as discrediting the lie-detector "as an instrument of utility and value", since "its usefulness has been amply demonstrated by detective agencies, police departments and other law-enforcement agencies conducting criminal investigations".

The appellate court case which came closest to holding lie-detector test

[65] 354 Mo. 181, 188 S.W. (2d) 43 (1945).

[66] Apart from the legal problems involved, it would, as the court points out, be very impractical to attempt to conduct a lie-detector test under court room conditions. The necessary test requirements of privacy and quiet are not present in a court room. Moreover, if the party or parties involved in the litigation were tested, there ordinarily would be no necessity to test the witnesses; a test of the principals themselves will usually provide a full and complete answer to the legal inquiry. Also see *infra* f.n. 68.

[67] 163 Kans. 622, 185 Pac. (2d) 147 (1947).

results admissable as evidence is *Boeche v. State*,[68] a 1949 decision of the Supreme Court of Nebraska. The defendant had been accused of cashing a bogus check. At her trial a cashier and a saleslady from the store where the check was cashed positively identified the defendant as the check-passer. Another store manager also identified the defendant as the person for whom he cashed another bogus check the same evening as the prior occurrence. On defendant's behalf her husband and several other relatives supported her alibi that at the alleged time of the check-passing she was in another town. Defendant's counsel also offered in evidence the testimony of a lie-detector examiner regarding the results of tests he had made on the defendant, which tests, in the opinion of the examiner, indicated the defendant's innocence of the offense. The trial court refused to admit the lie-detector test results. Upon appeal from her conviction the defendant contended that the trial court erred in refusing to admit the lie-detector test results in evidence. In reversing the case on other grounds, the majority of the Nebraska Supreme Court were of the opinion that the trial court was correct in its rejection of the lie-detector evidence. They thought that if such evidence were admitted, "the vital function of cross-examination would be impaired"; that while the examiner could be cross-examined regarding his qualifications and the procedures used, "the machine itself ... would escape all cross-examination". In addition to this rather vague objection about cross-examination "impairment", the majority of the court thought that the evaluation of lie-detector test results was "too subtle a task to impose upon an untrained jury". They also found that the test had "not yet received general scientific acceptance", and that "experimenting psychologists themselves admit that a wholly accurate test is yet to be perfected". However, at least one member of the Nebraska Supreme Court, Justice Chappell, thought that the time had arrived for the judicial acceptance of lie-detector test results. He expressed the view that upon proof of an examiner's competency and evidence of general scientific recognition, the test results should be accepted by the court. Justice Chappell was of the opinion that the failure of the judiciary to embrace scientific aids of this type "will only serve to question the ability of the courts to efficiently administer justice".

In the 1950 California case of *People v. Wochnick*,[69] involving a prosecution for murder, the trial court admitted in evidence the testimony of a lie-detector examiner regarding his conversation with the defendant and the results of a test (apparently a "peak of tension" test) in which the defendant had been shown five knives and asked whether he had seen each

[68] 151 Nebr. 368, 37 N.W. (2d) 593 (1949).
[69] 98 Calif App. (2d) 124, 219 Pac. (2d) 70 (1950).

knife before. According to the examiner the subject "reacted" to the knife used in the killing. The examiner also testified that on several tests involving the display of the five knives, the defendant kept his eyes closed (presumably for the purpose of avoiding any significant reaction when the fatal knife was placed before him). At the conclusion of the tests the examiner told the defendant: "If you can explain these things to me [apparently referring to the knife test] I wish you would". To this the defendant replied, "I cannot explain that". In its attempt to support the trial court's ruling in allowing the introduction of the test results and the examiner's conversation with the defendant, the prosecution contended on appeal that whatever error the trial court committed initially had been cured by its instruction to the jury to disregard any part of the examiner's statements regarding his interpretation of the test results. The prosecution also contended that the defendant's statement that he could not explain the reaction on the knife test was a tacit admission of having previously seen the fatal knife. Both contentions were rejected by the California Court of Appeal and the judgment of the conviction was reversed. The appellate court said that despite the trial court's instruction, "the evidence of the partial results of the lie-detector test with respect to the defendant's reaction upon being shown the murder weapon was indelibly implanted on the minds of the jurors and could not but have had a prejudicial effect". The appellate court also decided that the defendant's answer, "I cannot explain that", did not indicate a consciousness of guilt or an acquiescence of the truth of the examiner's statement regarding the reaction to the display of the fatal knife; consequently, the trial court erred in permitting the examiner to testify as to what he told the defendant regarding the fatal knife reaction.

In the 1950 North Dakota case of *State v. Pusch*,[70] the defendant offered in evidence the results of a lie-detector test as well as the testimony of a hypnotist, all to the effect that he was innocent of the crime with which he was charged. The trial court's ruling rejecting the evidence was sustained by the North Dakota Supreme Court.

The defendant in the 1951 Oklahoma case of *Henderson v. State*[71] unsuccessfully offered in evidence the results of both a lie-detector test and a "truth-serum" test to prove his innocence of a rape accusation. Upon appeal the Oklahoma Criminal Court of Appeals reviewed the various decided cases and some of the writings upon the subject. It concluded that "neither the lie-detector nor the truth-serum tests have gained that standing and scientific recognition nor demonstrated that degree of dependability to justify the courts in approving their use in the trial of criminal cases".

[70] 77 N. D. 860, 46 N. W. (2d) 508 (1950).
[71] 230 Pac. (2d) 495 (Okla. Cr. App., 1951).

In the 1952 Texas case of *Peterson v. State*,[72] the defendant, on trial for forgery, offered in evidence the testimony of a lie-detector examiner regarding the results of a test conducted on the defendant. The trial court refused to admit the test results as evidence, and upon appeal this ruling was sustained by the Texas Court of Criminal Appeals, for the following reasons: In the first place, stated the appellate court, the defendant had failed to make an offer of proof as to what the excluded evidence would have shown; and, secondly, since the test results are not admitted at the present time as evidence on behalf of the prosecution they cannot be used on behalf of the defendant.

The latest decision appears to be the Florida case of *Kaminski v. State*,[73] which involved an attempt at the indirect use of lie-detector test results. The prosecution's chief witness had been subjected to a rigid and effective cross-examination, after which the prosecutor tried to rehabilitate the witness' credibility by asking him whether he had taken a lie-detector test. The trial court permitted the question to be answered, but upon appeal this ruling was held to be improper. The Florida Supreme Court considered the trial court's ruling to be the equivalent of an outright admission of the test results in evidence, which it was not authorized to do.

Since all of the appellate court decisions have held lie-detector evidence inadmissible, we must conclude, therefore, that at the present time the test results have no judicial recognition. As will be subsequently explained, however, the one possible exception or qualification to this general statement is to be found in the view taken by some courts which have approved the admission of test results where the parties have entered into an agreement and stipulation to that effect.

WHAT SHOULD BE THE STATUS OF LIE-DETECTOR TEST RESULTS?

Are the results of lie-detector tests now ready for judicial recognition? In other words: does the present technique possess "a reasonable measure of precision in its indications", and is it an "accepted" one in the fields of science to which it belongs?

Although the present lie-detector technique, when used under the favorable conditions previously outlined, permits a very high degree of accuracy, there are other factors to consider before concluding that the time has now arrived for the admission of test results in evidence. First of all, consideration must be given to the fact that the technique is still in a relatively early

[72] 247 S.W. (2d) 110 (Tex. Cr. App., 1952).
[73] 63 So. (2d) 339 (Fla., 1953).
For a case in which a prosecutor's comment in his closing argument to the jury, about the defendant's lie-detector tests, was held proper because of the fact the defendant and his counsel had previously mentioned the tests, see People v. Weber, 401 Ill. 584, 83 N.E. (2d) 297 (1949)

stage of development. It has not yet become standardized as to test procedure, examiner qualifications, or even instrumentation itself. Much more remains to be done and accomplished before the courts should be urged to generally admit test results as evidence. Although a very high percentage of accuracy is attainable under fairly ideal conditions, the problem of judicial proof confronting lie-detector advocates is much the same as the difficulty facing many aspiring minor league baseball players. A player may hit very well against right-handed pitching, but if he is a frequent strikeout against left-handed pitching, he is usually not considered ready for major league play until he becomes adept at hitting both styles of pitching. The lie-detector technique is subject to somewhat comparable limitations in its present stage of development. Until the previously estimated accuracy is generally attainable, and a much higher degree of standardization achieved, the courts should continue to withhold judicial sanction of lie-detector test results.

The issue of judicial admissibility calls for a consideration of several important additional factors:

If lie-detector test results were admitted as legal evidence they would be offered and treated as proof of some very important phase of the case, usually the validity of the entire claim or contention of one of the parties. There would then be a tendency on the part of many judges and juries to accord conclusive weight and significance to the test results. It cannot be denied, therefore, that under such circumstances the admission of the test results as legal evidence would entail some risk even under the best of conditions—i.e., even when the proper instruments and methods have been used by experienced, competent, and honest examiners. The dangers of injustice would be considerably greater in instances where improper instruments or methods are used, or where the examiners are either incompetent or dishonest; and it must be reported that among the group of persons engaged in this type of work at the present time, there are some who are grossly incompetent and a few others who are unquestionably dishonest (and who would readily testify for the side that offered the larger fee).

It may be argued that there are somewhat similar dangers attending the use of many other types of scientific evidence, and that therefore this objectionable feature to lie-detector test results should be no bar to their admissibility. But, by and large, there is a valid distinction. In the first place, of course, most of the other types of scientific evidence usually pertain to some one particular phase of the case and are not ordinarily conclusive of the entire issue under litigation; therefore, there is less likelihood of injustice resulting from erroneous expert testimony. For instance, a toxicologist may find that there was poison in a murdered body, but other proof must be forthcoming as to who committed the act of poisoning; a firearms identification expert may conclude that a fatal bullet came from the accused person's gun, but other proof must establish the fact that it was the accused who fired the gun. Lie-detector evidence, however, would usually bear upon the crux of the whole case—e.g., is the defendant lying when he denies killing the deceased?; if he is, then he is guilty; if he is telling the truth, then he must be innocent. (There would be little or no reason to test any of the witnesses or other persons, since a test of the principals themselves would theoretically provide a full and complete answer to the legal inquiry.) Secondly, most of the other types of scientific evidence have been used over a longer period of time and are standardized as to instruments, methods, principles, and qualifications of the expert. The present lie-detector technique is not adequately standardized either as to instrumentation, or the manner in which the tests should be conducted, or the interpretation of the recordings; therefore, the courts would be unable to properly determine whether or not the results of some particular test should be admitted in evidence. Moreover, the essential qualifications for competent examiners have not been well enough established to permit a court to determine whether or not a certain examiner should be permitted to testify as an expert. Under such circumstances it would be relatively easy for incompetent or dishonest persons to represent themselves as lie-detector experts and be given an opportunity to render inaccurate or perjured testimony for the party by whom they are employed. Thirdly, in most other types of scientific evidence the situation is such that the opposing side in a legal controversy has a reasonable opportunity for exposing an incompetent or dishonest expert witness. The witness can ordinarily be required to present some observable basis for his conclusion (e.g., the indicated similarity between two specimens of handwriting)—something which the judge or jury can examine or consider in deciding what credence they are to place in the expert's conclusion; or else, in instances where there is no such observable basis, the expert can be required to state the principles, reasons, and facts upon which his conclusion is based, and these, of course, can be evaluated in the light of the recognized principles and procedures employed in his profession.

Lie-detector evidence would consist largely of an expert's opinion based upon a set of recordings which, in most instances, would be practically meaningless to anyone other than a person trained in the technique. A judge or jury ordinarily would have no opportunity to observe and understand the basis for the witness' opinion, because even if the recordings are produced in court they are frequently of such a nature that in the average case one witness could point out what he considers indications of deception while another with perhaps equal effectiveness could point out on the same records what he considers the indications of truthfulness. In such a situa-

tion the judge or jury would be at loss to properly evaluate the two opposing views. Moreover, in the present stage of the technique's development
there would be very little opportunity for exposing an incompetent or dishonest witness by cross-examining him with reference to any recognized
principles, procedures, and instruments employed by others within his
profession.

With regard to the second prerequisite for admissibility as legal evidence
—i.e., the "acceptance" in the fields of science to which the lie-detector
technique belongs—we must inquire into its status among psychologists
and physiologists.

Psychologists and physiologists will generally agree that there is some
basis in principle and theory for seeking to detect deception by recording
the physiological phenomena previously described, but there are not many
of them who have much confidence in the efficacy of the technique itself.
It must be reported, therefore, that at the present time the technique is
not an "accepted" one among the scientists whose approval is a prerequisite
to judicial recognition.[74]

As to why this is so there are a number of explanations. In the first place,
of course, even with all the necessary facts before them, members of the
psychology and physiology professions could, with some justification, decline to accept the lie-detector technique—in the sense that acceptance
would signify their confidence in the general reliability of the test results
and their approval of the practice of using the results as legal evidence.
Unfortunately, however, the two professions by and large have not been
sufficiently interested to investigate the possibilities of the technique or to
conduct their own independent research and experiments (except perhaps
as regards class room demonstrations); and for this reason they are actually
not prepared to offer an authoritative opinion upon the subject.[75] By tradi-

[74] The results of a recent survey suggest that at the present time the psychology
profession does not have an answer to the question of "general scientific recognition".
Very few professional psychologists have conducted actual case tests, and very few
have even familiarized themselves with the technique's efficacy in practical case
applications. See Cureton, E. C., "A Consensus as to the Validity of Polygraph
Procedures", which appears in "The Polygraphic Truth Test—a Symposium", 22
Tenn. L. Rev. 1, at p. 18 (1953).

[75] For an example of some "arm-chair" criticism by a group of psychiatrists, see
the resolution adopted by the Forensic Section of the American Psychiatric Association in 1944, and the discussion of the lie-detector technique in Eliasberg, V.,
Forensic Psychology (1946) 19 So. Calif. L. Rev. 349, at pp. 360–363. The resolution
is as follows:

    Whereas, modern psychopathology has discovered the nature of the feelings
      of guilt;
    Whereas, the defendant may legally refuse to submit to any of the lie detection
      tests and his enforced cooperation, as in other tests, e.g. intoxication tests,

tion their academic charts have omitted such adventurous paths as the one leading to the practical application of a lie-detector technique. Then, too, the practical workers in the field—the lie-detector examiners in various police departments and personnel laboratories—have failed to solicit or arouse the interest and cooperation of the academic psychologists and physiologists. Moreover, the sensational claims and cheap publicity on the part of some examiners have undoubtedly contributed to the present apathetic attitude of scientifically minded individuals, who prefer not to endanger their professional reputation by any such venture beyond the portals of respectable and conventional research and experimentation. In any event, and despite whatever the reasons might be, the lie-detector technique at the present time lacks not only the legally essential acceptance by psychologists and physiologists but also their active interest in the potentialities of the technique. For this latter situation the lie-detector examiners themselves must share a large portion of the blame.

It is generally recognized that our present legal methods and procedures for ascertaining the truth and administering justice are far from perfect and that therefore we should forever remain alert and eager for corrective measures and improvements. At the same time, however, we should not be too hasty in our acceptance of proposed innovations. In the case of the lie-detector technique such a cautious attitude will operate not only in the

---

may in some states, be held to violate the constitutional guarantee against self-incrimination;

Whereas, the hardened criminal is more immune to lie-detector tests than to the free interview and other recognized methods of clinical criminal investigation;

Whereas, the much vaunted confessions after the administration of the lie detector tests are (a) by no means particularly conclusive; (b) are by no means more reliable than the ordinary confession and (c) are not free from possible objections on the grounds of admissibility and voluntariness;

Whereas, the *pathological confession* (confession of the pathological innocent man) is likely to occur with the lie detector more often than with other methods;

Whereas the popular belief in the infallibility of the lie detector is apt to prevail unduly upon jurors and to lead to a belief in the machine rather than in conscientious deliberation;

Whereas, there is no conscience-robot and no diagnosis-robot;

Now, therefore, we the Forensic Section of the A. P. A., want to go on record as cautioning against advertising of the lie detector device. The section wants to point out that the machine can give valuable results only in the hands of thoroughly trained physicians and psychologists who will evaluate the data derived by applying other available methods and making use of all independently obtainable evidence. (Resolution quoted from Eliasberg, *op. cit. supra* at p. 362.)

best interests of the administration of justice but also to the ultimate advantage of the technique itself. A premature acceptance of the test results as legal evidence would undoubtedly occasion such a series of abuses and miscarriages of justice as to stigmatize forever the technique in the field of law as well as of science. It seems much wiser, therefore, to await a further development and standardization of the technique before admitting the test results as evidence in civil or criminal cases.

CONDITIONAL ADMISSIBILITY BASED UPON AN AGREEMENT AND STIPULATION BETWEEN OPPOSING ATTORNEYS PRIOR TO THE TEST

Under certain conditions and circumstances a possible exception may be made to the foregoing conclusions and recommendations regarding the admissibility of lie-detector test results. For instance, suppose the facts of a given case are such that (a) neither of the opposing attorneys is confident of the merits of his position, and (b) neither one is desirous of having a decision rendered upon the basis of the meager or equally contradictory evidence available to the court. Suppose further that the attorneys in the case, thus realizing the hazard of an unjust decision, agree between themselves (with the consent and approval of the respective parties, of course) and sign a stipulation to the effect that a lie-detector test shall be made of the parties in the case, by a designated expert, and that the test results shall be admitted into evidence without objection on the part of the party adversely affected. An excellent illustration of the type of case in which this situation might arise is one involving a paternity determination or bastardy proceeding. In such cases it is often extremely difficult for the presiding judge to arrive at a decision, and on many occasions his ultimate finding will be based upon nothing more than a guess or hunch on his part as to which side is telling the truth. Here is the type of case where lie-detector tests may be of considerable assistance and value, despite their possibility of error; and the desirability of their use under these conditions and circumstances has been recognized by a number of trial courts, particularly in the City of Chicago.[76]

In view of what has been stated previously with regard to the inadvis-

---

[76] As regards paternity determinations or bastardy proceedings it should be pointed out that blood grouping tests (of mother, child, and accused father) should be given priority over lie-detector tests. But since the blood grouping tests are helpful only where the alleged father can be *excluded* as a possible parent, and since there are many cases where the alleged father may still be innocent despite the fact that his blood type is that of a *possible* parent, the lie-detector tests can be resorted to for assistance in instances where it is not possible for blood grouping tests to solve the problem. Of course, where blood grouping test results indicate the impossibility of the accused person being the father of the child there is no need for any lie-detector tests.

ability of admitting lie-detector test results in evidence, how may we justify an exception merely because the opposing attorneys and parties agree between themselves to have the test made and to permit the introduction of the test results in evidence? It may be justified because of the following considerations:

1. Whenever opposing litigants and their respective attorneys are willing to resort to the use of lie-detector tests, it may be taken for granted that the case is a doubtful one—one in which the evidence on either side is not particularly convincing (e.g., a bastardy accusation and denial), and in which a decision reached on the basis of the available evidence would be more or less guesswork anyway. Therefore, since there already exists a considerable probability of an incorrect and unjust decision, there is a good reason for utilizing lie-detector test results which would certainly be more accurate than the guess or hunch of the judge or jury deciding the case in the absence of lie-detector evidence.

2. Whenever opposing attorneys agree upon the selection of an expert —and this, of course, is an essential element of the agreement and stipulation—we may safely assume that the person thus selected is an honest and competent examiner. A second and highly essential safeguard is therefore provided by this requirement—a safeguard which would not prevail under a system of general and unconditional judicial recognition of the lie-detector technique.[77]

Apparently the only appellate court decision directly in point as to the effect of a stipulation to admit the test results in evidence is a 1948 decision of the California District Court of Appeal in *People v. Houser*.[78] The court there held the defendant to be bound by the agreement he had made (with the attorney's consent and approval) to permit the test results to be admitted in evidence "either on behalf of the people or on behalf of the defendant". In its opinion affirming the defendant's conviction of a sex offense against a child, the court said, "It would be difficult to hold that defendant should now be permitted on this appeal to take advantage of any claim that (the examiner) was not an expert . . . and that such evidence was inadmissible, merely because it happened to indicate he was not telling the truth".[79]

---

[77] For a detailed description of a criminal case (assault with intent to murder) in which the lie-detector test results were admitted by stipulation, see article entitled "Detection of Deception Technique Admitted as Evidence", J. Crim. L. & Criminology 26: 262 (1935). Also see, as regards another similar case, *ibid.* 26: 758 (1936).

[78] 85 Calif. App. (2d) 686, 193 Pac. (2d) 937 (1948).

[79] Compare Le Ferre v. State, 242 Wis. 416, 8 N.W. (2d) 288 (1943), in which, for unspecified reasons, the court held that the state was not bound by the stipulation

A 1951 Michigan Supreme Court case, *Stone v. Earp*,[80] also involved the stipulation issue, but under a rather peculiar circumstance. During the course of a non-jury trial to determine whether the plaintiff or defendant was the owner of a certain motor vehicle, the trial judge made the following announcement: "I am not going to decide this case until your clients take a lie-detector test". He then continued the further hearing of the case. When the trial resumed, the judge inquired of each attorney whether he was agreeable to having his client take the test. Each one expressed his consent. The tests were conducted in a private room and the court then received the testimony of the examiner, who stated that the results of his examination indicated that the plaintiff was lying. Upon appeal the plaintiff contended that the trial judge erred in giving any consideration and weight to the lie-detector examiner's opinion. In this the Michigan Supreme Court concurred, but it also held that the error thus committed was not prejudicial because of the preponderance of other evidence in support of the same conclusion reached by the examiner. The court did indicate in its opinion, however, that the test results would still be considered inadmissible even if the judge had not suggested the test himself and the parties had on their own initiative entered into the agreement and stipulation. That appears to be the effect of the following statement in the court's opinion: "We are not unmindful of the fact that at the direction of the trial court, the parties agreed to submit to the test. But whether by voluntary agreement, court decision, or coercion, the results of such tests do not attain the stature of competent evidence".

There seems to be no substantial reason why an agreement and stipulation to admit lie-detector tests in evidence should not be upheld. The final decision, however, might well be left to the sound discretion of the trial court. If it should appear to the trial judge, therefore, that the circumstances of a particular case did not warrant such a procedure, or if he knew or had any reason to believe that the expert in the case was not properly qualified, he would have the discretionary right to ignore the agreement and stipulation and decline to accept the lie-detector evidence.[81]

regarding the admissibility of the test results. An unusual situation was involved in this case, however, and the decision does not seem to be controlling upon this point.

Also see Orange v. Commonwealth, 191 Va. 423, 61 S.E. (2d) 267 (1950), in which a defendant sought to introduce the results of a "truth serum" test made pursuant to an agreement with the prosecuting attorney. The court there held that the results were properly excluded since the agreement to have the test made did not provide that the results of the test would be admissible in evidence. It appears that the court would have admitted the results if there had been a stipulation to that effect.

[80] 331 Mich. 606, 50 N.W. (2d) 172 (1951).

[81] This proposal is consistent with the existing view regarding stipulations generally: Electric Park Co. v. Psichos, 83 N.J.L. 262, 83 Atl. 766 (1912). Also see People v. Pearson, 107 Pac. (2d) 463 (Calif., 1940).

Attorneys contemplating a lie-detector test agreement and stipulation may find it helpful to consider the following suggested form, based upon a hypothetical case situation:

It is hereby agreed and stipulated between the defendant, Jack Snow, and the prosecuting attorney of Oak County, Alaska, Paul Rain, that the said Jack Snow shall submit to a lie-detector examination, to be given by Henry Spring of Podunk, Oregon, on or about January 5, 1954, in Salmon Flat, Alaska, for the purpose of determining whether the said Jack Snow burglarized the Alaska Historical Museum on April 6, 1952, for which offense Jack Snow is presently under indictment.

It is further agreed and stipulated that the results of the lie-detector examination, in the form of an opinion by the examiner, Henry Spring, may be offered in evidence on behalf of the defendant or on behalf of the prosecution. In presenting his opinion the examiner may exhibit and explain to the court and jury the various recordings obtained as part of the test procedure. He may also describe the instrument used, explain the nature of the test, and state the reasons which form the basis for his opinion that the said Jack Snow is either lying or telling the truth about the offense for which he is charged.

The expenses, if any, for the examination and for the testimony of the examiner, Henry Spring, shall be borne by [the county, or the defendant].

If the test results and the examiner's opinion are offered as evidence by either party to this agreement and stipulation, the opposing party shall have a right to cross-examine the lie-detector examiner with respect to the manner in which he conducted the test, his own training and experience, and also regarding the lie-detector technique's limitations and possibility of error. The trial court's discretion shall prevail as regards the privilege of inquiring into any other matter on cross-examination.

If the case is tried by a jury, the court shall be requested to instruct the jury regarding the terms of this agreement and stipulation. The court shall also be requested to further instruct the jury that they should not accept the test results and the examiner's opinion as conclusive of the issue before them, but that they are privileged to consider the results and the examiner's opinion along with all the other evidence in the case and give the lie-detector evidence whatever weight and effect they think it resonably deserves.

In consenting to this lie-detector examination the defendant knows and understands that he is under no legal compulsion to do so.

Agreed and stipulated this ——— day of ———, ———.

———————————
Defendant

———————————
Counsel for Defendant

———————————
Prosecuting Attorney

LEGAL STATUS OF CONFESSIONS, ADMISSIONS, AND OTHER EVIDENCE OBTAINED BY THE USE OF A LIE-DETECTOR

In view of the inadmissibility of lie-detector tests results generally, what is the legal status of confessions, and other evidence obtained in consequence of the use of a lie-detector?

The Supreme Court of Pennsylvania had occasion to pass upon this question in *Commonwealth v. Hipple*,[82] a case in which the defendant had confessed to a murder after having been given a lie-detector test. His counsel objected to the admissibility of the confession because of the fact that the instrument had been used and also because the defendant had been told by the investigating officers that "you can lie to us but you cannot lie to this machine". In upholding the trial court's ruling in admitting the confession the Pennsylvania Supreme Court held that since no promises, force, or threats had been employed in obtaining it, the mere use of the instrument did not render the confession inadmissible. The court also stated that even if the officers' comments regarding the defendant's inability to "lie to the machine" could be considered a trick, that fact alone would not nullify the confession, because of the general rule pertaining to confessions procured "by a trick or artifice not calculated to product an untruth".[83]

Similar views have been expressed by the Supreme Courts of Ohio, Wisconsin, and California.[84]

Contrary to the usual contention of defense attorneys, the use of a lie-detector does not of itself constitute a "third degree" practice. The temporary discomfort produced by the blood pressure cuff is too slight to warrant objection, and the test procedure is of such a nature that it is extremely improbable that it would encourage or compel a person to confess a crime which he did not commit. Nevertheless, the technique is subject to abuse, in the same way that any medical instrument may be used for

[82] 333 Pa. 33, 3 Atl. (2d) 353 (1939).

[83] For another Pennsylvania case in point, see Comm. v. Jones, 341 Pa. 541, 19 Atl. (2d) 389 (1941). Regarding the legality of trickery and artifice in inducing confessions, see *infra* p. 222.

[84] State v. Collett, 144 Ohio 639, 58 N.E. (2d) 417 (1944); State v. DeHart, 242 Wis. 562, 8 N.W. (2d) 360 (1943); and People v. Hills, 30 Calif. (2d) 694, 185 Pac. (2d) 11 (1947).

In the Hills case, the defendant had confessed killing his wife and had led the police to the grave where he buried her. At the trial defendant's counsel made no objection to the introduction of the confession in evidence, which the appellate considered as a waiver of his right to raise the point on appeal. The court did indicate, however, that even if a proper objection had been made its decision would still be the same, since the lie-detector examination and other police activities did not constitute any mental or physical coercion. Also see State v. Lowry, *supra* note 67, in which the court said that admissions and confessions obtained as a result of lie-detector tests, if otherwise competent, have generally been admitted, "and no reason now appears why they should not be admitted". And in Henderson v. State, *supra* note 71, the court said that it was legally proper to use the lie-detector technique as an investigative aid and that a confession so obtained could be used as evidence, provided the test results themselves are not directly or indirectly offered in evidence.

unethical purposes. For instance, in the Colorado case of *Bruner v. People*,[85] a lie-detector test was given to a subject who had previously been interrogated very extensively over a period of many days. The lie-detector test and the subsequent questioning by the examiner was alleged to have lasted from about noon until three-thirty the next morning, at which time the defendant confessed to killing his wife. Upon his trial for murder the defendant contended (and his testimony in this respect was uncontradicted) that for about twelve hours the "machine was left on continuously ... except for one period when he removed it because his whole arm became bloodshot"; that during this twelve hour period he was not permitted to use a toilet; that he was told that such treatment would continue "until a favorable statement was obtained"; and that the lie-detector operator used profane and insulting language and told him that he should be given "a little Chicago treatment" (third degree). Because of such attending factors, which the Colorado Supreme Court rightfully assumed to be true, in the absence of a contradiction by the State's witnesses, the defendant's confession was held to be involuntary and therefore inadmissible.[86] The Colorado Supreme Court was of the opinion that the defendant "was justified in assuming that [the examiner's] treatment would continue until such time as defendant was physically and mentally exhausted and in this condition make a confession of guilt".[87]

The Illinois Supreme Court has held a confession to be inadmissible in evidence when obtained from a subject as she was about to be given a lie-detector test which she had previously refused to take, but to which she had been ordered to submit by the prosecuting attorney and police in-

[85] 113 Colo. 194, 156 P. (2d) 111 (1945).

[86] The lie-detector examiner involved in this case informed the writers that at the time of trial he was in the armed forces overseas and was therefore unavailable to the state as a witness. The court's opinion, however, does not disclose any accounting by the state of the unavailability of the witness.

[87] Another case in which the court considered the lie-detector technique to have been improperly used is Prince v. State, — Tex. Cr. R. —, 231 S.W. (2d) 419 (1950). The defendant had been interrogated at various intervals for about two and a half days as a murder suspect, during which time he was taken a distance of 280 miles for a lie-detector test. After being returned to his city he confessed the murder. During all this time he had not been formally charged or given a preliminary hearing. Upon appeal from his conviction, the Texas Court of Criminal Appeals held that the use of a confession obtained as a result of investigative procedures of the sort employed by the police in this case constituted a violation of due process. For another case in which a lie-detector examination was involved in a series of events and occurrences which, in terms of their total effect, were considered illegal, see Refoule v. Ellis, 74 Fed. Supp. 336 (1947). A Federal court in this case granted an injunction against certain police officials to restrain them from using harassing investigative procedures in violation of the Federal Civil Rights Act.

vestigators.[88] On the other hand, however, the mere fact that the suspect expected to be given a test, and for that reason confessed, does not affect the admissibility of the confession.[89]

In laying the legal foundation for the admissibility of a confession obtained by a lie-detector examiner, a prosecuting attorney is confronted with a task requiring considerable caution. Although the foregoing cases clearly establish the validity of such a confession, the lie-detector test results are not admissible in evidence. In order to obtain the advantage of the confession and at the same time avoid the risk of error with respect to the test results themselves, the procedure usually followed is to introduce as a witness the examiner to whom the confession was made, and by him lay the foundation for the admissibility of the confession by merely proving its voluntary character (i.e., the absence of any threats, force, or objectionable promises); and all this without any mention of the fact that a lie-detector had been used. In this way the prosecution will avoid any danger of reversible error occasioned by the introduction of lie-detector evidence. The choice will therefore rest with the defense attorney as to whether or not he cares to inject the lie-detector issue into the case for the purpose of attempting to show that it was a torture device which compelled the defendant to confess.

The pitfall awaiting a prosecutor in cases of this type is illustrated in the recent Oklahoma case of *Leeks v. State*.[90] Although the examiner, in relating the defendant's confession, did not specifically testify about the test results, he did state that he told the defendant that the test results would be disclosed to the investigating officers. This was held to be the equivalent of the unauthorized admission in evidence of the test results themselves. On the other hand, however, a very liberal view was taken in a 1951 Federal appellate court case regarding the propriety of an examiner's discussion of the lie-detector test and test results while testifying as to the defendant's confession following the test. In *Tyler v. U.S.*,[91] in which the defendant was

[88] People v. Sims, 395 Ill. 69, 69 N.E. (2d) 336 (1946).

[89] Pinter v. State, — Miss. —, 34 So. (2d) 723 (1948). The defendant in this case testified that while en route to jail, as a murder suspect, he overheard someone discuss the existence of a lie-detector. He said that this statement about a lie-detector "scared him" and thereby rendered his ensuing confession involuntary. The Mississippi Supreme Court held that even if such statements about the instrument had been made, which the prosecution denied, the fear expressed by the defendant was "not a fear of the machine but of its capacity to elicit the truth". Consequently, according to the court, "It was, therefore, a fear of the truth and its consequences", and "a desire to anticipate, by voluntary disclosure, the supposed revelation of a 'lie-detector', had its origin in the mind and conscience of the defendant, and is not an undue influence".

[90] — Okla. Cr. R. —, 245 Pac. (2d) 764 (Okla. Cr. App., 1952).

[91] 193 Fed. (2d) 24 (1951). Cert. denied, 72 S. Ct. 639 (1952).

on trial for a murder committed in Washington, D.C., the prosecution offered as a witness a lie-detector examiner who testified to the following effect: After describing the test procedure, he stated that the defendant attempted to "beat the machine" by abnormal breathing, and that the defendant admitted making such an effort; the examiner then ran another test, after which the subject was advised that the test indicated he was lying and the examiner proceeded to interrogate him; and that about an hour later the defendant confessed. His confession was reduced to writing and signed by him. To all of this testimony the defendant objected. The trial judge over-ruled the objections but at the same time he instructed the jury that the examiner's statement that he told the defendant he was lying "is not admitted as evidence of any alleged lying of the defendant, but merely as evidence bearing upon the question whether the confession was, in fact, voluntary". The Court of Appeals for the District of Columbia Circuit sustained this ruling and action of the trial court and held that although lie-detector test results are inadmissible as evidence, the test procedure and what the examiner told the defendant had a material bearing upon the vital question of the voluntariness of the confession. Considerable significance was attached to the trial court's "clear and positive instruction to the jury, holding the evidence within proper bounds". The appellate court also commented upon the fact that the examiner's testimony did not reveal either the nature of the test questions or the defendant's answers, "so there was nothing to indicate to the jury what particular statements [the examiner] had reference to when he told [the defendant] there were indications he was lying".

In view of the many qualifying circumstances and conditions surrounding the admission of the examiner's testimony regarding the lie-detector tests and the results indicating lying, the above *Tyler* case cannot be considered as a reliable case precedent even for the admission of test results in support of a confession's admissibility.

OTHER LEGAL PROBLEMS FOR POSSIBLE FUTURE CONSIDERATION

If and when lie-detector test results are declared to be competent legal evidence, questions soon will arise as to whether or not an accused person in a criminal case may be compelled to submit to a test, or as to whether or not the party litigants in a civil case, or the witnesses in either type of case, may be required to subject themselves to a test.[92]

[92] The answer to the auxiliary question regarding comment upon, or an inference from a person's refusal to take a test will depend upon the answer to the primary question as above stated. At present, a refusal to submit to a test cannot be used as evidence of a consciousness of guilt. See State v. Kolander, — Minn. —, 52 N.W. (2d) 458 (1952). Also see State v. Zeler, 230 Minn. 39, 41 N.W. (2d) 313 (1950), in which a

As previously stated, during the course of a lie-detector test it is not necessary for the person being examined to discuss the matter under investigation, except in so far as he responds to the examiner's questions by either "yes" or "no"; and even these verbal answers may be dispensed with without materially affecting the test results. Therefore, since the physiological reactions obtained by the technique, and even the "yes" and "no" answers, are not used testimonially—that is, as "statements of facts to show their truth"—it may be argued that there should be no legal obstacle to a compulsory examination of this nature. The situation in all essential respects may be considered analogous to that involved in cases in which an accused person is compelled to stand up in court for purposes of identification; or to make footmarks for comparison with those found at the scene of a crime, or to give impressions of his fingerprints for the same purpose; or to submit to a physical examination for scars, wounds, and other identifying characteristics.[93] On the other hand, however, the courts may find a sufficient "volition of the will" to conclude that a silent answer is the equivalent of a verbal one.[94]

The rule with regard to the power of a court in a civil case to compel one of the parties to submit to a medical or physical examination (e.g., for the purpose of determining the extent or the existence of alleged injuries) should apply with equal force to the question as to whether or not a party litigant in a civil case may be compelled to submit to a lie-detector test to determine the truthfulness of his assertions.[95] In any event, there are no

witness' impeaching statement contained a reference to the defendant's refusal to take a test. One of the defendant's witnesses, while under cross examination, complained that all of the questions which had been asked her in the prior statement were confusing and purposely designed to confuse her. To offset this assertion the prosecution introduced all of the witness' statements in evidence. The statements "contained references to the defendant's refusal to take a lie-detector test and truth serum", and the defendant contended that the use of the statements containing such references constituted reversible error. Upon appeal the Minnesota Supreme Court held that since the defendant did not request the court to instruct the jury to disregard the references to the lie-detector and truth serum, he could not now claim error in their admission.

[93] For a more detailed discussion of this self-imcrimination issue see Inbau, F. E., *Self-Incrimination—What Can an Accused Person be Compelled to Do?* 66–68 (1950). Also see, upon this point (as well as upon the general problem of the legal application of deception tests), McCormick, C. T., "Deception Tests and the Law of Evidence" (1927), 15 Cal. L. Rev. 484.

[94] A similar line of reasoning was used in a case involving the issue of whether a compulsory handwriting specimen constituted a violation of the privilege. See Villaflor v. Sumners, 41 Phil. Is. 63 (1920), and a discussion of this case in Inbau, *op. cit. supra* note 93 at p. 46.

[95] As to compulsory physical examinations there is a division of authority, with the majority view favoring the right to such examinations. See Schroeder v. C.R.I.

constitutional prohibitions placed upon such a practice in civil cases,[96] and either the courts or the legislatures could provide for compulsory lie-detector tests if they so desired. And the same rule might be applied to witnesses, although there are some practical objections to an unlimited extension of the principle in that direction.[97]

& P. Ry., 47 Iowa 375 (1877), and compare Union Pacific Ry. v. Botsford, 141 U.S. 250, 11 Sup. Ct. 1000, 35 L. Ed. 734 (1891). Also see annotations in 51 A. L. R. 183 *et seq.*

[96] See Rule 35 of the Federal Rules of Civil Procedure, which permits the federal courts to order a physical or mental examination where "the mental or physical condition . . . is in controversy". Also see Sibbach v. Wilson, 312 U.S. 1, 61 Sup. Ct. 422, 85 L. Ed. 479 (1941), and (1945) 40 Ill. L. Rev. 113.

[97] To permit either party to compel all his opponent's witnesses to submit to a lie detector test might well lead to intolerable confusion and delay, unless the technique is eventually developed, refined, and simplified far beyond present expectations. Perhaps practical considerations would necessitate a restriction to the use of the test on the parties alone; or perhaps as regards the use of the test on witnesses the matter could be left to the discretion of the trial judge. At the present time, of course, all these problems are of an academic nature since the technique itself has not been approved even in cases where the examination is submitted to voluntarily.

(For up-to-date future developments respecting the legal aspects of lie-detector test results, the reader is referred to the Journal of Criminal Law, Criminology, and Police Science, a bi-monthly publication of Northwestern University School of Law. This Journal is also the most probable source of information regarding future scientific developments in the field of lie detection.)

PART II

Criminal Interrogation

The detection of deception is only one part of the task that confronts a criminal interrogator. There still remains the problem of what to do and how to proceed to elicit from an untruthful subject the desired information. And the problem is essentially the same for the interrogator who has had the assistance of a lie-detector as it is for one who has had to depend upon other sources or methods for ascertaining the fact or probability of the subject's deception.

Ordinarily it is no simple matter to obtain a confession of guilt, and in some instances difficulties are also encountered in obtaining helpful information from witnesses or other prospective informants. The task is one that usually requires considerable patience and effort. Nevertheless, there are certain interrogation principles, methods and procedures which, when properly applied, tend to lessen the interrogator's burden and at the same time render the interrogation more effective than would otherwise be the case. In the ensuing discussion a number of such principles, methods and procedures are recommended. Their usefulness and application in no way depend upon the aid of a lie-detector. As a matter of fact, they are here presented primarily for the average criminal interrogator who may be equipped with nothing more than his own good common sense and a fair understanding of human nature.

Privacy

The principal psychological factor contributing to a successful interrogation is privacy. This we all seem to realize in our own private affairs, and yet in police interrogations its importance is generally overlooked. For instance, in asking a personal friend to divulge a secret, we carefully avoid making the request in the presence of other persons, and seek a time and place when the matter can be discussed in private. But in criminal interrogations, where the same mental processes are in operation, and to an even greater degree, police interrogators generally seem to lose sight of the fact that a suspect or witness is more apt to divulge his secret in the privacy of a room occupied by only two persons than in the presence of five, ten, or twenty.

Three cases with which the writers are familiar serve well to illustrate this point.

In a small mid-western town a citizen of the community was being questioned concerning the killing of his wife, who had been shot on a lonely road not far from a main highway. According to the husband's story, while he and his wife were riding in their automobile they were held up and robbed by a man who then fired upon the deceased when she called for help. This account, though plausible enough, did not satisfy some of the authorities, particularly the state's attorney. Suspicion was directed toward the husband as being the actual killer. For several hours upon two or three different occasions during the twenty-four hours following the shooting, the husband was subjected to considerable questioning—*but always in the presence of several persons*. Later, at the request of the state's attorney, one of the writers interrogated the suspect. A private room was selected for this purpose, and all persons were excluded except the suspect and the interrogator. Although a lie-detector test was given, it really was unnecessary, because from the very moment the suspect entered the room he displayed every indication of guilt, and from the very outset it appeared quite evident that here was a man who *wanted* to tell someone his troubles. He had experienced a very unhappy married life—meddling relatives, sexual incompatibility, ill health, another woman, etc. Now he wanted some sympathy; and he wanted to be told that the shooting of his wife was something which anyone else might have done during his weaker moments under similar circumstances. It was essential, however, that he be alone with the person who was to listen to his troubles and offer him the sympathy his mind so craved. Up to the time of his discussion with this interrogator he had not had this opportunity; but when the opportunity presented itself, he very soon told the real story of how and why he killed his wife.

This was the easiest sort of case. It should have been unnecessary for the local authorities to seek outside assistance, and certainly no lie-detector should have been required. All that was really needed was a little privacy.

Another case in point involved an investigation into the rape and murder of a young girl who had been employed as a hostess in a cafeteria. Her nude body had been found in a ditch by the side of a road the morning after the night of her disappearance while on her way home from work. She was last seen in the company of a bus-boy employee of the same restaurant in which she served as hostess. The bus-boy stated he had merely walked to the streetcar with her and saw no more of her after that.

In an effort to obtain information concerning the character and habits of the deceased, and the relations between her and the bus-boy—in so far as such information might furnish some clue to her murderer—the local authorities began questioning other employees of the restaurant. This was undoubtedly a good starting point, but the procedure followed deserves no recommendation. In the presence of *eighteen* persons, gathered in the office of the chief of police, five waitresses from the restaurant were asked to divulge any confidential information they might have as to the character and habits of the deceased and of the bus-boy, who upon several occasions had been the escort and companion of one or two of these girls. In answer to questions as to the character and habits of the victim the waitresses invariably replied, "She was a good girl". When questioned about the boy, and as to his behavior when alone with a girl, the answer was: "He is a good boy; on dates he behaves like a gentleman". What other sort of answers could be expected?—even if the victim had been a girl of very loose morals or the boy a rake of the first order. It so happened, however, that other more thorough investigation resulted in a solution of the crime, clearing the bus-boy and confirming the good moral character of the victim. But suppose one or more of these five girls had possessed valuable information as to the victim or the bus-boy? Was it not expecting too much of them to ask for confidential information in the presence of eighteen persons, whose number included several local politicians of the town, and a few curious spectators having no official connections either with the city or the case itself?

In the famous Degnan murder case in Chicago (1945–46), the importance of privacy was impressively indicated—*by the murderer himself!* William Heirens, a 17 year old college student, was accused of the brutal killing of 6 year old Suzanne Degnan. His fingerprints were found on a ransom note left in the Degnan home; the handwriting on the note was identified as his; and there was also evidence that he had killed two other persons and committed twenty-nine burglaries. His attorneys, to whom he apparently admitted his guilt, advised him to confess to the prosecuting attorney and thereby afford them an opportunity to save him from the electric chair.

Arrangements were made by Heirens' counsel with the Cook County State's Attorney to take Heirens' confession, but at the appointed time and place Heirens refused to confess. The reason for his last minute refusal appears in the following headline from the Chicago Daily News of August 2, 1946: "*Youth asks Privacy at Conference. Blames Refusal to Talk on Large Crowd at Parley*". The newspaper account further stated: "It was learned that Heirens balked at a conference arranged for last Tuesday because [the prosecuting attorney] had invited almost 30 law enforcement officers and others to be present. . . . It was at the conference between the youth and his lawyers that he told them for the first time that there were 'too many' present on Tuesday. He said he would go through with the plan to offer the confession in an attempt to escape the electric chair if it were under different conditions. The State's Attorney told reporters that he had invited the police officials to the conference because they had all played a leading part in the investigation and he felt they should be 'in on the finish'."

Another Chicago newspaper, the Chicago Times of August 2, 1946, reported: "It was hinted the original confession program was a flop because the youth was frightened by the movie-like setting in [the State's Attorney's] office. Presumably he was frightened out of memory, too. To every question about the murders he answered 'I don't remember'. His self-consciousness reportedly was deepened by the presence of several members of the police department, especially [the police officer] whose handiness with flower pots as weapons brought about Heirens' exposé in a burglary attempt".

At the second setting for the taking of Heirens' confession the number of spectators was reduced by about half the original group, but a reading of the confession gives the impression that Heirens, though admitting his guilt, withheld—for understandable reasons—about fifty per cent of the gruesome details and true explanations of his various crimes.

It is indeed a sad commentary upon current police interrogation practices when a seventeen-year-old boy has to impart an elementary lesson to top-ranking law enforcement officials to the effect that it is psychologically unsound to ask a person to confess a crime in the presence of thirty spectators.

To illustrate further the desirability of privacy in a criminal interrogation, let us refer to a commonplace experience. X may tell his troubles and his secrets to his friend Y, and he may tell the same thing to his other friend Z; but he is less likely to do so if he must talk to them at the same time and in each other's presence. As to why this is true we may differ in explanations; but we must agree, after recourse to our everyday experiences, that this is usually the case.

Lack of privacy during a criminal interrogation is comparable to a situation in which a surgeon tries to perform a serious operation out on a public street rather than in a properly equipped operating room. Each one has about an equal chance of a successful performance.

In the interrogation of a female subject, however, it is advisable to have another woman in a position to hear and observe the proceedings. This practice will enable the interrogator to protect himself from a false accusation of indecent conduct or proposals which might be charged by the subject for the purpose of diverting attention from the principal offense, or because of some other reason such as her own psychopathic thinking or behavior.

COOPERATION AMONG INVESTIGATORS

The writers are aware of the practical difficulties a criminal investigator will encounter in arranging for a private interrogation even after he is convinced of its desirability. In a case of any importance each investigator wants to be present when a suspect "cracks" or when an informer or a witness divulges valuable information. He wants to improve his efficiency rating or otherwise demonstrate his value to the department or to his office; and the publicity in his community is considered of value—to say nothing of the satisfaction to his ego. All this is perfectly understandable and nothing more than the reaction of a normal human being. But it is something which to some extent must be controlled in the interest of efficient police procedure.

Privacy in interrogations can be maintained without denying to any investigator assigned to the case the credit due him for his efforts. An understanding may be reached among the various investigators to the effect that if a "break" comes when any of them have absented themselves from the interrogation room for the purpose of insuring privacy between the interrogator and the suspect or witness, they will all share the credit for what ever results the interrogator himself obtains. Perhaps this suggestion may seem naïve and impractical, but the writers have seen it operate successfully in a number of instances, and under the most trying conditions. For example, in one community where the prosecuting attorney and the sheriff were members of opposing political parties they followed such a procedure, and their teamwork and cooperation simplified their respective duties to an immeasurable extent. Neither one hesitated to cooperate with the other because each knew that the other would not seek any publicity to the exclusion of his co-worker.

The investigator who gains the reputation of publicity seeker in his case-work will soon find it difficult to obtain the proper cooperation from his fellow officers. His own work then becomes considerably more of a burden when he has to operate alone; and, as most of us fully realize, criminal investigation is not a one-man job. Of course, there are investigators who are more capable than their colleagues; but, just as a star halfback on a football team needs the blocking of his teammates, the best of investigators must have the cooperation and assistance of other workers if he is to operate successfully. Consequently, in the interest of his community, as well as for his own selfish desires, the interrogator should make every effort to secure and maintain the respect and cooperation of his fellow workers by sharing with them credit as well as responsibility. Eventually his true merit and value to his department, office, and community will become known and recognized by his superiors and also by those members of the public who can be of most help to him in shaping his future career.

No set rules can be outlined for overcoming this practical difficulty of having investigators seemingly sacrifice their own interest in being present during an interrogation. Each community presents its own distinctive problems. It may be a sheriff-prosecuting attorney relationship; or that between a sergeant and patrolman; or between a homicide squad and district detectives. But it is a problem which should and must be worked out in the interest of efficient investigation.

The Interrogation Room

In providing for privacy during interrogations it is advisable to select some quiet room with few or none of the usual police surroundings, and containing as few distractions as possible. If existing facilities permit, a special room, or rooms, should be set aside for this purpose.

The less there is in the surroundings of an interrogation room to remind a criminal offender, suspect, witness, or other prospective informant that he is in police custody or in jail, or that the penitentiary awaits, the more likely is he to make a frank statement or to supply the interrogator with the desired information. To this end, therefore, it would be well to select a room without barred windows, or better yet, one without any windows at all. If windows cannot be avoided, then the bars should be dispensed with in favor of some sort of ornamental grill work which would be just as effective for preventing possible escapes during the temporary occupancy of such a room.[98] (As to the ventilation of a windowless room, a mechanical blower and exhaust system could be used without much difficulty or inconvenience.)

The interrogation room should contain no ornaments, pictures, or other objects which would in any way distract the attention of the person being interviewed. (In any event, if pictures or ornaments are used, they should not be placed in that part of the room faced by the subject during the interview.) And the lighting fixtures of the room should be arranged in such a way as to provide good but not excessive or glaring illumination of the subject's facial features.

No telephone should be present in the interrogation room. Its ringing or use would constitute a serious distraction.[99]

[98] One police department interrogation room, located on the first floor of the police building, was purposely arranged with open unbarred windows so as to invite "escape" into an adjoining yard from which no further flight was possible. It was found that once a guilty subject had made an unsuccessful attempt to escape his confession usually followed soon thereafter.

[99] The importance of a proper physical setting and privacy during an interrogation is generally recognized by interviewers in non-criminal investigations. See Bronner, A. F., "Techniques in Interviewing", *Federal Probation*, July-Sept. 1943, at p. 12: "The physical setting in which interviewing takes place colors success or failure in

Preliminary Preparations

Prior to the interrogation, the interrogator should become thoroughly familiar with all the facts and circumstances of the case which are known up to that time. To ignore or disregard such previously obtained information is to lose, for one thing, information which might permit the detection of the subject's deception more readily than would otherwise be the case; and such an omission would also tend to lead the interrogator into a maze of non-essential and irrelevant matter which might otherwise be avoided.

In addition to familiarity with the case itself, it is advisable for the interrogator to obtain as much information as possible concerning the past life and history of the subject—particularly so if he is considered to be the guilty offender or suspect. Information of this sort will permit the interrogator to more readily engage a reticent subject in conversation; and a display of such knowledge tends to create a psychological advantage in favor of the interrogator. It is impressive for any subject to realize that the interrogator is thoroughly prepared for his interview—and in the case of a lying or guilty subject it renders his task of guilt concealment or lying all the more difficult. Moreover, such information is in itself very helpful to the interrogator in ascertaining which interrogation tactics and techniques are likely to prove most effective.

Attitude and Conduct of the Interrogator

It is a difficult matter to attempt to formulate and propose any set rules with regard to the attitude and conduct of an interrogator during his interview with the subject. Much of this will depend, of course, upon the circumstances of each particular case, but in general the following recommendations seem appropriate and valid:

(1) Avoid creating the impression that you are an investigator seeking a confession or conviction. It is far better to appear in the role of one who is merely seeking the *truth*. In this respect an interrogator's civilian dress is to be preferred to a uniform. If the uniform cannot be avoided altogether, the coat, star, and holster should be removed for the period of the interrogation.

(2) Keep pen and paper out of sight during the earlier stages of an interrogation, and, as a general rule, minimize the extent of note taking thereafter. By recording the subject's statements or comments during the course of an interrogation, the interrogator places before the subject a more

---

establishing rapport (a relationship of trust and confidence) and hence is of importance. Quiet, privacy, freedom from interruption—by people or telephone or outside noises—are all taken into account. Only when they exist can the interviewee be frank and feel the interviewer is genuinely interested".

or less grim reminder of the seriousness of the situation or of the legal significance or implication of an incriminating remark. As a general rule, therefore, it is preferable to reserve the written statements or note-taking until the conclusion of the interrogation. (This recommendation is not intended to apply, however, to the routine taking of statements at crime scenes; and there are, of course, other occasional exceptions.)

(3) Such realistic words or expressions as "kill", "steal", and "confess your crime" should not be used by the interrogator. It is much more desirable, from a psychological standpoint, to employ milder terminology like "shoot", "take", and "tell the truth".

(4) The interrogator should sit fairly close to the subject, and between the two there should be no table, desk, or other piece of furniture. Distance or the presence of an obstruction of any sort seems to afford the subject a certain degree of relief and confidence not otherwise attainable.

(5) The interrogator should avoid pacing about the room. To give undiverted attention to the person being interrogated makes it that much more difficult for him to evade detection of deception or conceal his guilt.

(6) The interrogator should avoid or at least minimize smoking, and he should also refrain from fumbling with a pencil, pen, or other room accessories, for all this tends to create an impression of lack of interest or confidence. As to the smoking, there is an addition reason for its avoidance. If the interrogator is not smoking, the subject is less likely to attempt to resort to a smoke in an effort to relieve his emotional tension or to bolster up his resistance to an effective interrogation; and if such a request to smoke is made, the interrogator may with much justification and fairness suggest that the subject postpone his smoking until he leaves the interrogation room. However, if the interrogator must smoke, he should start off by offering a cigarette to the subject and then minimize his and the subject's smoking as much as possible. To smoke without permitting the subject to do so would prevent the establishment of the relationship of trust and confidence so essential to a successful interrogation.

(7) The interrogator should adapt his language to that used and understood by the subject himself. In dealing with an uneducated ignorant subject the interrogator should use simple words and sentences. And where, for instance in a sex case, the subject uses slang and commonplace expressions and gives evidence of his lack of knowledge of more acceptable terminology, the interrogators should resort to similar expressions. This can be done in a reserved manner without the loss of the subject's respect for the position occupied by his interrogator.

(8) Since the interrogator should always occupy a fearless position with regard to his subject and to the conditions and circumstances attending the

interrogation, the subject should not be handcuffed or shackled during his presence in the interrogation room. For similar reasons the interrogator should not be armed. In other words, the interrogator should face the subject as "man to man" and not as policeman to prisoner.

In dispensing with these various precuationary measures, others may be substituted with comparable assurance that no escape will occur or that no physical harm will come to the interrogator as a result of such omissions. For instance, where circumstances so warrant, a guard may be placed outside the door of the interrogation room, on the alert for an attempt to escape or for possible acts of violence toward an unarmed interrogator.

The "Sizing-up" and Classification of Subjects for Interrogation Purposes

An interrogator's success will depend to a considerable extent upon his ability (1) to "size-up" his subject, and (2) to select and effectively apply the interrogation tactics and techniques most appropriate for the occasion. As to the first phase of the task—the "sizing-up"—there is not much an experienced interrogator can offer in the form of written instructions to less experienced persons. Even with the opportunity of utilizing actual case demonstrations for instruction purposes, the development of this ability to "size-up" a person must remain largely a matter of practical experience, although even then the degree of efficiency attainable by the interrogator will be dependent to some extent upon his own native ability and capacity for such psychological insight.[100] However, with regard to the selection and application of available tactics and techniques, an experienced interrogator's recommendations may be reduced to writing and thereby rendered of value to other interrogators not possessed of comparable experience or training.

Rather than offer to the reader a random and generalized discussion of various interrogation tactics and techniques, an effort has been made to organize and classify the following material so as to render it of greater practical utility. First of all, there is a major classification on the basis of the subject's presumed relationship to the offense in question—that is, whether he is considered as (1) a suspect or (2) merely as a witness or other prospective informant. Consequently, in conformity with this primary classification, one part of the following discussion of interrogation methods

---

[100] "The skilled interviewer utilizes different approaches and methods with different persons interviewed, gaining, with experience, such rapid fire impressions of his various clients that his way of beginning each interview seems almost intuitive. . . . Skill in this grows with one's own thoughtfulness and desire to improve technique through self-awareness and self-criticism". Bronner, A. F., *supra* note 99 at p. 11.

will deal with *Suspects* and the other part will be devoted to *Witnesses and Other Prospective Informants*.

The Interrogation of Suspects

There are two general groups of suspects:

1. SUSPECTS WHOSE GUILT IS DEFINITE OR REASONABLY CERTAIN; and
2. SUSPECTS WHOSE GUILT IS DOUBTFUL OR UNCERTAIN.

In dealing with suspects whose guilt is definite or reasonably certain, the interrogator will usually make known his belief in the suspect's guilt and attempt from the very outset to secure a confession or incriminating statement. On the other hand, with suspects whose guilt is doubtful or uncertain, the interrogator must "feel his way around" until he arrives at a decision of guilt or innocence. This difference in objective and interrogation approach obviously necessitates a separate discussion of the interrogation techniques to be used upon each group of suspects.

SUSPECTS WHOSE GUILT IS DEFINITE OR REASONABLY CERTAIN

In addition to a division of suspects into the above two groups on the basis of probability of guilt, a further classification is required, for interrogation purposes, of suspects whose guilt is definitely or reasonably certain. This latter classification, however, is in terms of the nature of the offense committed, the motivation, and the offender's reaction to its commission. These various factors have been found to determine a suspect's responsiveness to an interrogation. For interrogation purposes, therefore, criminal offenders fall into one or the other of two general groups:

A. "Emotional Offenders"—persons who commit crimes in the heat of passion, anger, or revenge (e.g., assaults; killings; rape, or other sex offenses; etc.), and also persons whose offenses are of an accidental nature (e.g., the hit-run motorists). This group also includes some first offenders in other types of cases.

The "emotional offender" usually has a feeling of remorse, mental anguish or compunction as a result of his act. He has a sense of moral guilt. His conscience "bothers" him, and he has difficulty resting or sleeping, and because of this feeling of guilt the most effective interrogation approach to use on him is one based upon *sympathetic considerations* regarding his offense and present difficulty.

B. "Non-emotional Offenders"—persons who commit crimes for financial gain (e.g., larceny, robbery, burglary, and killings for money reasons), and particularly offenders who are recidivists or repeaters. In contrast to the "emotional" offender, this type of offender usually has no moral guilt, no troubled conscience. He does not lie awake at night grieving over the harm or hurt he has inflicted. His only concern is usually, "Am I going to get caught"? That being so, there is little to be gained by a sympathetic interrogation approach. The most effective method to employ on him is to convince him that his guilt is already established or that it will be before long, and that therefore he might just as well tell the truth. In other words, the interrogator should make a *factual analysis* of the suspect's predicament and appeal to his common sense and reasoning rather than to his emotions.

In classifying criminal offenders into these two groups, and in enumerating the foregoing types of offenders who are classified as members of one group or the other, we do not intend to convey the impression that all offenders possess exclusively the characteristics of either one or the other of the two groups, or that an interrogator in any given case should confine his interrogation tactics and techniques to the set generally considered more effective for the group into which he places his particular subject. There is, of course, no strict line of demarcation between the two groups, or between the various interrogation methods which are considered more appropriate for the one group or the other. For instance, in classifying as members of the second group those offenders who commit crimes for mercenary gain, this does not mean that all persons who steal are devoid of any feeling of remorse, mental anguish, or compunction over their offensive behavior. Likewise, in recommending for the first group a certain tactic or technique, we do not in any sense of the word imply that all members of the second group are impervious to a similar approach and that in no case should it be tried on members of the latter group. In listing these various tactics and techniques we are only stating what appears to be the general rule in dealing with such offenders. As to the exceptions to be considered, or as to the selection of particular tactics and techniques from either or both sets subsequently discussed, the interrogator must resort to his own ingenuity—to his psychological insight and ability to "size-up" his subject.

"Emotional Offenders"

Interrogation of Offenders Whose Offences Produce in Them a Feeling of Remorse, Mental Anguish, or Compunction; and upon Whom a Sympathetic Approach is Usually the Most Effective Interrogation Tactic or Technique for Eliciting an Incriminating Statement or Confession

TYPICAL SUBJECTS: Persons who have committed crimes while in the heat of passion, anger, or revenge; first offenders in many other types of cases; and also accidental offenders.

Although this group of offenders is characterized—and distinguishable from the second group—by a more impelling urge to confess in order to attain the consequent mental relief and comfort, it must be understood that very often the desire to avoid the legal consequences of their offensive behavior persists nevertheless as an opposing factor. Moreover, given sufficient time for their wounds of conscience to heal, and if permitted to feel confident that their offensive behavior is and will remain undetected, or at least uncertain in the minds of the investigators, members of this group may and often do become less emotional and more rational regarding their wrongdoing. Eventually the urge to confess for the sake of mental relief and comfort may subordinate itself to the urge to avoid legal consequences; and then the offender will begin to react in much the same manner as a confessed criminal who later (e.g., at or preceding the time of his court trial) experiences a recurrence of the urge of self-preservation and once more denies his guilt, retracts his confession, and seeks to avoid legal sentence and punishment. It is usually necessary, therefore, that the interrogator do more than merely sympathize with the offender and wait for the urge to confess to overcome his urge of self-preservation. An effort must be made to have even this type of subject believe or realize that his guilt has been detected and that therefore it is useless for him to deny it. To this end it is effective for the interrogator to display an air of confidence in the subject's guilt; to point out the circumstantial evidence against him; and also to call attention to his physiological and psychological symptoms of guilt. The manner in which this may be accomplished is discussed in the first three of the following described tactics and techniques.

(The sequence in which these various interrogation methods are listed and discussed conforms to the order in which they are usually employed in actual case applications. The lettering is used merely for reference purposes and is not intended to signify a routine, unalterable application of these tactics and techniques.)

A. DISPLAY AN AIR OF CONFIDENCE IN THE SUBJECT'S GUILT

By an "air of confidence" we do not mean a supercilious or bullying attitude, but rather one which will convey to the subject the impression that the interrogator is "sure of himself" and that he "means business". As part of this impression, of course, the interrogator must give no indication that he is being influenced by what the subject may state in behalf of his innocence; and this should be so even when the interrogator actually realizes the reasonable implication of possible innocence in some fact or evidence presented by the subject. In other words, the subject should be required to extend himself to the limit in order to avoid detection or confession, for during the course of his efforts toward that end he is more vulnerable to the tactics and techniques designed to produce the desired information.

B. POINT OUT THE CIRCUMSTANTIAL EVIDENCE INDICATIVE OF GUILT

It is usually very effective to enumerate during the early stages of the interrogation the various facts and circumstances indicative of the subject's guilt. While this is being done, however, the interrogator should not pause for any of the subject's possible explanations until these facts and circumstances have been completely enumerated and finished off with a comment to the effect that there are also other indications of guilt in addition to the ones stated.

Except in the occasional case where the interrogator may see some particular advantage in letting the subject attempt an early explanation of the evidence against him (e.g., where there is some indication that the subject will make a remark contradictory to one previously made), it is better to show no interest whatsoever in anything the subject has to say to refute the indications of guilt. Later, of course, the interrogator can always change his tack and let the subject go into as much detail and discussion as he chooses, but during the initial stages of the interrogation it is preferable that the subject's explanations be brushed aside as inconsequential.

As a defensive measure some offenders attempt to ward off the effects of the interrogator's accusations and enumerations of facts and circumstances of guilt by entering into a prolonged and detailed dissertation upon their innocence. To permit them to do so will merely make it more difficult to break down their mental resistance later on during the interrogation. By stopping short any such attempted dissertation the interrogator will deprive this type of subject of his most effective weapon of defense, both as to his own urge to confess and also to the interrogator's tactics and techniques as well.

C. CALL ATTENTION TO THE SUBJECT'S PHYSIOLOGICAL AND PSYCHOLOGICAL "SYMPTOMS" OF GUILT

An offender who is led to believe that his appearance and demeanor are betraying him is thereby placed in a much more vulnerable position. His belief that he is exhibiting symptoms of guilt has the effect of destroying or diminishing his confidence in his ability to deceive, and it tends to convince him of the futility of further resistance. This attitude, of course, places him much nearer the confession stage.

This technique of calling attention to various physiological and psychological phenomena as "symptoms" of guilt may be utilized somewhat as follows; but the reader should bear in mind that, with one possible exception, none of these phenomena is a reliable indication of guilt.

(1) Pulsation of Carotid Artery

Although an accelerated pulsation of the carotid artery in the neck is experienced by some innocent persons as well as by a certain number of guilty ones, such a phenomenon exhibited by a guilty subject can be commented upon to good advantage. In doing so, the interrogator, pointing to the pulsations beneath the skin, may remark: "You are so disturbed and conscious of your lying that this artery in your neck is pumping away so fast it can be seen clear across the room; that sort of thing doesn't happen when a man is telling the truth, regardless of how nervous he may be".

(2) Excessive Activity of the "Adam's Apple"

For much the same reason, and in much the same way as with (1) above, it is well to comment upon the over-activity of a subject's epiglottis or "Adam's apple". The fact that an acceleration of its up and down movement is experienced by many offenders when questioned—and particularly when first accused—is well recognized among experienced interrogators.

(3) Dryness of the Mouth

A fairly reliable symptom of deception is a condition describable as "dryness of the mouth". It may be observed in a subject by his swallowing motions accompanied by repeated attempts to wet the lips, which are sometimes so dry and sticky that upon parting they emit a smacking sound. (This condition is apparently due to an inhibition in the functioning of the salivary glands, thereby producing a deficiency of saliva in the mouth.)

Whenever this condition is observed the interrogator should call it to the subject's attention by first asking the question—"Your mouth's very dry, isn't it?" After receiving the usual affirmative reply, it is well to supplement this question with another—"Feels like you have a mouthful of cotton, doesn't it?" Then the interrogator should comment as follows: "That's the result of your lying; the glands in your mouth which produce the saliva are not functioning properly—they've just about quit for the time being; you can drink all the water your stomach can hold without getting any relief. There's only one remedy, and that is to tell the truth".

(4) Inability to Look the Interrogator "Straight in the Eye"; Swinging One Leg over the Other; Tapping on the Chair; etc.

When a subject fails to look the interrogator "straight in the eye", or when he exhibits a restlessness by leg swinging, hand tapping, foot wiggling etc., it is well to comment upon these characteristics as indications of a disturbed mental condition inconsistent with the subject's protestations of innocence.

(5) The "Peculiar Feeling Inside"

When interrogating a subject of the type now under discussion, it is advisable to remind the subject that he "doesn't feel very good inside", and that this "peculiar feeling" (as if "all his insides were tied in a knot") is the result of a troubled conscience. While making this statement it is well for the interrogator to touch or tap the subject's abdomen, as though it were the repository for the conscience to which the interrogator refers.

(6) Swearing to the Truthfulness of Assertions

Quite often a guilty subject will invoke such expressions as "I swear to God I'm telling the truth", "I hope my mother drops dead if I'm lying", "I'll swear on a stack of Bibles", etc. Although expressions of this type cannot be considered as reliable symptoms of deception, they frequently are used by guilty subjects in an effort to lend forcefulness or conviction to their assertions of innocence. Consequently, whenever the subject swears to the truthfulness of his statements, or, better yet, whenever he starts to raise his hand with that apparent purpose in mind, the interrogator should comment upon the psychological significance of this conduct somewhat as follows: "Put your hand down! When you're telling the truth I'll know it; you won't have to swear to it. Your swearing is just added proof you're not telling the truth. In my experience I've found that people who are telling the truth don't swear to it. For them it's not necessary. You and others who aren't telling the truth, however, know you're not truthful and you realize we know it. So you try to make your story convincing by swearing to it. Well, that sort of stuff doesn't work; we're wise to it, because it's been tried so many times before. Listen, when a man is telling the truth he doesn't have to swear to it—because it sounds like the truth, and he looks like a truth-telling man when he says it. But with you, well, you know you don't sound convincing; you know I don't believe you, so in desperation you use such an expression in an effort to bolster up your story."

(7) "Spotless Past Record"—"Religious Man"

The same psychological motivation as with swearing is involved in the use of such expressions as "I have a spotless past record" or "I'm a very religious man; I couldn't do anything like that". In instances where expressions of this type are used, the interrogator should counter with comments to the effect that even assuming that to be true he knows that the subject is still responsible for the act under investigation. Moreover, the interrogator should point out to him the reason for his assertions of good past record or religious nature—that they are made in an effort to lend support to statements which he knows, and realizes the interrogator knows, to be false.

(8) "Not That I Remember" Expression

Very often a lying subject will resort to the use of "not that I remember" when answering certain questions pertaining to facts or events which, in view of their nature, or the time and place of occurrence, might reasonably be expected to have been so definitely impressed upon the subject's mind that an unequivocal "yes" or "no" answer should be forthcoming instead of a "not that I remember" one. In such instances it is well for the interrogator to comment somewhat as follows, immediately after the qualified answer is given: "What do you mean, 'not that I remember'? This thing (fact, event, etc.) is sufficiently important (or else the circumstances under which it occurred were such) that you remember very definitely whether it is or isn't, or whether it happened or didn't happen (etc.). There is no 'if', 'but', or 'not that I remember'. However, I'll tell you why you're saying 'not that I remember'. It's because you're not telling the truth and you find it easier to tell half a lie than to tell a whole one. It's easier for you to say 'not that I remember' than it is to say 'yes' or 'no'. You can't muster enough courage to tell an outright untruth, but you are able to pull yourself together to utter half a one. And I know from my experience that whenever a man uses the expression 'not that I remember', he's not telling the truth, for otherwise he'd say 'yes' or 'no' and let it go at that".

D. SYMPATHIZE WITH THE SUBJECT BY TELLING HIM THAT ANYONE ELSE UNDER SIMILAR CONDITIONS OR CIRCUMSTANCES MIGHT HAVE COMMITTED A SIMILAR OFFENSE

In applying this technique the interrogator should be careful not to violate the legal prohibition against making promises of immunity or diminution of punishment as an inducement for confessing. But there is no legal objection to extending sympathy to an accused person in an effort to obtain from him an incriminating statement or confession of guilt.

An offender of the type now under consideration derives considerable mental relief and comfort from an interrogator's assurances that anyone else under similar conditions or circumstances might have committed a similar offense. He is thereby enabled to at least partially justify or excuse in his own mind his offensive act or behavior. Yet there still remains the realization that a wrong has been committed or a "mistake" made, which has been injurious or damaging to another person. This self-condonation, therefore, does not completely satisfy the offender's desire for relief from a troubled conscience. As a matter of fact, the comfort derived from the interrogator's assurances that another person might have committed a similar offense merely offers an added inducement to him for obtaining the greater degree of relief and comfort attending a confession of guilt. While the subject is in such a frame of mind, the solicitations of a sympathetic interrogator seem to cast a shadow over the subject's previously clear vision of the legal consequences of an exposure of his guilt.

An illustration of the type of case in which this technique may be used very effectively is one involving the interrogation of a "hit-and-run" driver in an automobile accident. For instance, by making a "hit-and-run" driver believe—and often rightly so—that anyone else under similar conditions of panic might also have fled from the scene, he is afforded an opportunity to "square himself" with his own conscience. And at the same time his realization that he was less savage-like in his behavior than he first assumed himself to be renders his task of confessing a much easier one than would otherwise be the case. In the sense in which Orientals use the term, he is thus permitted to "save face".

In addition to utilizing this technique for the purpose of justifying or excusing the offense itself, the interrogator should pursue a similar course with regard to the subject's conduct in previously denying his guilt to the investigating officers or to the present interrogator during the initial stage of the interrogation. Therefore, in an effort to pave the way for an incriminating statement, the subject should be told that neither the interrogator nor any of the investigators resents his previous or persistent lying up to the present time—since anyone else, including themselves, probably would have done likewise under similar circumstances—but that now, after the subject's situation has been outlined to him, and after he has had an opportunity to think the matter over, he should proceed to tell the truth. By this assurance the interrogator removes another barrier from the subject's mind —namely, the deterrent effect of his previous lies told to a person (or persons) to whom he now desires to be truthful.

E. REDUCE A SUBJECT'S GUILT FEELING BY MINIMIZING THE MORAL SERIOUSNESS OF HIS OFFENSE

Although this technique is of value in many types of cases it is particularly effective in sex cases, in which it is desirable for the interrogator to pursue a practice of having the subject believe that his particular sexual irregularity is not an unusual one, but rather one which occurs quite frequently, even among so-called normal and respectable persons.[101] The sub-

[101] In this connection it has been found effective to comment as follows: "We humans are accustomed to think of ourselves as far removed from animals, but we're only kidding ourselves. In matters of sex we're very close to most animals, so don't think you're the only human being—or that you're one of the very few—

ject might also be told that the interrogator has worked on cases much worse than the present one and has heard many persons relate experiences much more offensive than any the subject can talk about.[102] Another effective line of discussion is to tell the subject that the interrogator himself has been tempted to do, or almost or actually did do, the very sort of thing of which the subject is accused. The more the sex offender is led to believe that in a moral sort of way he is not much different from the interrogator and other "normal" and "respectable" people, the easier it becomes to confess his guilt.

The application of this technique in the interrogation of the murder-rapist, Jerry Thompson, was instrumental in eliciting his confession of the killing of his last rape victim. During Thompson's interrogation, the interrogator told him that his rape-murder was no worse than the many other ordinary rapes he had committed (and to which he had confessed during an earlier period of his interrogation). He was told that in the one case where death had resulted he merely "got a tough break"—as was true to a considerable extent, because from all indications Thompson apparently merely wanted to subdue his victim's resistance rather than kill her. (He had choked and slugged the victim in a fit of passion, which was his usual practice with others, but in this particular instance the girl failed to recover consciousness soon enough; so he assumed she was dead, and disposed of her body by throwing it from his automobile. To his later regret, Thompson realized—and perhaps correctly so—that the victim was probably killed only when thrown from his car, and therefore her life might have been spared if he had only given her sufficient time to recover from the effects of his prior acts of violence.) During an interview which one of the writers had with Thompson a few days before his execution, Thompson stated that at the time of his interrogation just prior to his confession he had been very much comforted by the interrogator's remarks regarding the "no worse" aspect of his present offense in comparison with his previous ones.

who ever did anything like this. There are plenty others, and these things happen every day and among many persons, and they will continue to happen for many, many years to come". In appropriate instances, with the so-called "intellectual" type of subject, it may be helpful to support these statements by referring to the studies of Dr. Alfred C. Kinsey of Indiana University. See Kinsey, A. C., Pomeroy, W. B., and Martin, C. E., *Sexual Behavior in the Human Male* (1949).

[102] At this point it is well for the interrogator to state: "I know it's somewhat embarrassing for you to tell what happened. That's only natural. But go right ahead and talk to me just the same as if you were in a doctor's office telling him about some stomach ache or pain. I've listened to many a man's troubles for many years. That's my job. I've made a study of this problem and I thoroughly understand what the difficulty is; so go ahead and be perfectly frank with me. You won't surprise or shock me with anything you might say because I've heard the same thing, and a lot worse, related time and time again".

As previously stated with respect to Technique D, the interrogator must avoid any expressed or intentionally implied statement to the effect that because of the minimized seriousness of the offense, the subject is to receive a lighter punishment. Nevertheless, there is no legal objection to minimizing in the subject's mind the moral seriousness of the offense in his particular case.

F. SYMPATHIZE WITH THE SUBJECT BY CONDEMNING HIS VICTIM, OR HIS ACCOMPLICE, OR ANYONE ELSE UPON WHOM SOME DEGREE OF RESPONSIBILITY MIGHT CONCEIVABLY BE PLACED FOR THE COMMISSION OF THE CRIME IN QUESTION

The psychological basis for this suggested technique can be appreciated quite readily by anyone who will reflect upon his own non-criminal wrongdoings and upon the occasions (particularly during childhood) when he had to "own up" to them. In such instances there is a natural inclination to preface the admissions with a condemnation of the person or thing offended against, or with a statement purporting to place part of the blame on someone else. And the same mental forces are in operation in matters involving criminal offenses—only to an even greater degree because of their more serious nature.

In view of the fact that such self-condonation so frequently accompanies a confession of guilt—with the offender seeking by this means to more or less justify or excuse the offense in his own mind—it seems only reasonable to presume that an interrogator's condemnation of the offender's victim, accomplice, etc., would prove to be effective in provoking or expediting such confessions. Moreover, actual experience has demonstrated this to be so.

The following description of several cases and case situations illustrates the manner in which this technique can be applied.

(1) Condemn the Victim

Some outstanding examples of the effectiveness of this technique are to be found in sex cases involving offenses in which the victims are children. In such cases, when an adult offender makes his confession he almost invariably places the blame upon his victim, even though the victim may be only a six-year-old child. The presence of this trait should in itself suggest the technique to be used in the interrogation of offenders of this type— namely, the condemnation of the victim.

In one of the writer's cases, which involved the interrogation of a fifty-year-old man who was accused of having taken indecent liberties with a ten-year-old girl, the subject was told: "This girl is well-developed for her age. She probably learned a lot about sex from the boys in the neighborhood. And knowing what she did about it she may have set about deliberately to excite you to see what you would do". The offender then confessed, but, true to the characteristics of his group, he attempted to place the blame on the child. Even if this were so, however, he would still be just as guilty in the eyes of the law.

This interrogation technique can be used advantageously in other types of sex cases—for example, in one involving a forcible rape—by suggesting to the subject that the victim may have been to blame for dressing or behaving in such a way as to unduly excite a man's passion.

In embezzlement cases—and here we refer particularly to first offenders and to those whose motive arises more or less from a need or fairly reasonable desire for more money than is represented by their salary, rather than from a scheme to "get rich quick"—it is well to condemn the employer for paying inadequate and insufficient salaries, or for some unethical practice which may have created a temptation to steal.

(2) Condemn the Accomplice

For much the same reason that a youngster with a baseball bat in hand alleges to an irate home-owner near the playing field that "we" (he and his teammates) broke the window—rather than stating that "I" did it (meaning the batsman who struck the ball its damaging blow)—the criminal offender is naturally inclined to have someone else share the blame for the commission of the crime in question. Any line of interrogation, therefore, which tends to lift from him some of the burden he bears for his criminal act will make him that much less reluctant to confess his guilt.

Here again, however, the interrogator must proceed cautiously and refrain from making any comments to the effect that the blame cast on an accomplice thereby relieves the subject of legal responsibility for his part in the commission of the offense. By suggesting the application of this technique we merely recommend a moral condonation in the form of expressions of sympathy for the subject's "unfortunate" experience in having been influenced" by his "criminally-minded associate".

The manner in which this technique may be utilized is aptly illustrated in the following description of an interrogation of a property owner who was accused of arson. The subject had invested heavily in a real estate project which, as it neared completion, seemed doomed as a financial failure. In charge of the property in question was a handy-man whose mental capacity was somewhat deficient. After a fire of suspicious origin, in which a large and heavily insured house was destroyed, the handy-man, upon being questioned by investigators, confessed that he set fire to the place at the request of the owner. On the basis of this confession, together with the evidence that the fire was of incendiary origin, the owner was arrested and charged with the offense. At first he denied his guilt, and he continued to do so even when confronted with the testimony of his employee. However, during a subsequent interrogation period, another interrogator proceeded to apply the above suggested technique of condemning the accomplice. The interrogator's expressions in this respect were somewhat as follows: "We all know—and you know—that there's considerable truth to what your employee says about the fire. We also know that a man of your type may not have done such a thing had it not been suggested or hinted at by someone else. It looks to me that this fellow you have working for you may be the one who conceived this idea. He knew you were having a tough time financially, and he probably wanted to be sure his pay would go on, or perhaps he was looking for even more than that. For all I know he might have framed this whole business so as to get you in trouble. Maybe he wanted to get even with you for something he thought you had done to him. That I don't know, and we won't know the true explanation unless you tell us. We know this much: the place was set afire; your employee did it; he says you told him to do it; and this we'll have to believe unless you can give us another explanation". (Along with all this, of course, the interrogator also freely applied the previously described Techinque D.) After an hour or so of such conversation, the subject admitted he knew the property was to be set afire and had approved of the burning. At first he insisted, as the interrogator had indicated as a possibility, that it was the employee's idea, etc. This version, of course, was false; nevertheless, for a few minutes the interrogator permitted the subject to bask in the sunshine of this partial and reflected guilt, and to derive therefrom the attending mental comfort and relief. However, soon thereafter the interrogator began to point out the lack of logic and reasonableness in the subject's accusation of his employee. The subject was told that he still did not look as relieved as a man who had told the whole truth. Then the interrogator proceeded to explain sympathetically that by coming out first with only part of the truth he was doing what all human beings do under similar circumstances. Finally, as a climax to such comments, the interrogator urged the subject to "tell the whole truth". He then admitted that the idea of burning the building was his own, and that the rôle of the tempted and misguided individual was played not by him but rather by his accomplice. Nevertheless, for the purpose of inducing the subject to begin his confession, it was very effective for the interrogator first to blame the accomplice.[103]

[103] The effectiveness of this technique of condemning an accomplice was recognized during the Spanish Inquisition. The inquisitors were instructed to address suspects as follows: "You have behaved with credulous simplicity toward people whom you believed good and of whom you knew no evil. It might well happen to much wiser men than you to be so mistaken". Sabatini, R., *Torquemada and the Spanish Inquisition* 175.

(3) Condemn Others

In addition to victims and accomplices, there are others who may be condemned to good advantage. Toward this end the interrogator in some instances may find it effective to cast blame on government and society for permitting the existence of social and economic conditions which are conducive to the commission of crimes such as that for which the offender is accused. On other occasions the offender's parents, wife, etc., may be alleged blameworthy for the offender's conduct. Numerous other possible recipients of the interrogator's condemnation might be mentioned, but the following case description will suffice to illustrate the application and effectiveness of this technique.

In the interrogation of an accused wife-killer (the one referred to in the previous discussion of privacy), the interrogator proceeded to condemn the wife's relatives who were known to have meddled in the offender's marital affairs. They were blamed for having deliberately set about to render the subject's married life an unhappy one. At one point the interrogator remarked that probably the relatives themselves should have been shot. During the discussion the interrogator did not spare the wife either—nor wives in general. The subject's wife was alleged to be a provocative, unreasonable, and unbearable creature, a woman who would either drive a man insane or else to the commission of an act such as that perpetrated by the subject. In this respect, however, the interrogator stated that the subject's wife was "just like most other women". The subject was also told that many married men avoid similar difficulties by becoming drunkards, cheats, and deserters, but unfortunately the subject tried to do what was right by sticking it out, and it got the better of him in the end. All of this, of course, rendered the subject's offense less reprehensible in his own mind —and his self-condonation finally overcame his desire to avoid an exposure of his guilt.

G. EXPRESS FRIENDSHIP IN URGING THE SUBJECT TO TELL THE TRUTH

Although expressed friendship is an essential factor in the successful application of several of the preceding techniques, under the present title we wish to suggest certain specific overtures which may be made in this direction.

(1) Extend Sympathy by Such Friendly Gestures as a Pat on the Shoulder or Knee, or by a Grip of the Hand

It is surprising to observe how effective such a gesture can be in obtaining a confession. Coming as a climax to a series of sympathetic expressions constituting the basis for the previously employed techniques, a gesture of this sort may produce a flood of tears along with the confession of guilt.

(2) Tell the Subject that Even if He Were Your Own Brother (or Father, Sister, etc.) You Would Still Advise Him to Speak the Truth

A statement to this effect helps to establish the subject's confidence in the interrogator and thereby renders it easier for the subject to tell the truth.

(3) Urge the Subject to Tell the Truth for the Sake of His Own Conscience, Mental Relief, or Moral Well-being, as well as "for the Sake of Everybody Concerned", and also Because It Is "the Only Decent and Honorable Thing to Do"

In urging or advising an offender to tell the truth the interrogator must avoid expressions which the courts of his state may consider objectionable on the grounds that they constitute illegal promises or threats. However, by speaking in generalities such as "for the sake of your conscience", or "for the sake of everybody concerned", etc., the interrogator can remain within permissible bounds.

A line of discussion which has been used to good advantage on many occasions (particularly in sex cases) is one in which the subject is advised that by telling the truth he performs somewhat of a mental operation on himself —an operation equally as important and necessary as the removal or destruction of injurious tissue in a cancer patient. In this respect it is helpful to draw a circle on a piece of paper, mark off a small area on the rim of it, and tell the subject that in effect the marked-off portion represents a piece of infected tissue on his mind or soul which, if unarrested and unremoved, will continue to spread and produce other and more serious offenses than the one for which he is now accused. He should then be told that there is only one way that the necessary mental operation may be performed, and that is by telling the truth.

"For the sake of everybody concerned" is an expression which lends itself to many interpretations conducive to truth-telling. One consideration which it seems to bring to mind is the suffering of the victim or of his dependents, etc., or the wrong committed against other persons adversely affected as a result of the offender's conduct. It is advisable, therefore, to briefly mention these consequences for the purpose of placing the subject in a more regretful mood.

The expression "It's the only decent and honorable thing to do" appears to constitute somewhat of a challenge for the offender to display some evidence of decency and honor. This is particularly so in sex cases where, in the absence of a plea of guilty, it would become necessary for the victim to undergo the ordeal of publicly relating the details of the offense committed against her; and in such instances it is occasionally helpful to ask the subject how he would like to have his own sister or mother appear in court as his victim may have to do. In playing upon this potential weakness, if the subject happens to be a religious person discuss with him the tenets of his particular creed. Mention to him the fact that his religion becomes meaningless unless he tells the truth with regard to the offense in question. Likewise, if he belongs to a fraternal order, appeal to him in its name. It is also quite helpful if the interrogator can state that he or his parents or close friends belong to the same church or fraternity and that therefore he, the interrogator, knows and appreciates what the subject's moral obligations are in the present situation.

(4) Let the Subject Talk of His Misfortunes and Troubles in General; Listen and Console as a very much Interested and Understanding Friend

This technique is particularly appropriate in a case such as the following one. In the interrogation of a subject about twenty-two years of age who was accused of rape (while in an intoxicated condition), the interrogator encountered considerable difficulty because of the subject's attitude of despair and resignation. He would merely deny he committed the offense and then say, "I don't care whether you believe me or not; I'd just as soon go to jail as not because there's nothing for me to look forward to in this world anyway". In view of such an attitude the interrogator had only one course open to him, so he gave the subject a pat on the knee, told him life must have treated him rather roughly, and then asked to hear about his troubles and misfortunes. The subject than proceeded to discuss them quite freely. He related a truly pathetic story: an adulterous mother, a bootlegging and brutal father, a very unhappy childhood, etc., all of which drove the subject to reckless living and drink. After a brief period of attentive listening and consolation on the part of the interrogator, the subject seemed so relieved and comforted over his general troubles and misfortune that he went into a discussion of the rape charge and made a full confession.

In this case it was absolutely necessary first to get the subject out of his doleful mood—to get him talking. This, of course, called for the exercise of considerable patience on the part of the interrogator, but in the end it was worth the effort.

(5) The "Friend and Enemy" Act

A display of friendship may at times be rendered more effective by combining with it the efforts of another interrogator who pretends to be very much displeased with the offender and with his conduct in denying his guilt

The technique may be applied somewhat as follows: Interrogator *A*, after sympathizing with the offender and being friendly throughout his part of the interrogation, leaves the room, expressing his regrets and disappointment over the subject's refusal to tell the truth. Then in comes Interrogator B who proceeds to condemn the subject in an unfriendly manner. A little later, at the height of B's deliberate condemnation, A re-enters and opposes B's unfriendly behavior and tells him to leave so that A and the subject can "talk things over"—whereupon B makes another uncomplimentary remark about the subject and slams the door shut as he leaves the room. Following this, A resumes his interrogation in a mild and friendly manner.

This "friend and enemy" act seemingly tends to cause the subject to lose the equilibrium which previously maintained a favorable balance between his thinking processes and his urge to release the emotional tension created by his resistance to an exposure of guilt. Moreover, the contrast between the tactics used by each interrogator tends to accentuate the friendliness of the one, and to thereby render his efforts more productive of fruitful results than otherwise might have been the case.

This technique was effectively applied in a case in which a state police captain and a state trooper were interrogators, with the captain playing the "unfriendly" rôle. As the captain left the room and the "friendly" trooper entered, he told the subject that nothing would please him more than to have the subject tell him, the trooper, the whole story so that he could "show up" the captain. The subject thereupon related his confession—in order "to get even with" and show his contempt for the "unfriendly" captain.

Although the "friend and enemy" act is usually performed by two persons, the same effect often can be obtained by a single interrogator working alone. This means, of course, that he plays the parts of both "Dr. Jekyll and Mr. Hyde", but it is surprising how well he can discard the one rôle as he changes into the next. A brief absence from the interrogation room usually suffices to break off the one rôle from the other.

H. INDICATE TO THE SUBJECT, AS A REASON FOR TELLING THE TRUTH, THE
   POSSIBILITY OF EXAGGERATION ON THE PART OF HIS ACCUSERS

In many instances where an offender is accused by his victim, or by a witness to the crime, the interrogator should tell the subject that even though there must be a basis for the accusation there is the ever present possibility of exaggeration—which can be determined only by first obtaining the offender's own version of the occurrence in question. For example, in a case where the subject is accused of rape—and he denies not only the rape but even the act of intercourse itself—it is effective to interrogate the subject somewhat as follows: "We know that there's some truth to what the girl says. We also know that you're not telling the whole truth, so as matters now stand, we have to take the girl's story as being the absolute truth—even though she may be lying about certain things. For instance, perhaps she had intercourse with you voluntarily, and then after it was all over she became worried, and in order to ease her own conscience or to have an explanation in case she became pregnant, she concocted a rape story. If this is what happened, we have no way of finding out—unless we hear your explanation. Now I'm not saying that this is what happened. I'm merely looking at this from all possible angles, but in any event we're interested in the truth. If the truth is what she states, we want to know it; on the other hand, if it's anything less than that, we're just as anxious to find that out. My advice to you, therefore, is to tell the truth". (All this may be preceded or supplemented, of course, by a condemnation of the victim, or of women in general, etc., as previously suggested in Technique F.)

After an offender has succumbed to this technique, he may try to cling to his partial admission as representing the whole truth; but once he has acknowledged the fact that previously he had lied to the interrogator, it becomes very difficult for him to continue his resistance. He then can be told that if his present admission represented the complete truth he would not have delayed so long in stating it, and that he still does not have the relieved look, etc., of a man who has told the whole truth.

I. RATHER THAN SEEK A GENERAL ADMISSION OF GUILT, FIRST ASK THE SUBJECT A QUESTION AS TO SOME DETAIL PERTAINING TO THE OFFENSE

A properly conducted interrogation based upon the application of techniques such as those previously discussed will ordinarily have the effect of producing in the subject moments of bewilderment or mental inactivity, during which his struggle to avoid exposure will be partially overcome by (or temporarily deadlocked with) his impulse to confess. At such times a question as to the reason why the crime was committed, or as to some circumstance surrounding its commission, constitutes an effective technique for eliciting a confession.

Illustrative of the application of this technique are the following questions which may be asked in a fatal automobile accident case of a "hit-and-run" driver who has steadfastly denied even being present at the accident scene: "How fast were you going when you reached the intersection?", or "Where was the pedestrian when you first saw him?"[104] However, the effectiveness of such questioning can be enhanced considerably by appending to them, or supplementing them with, concrete suggestions of possible explanations or excuses. For instance, in the interrogation of a murderer in a shooting case, the interrogator may ask, "How did the

---

[104] Note that these two questions deal with events prior to the accident. In such form they are probably more advantageous, psychologically, than questions referring to events at the time of or subsequent to the crime itself, such as the hitting or the running away.

shooting occur?—Were you just trying to scare him with the gun and it went off accidentally?" Or, in an embezzlement case, the question might be, "What did you need the money for—to pay some medical bills?"

Questions of this type asked at the proper psychological moment possess a number of features which make them much more effective than inquiries or solicitations calling for an outright or general admission of guilt (e.g., "Yes, I did" in response to the question, "You killed him, didn't you?"). In the first place, by delving into details as to why, how, when, and where, the interrogator effectively displays a greater degree of certainty in the subject's guilt—for otherwise there would be no interest in details—and this, in itself, has a tendency to break the subject's resistance. Then there is the very desirable element of surprise in a question of this type. It catches the subject off his guard at a very crucial time, and it stimulates to greater activity the already aroused impulse to confess. Also, a question as to detail, when put to a subject who feels impelled to confess but who is thwarted by the task of bursting forth with the complete admission all at once, offers an opportunity for him to preface or combine his admission of guilt with whatever excuses or explanations he cares to make in an effort to ease his conscience, as well as to have the interrogator believe that the crime is less odious or less reprehensible than is actually the case.[105] Moreover, an inquiry as to a detail of the offense implies a rather sympathetic attitude on the part of the interrogator—the impression that he is not particularly interested in a confession but rather in ascertaining and understanding the reasons for the offender's behavior, or in being informed of the circumstances or conditions which contributed to the consummation of the deed.

Occasionally, in the application of this detail question technique, the interrogator will encounter a subject who may grasp any one of the suggested explanations or excuses and persist thereafter in relying upon it for his legal defense, even though it may not represent the truth. But once the subject has admitted the act itself the interrogator can almost always follow through successfully and obtain the accurate version by pointing out to the subject the flaws in the explanation or excuse given. Nevertheless, despite such eventualities, the tactical advantages to be gained from any admission which contradicts the subject's previous denials will sufficiently compensate for the risk involved in procuring the initial admission by suggesting possible explanations or excuses.

The psychological principles involved in the foregoing problems are also applicable to other situations of somewhat similar nature. For example, where the interrogator has reason to believe that the subject possesses or

---

[105] In the words of the great Hans Gross: "It is merciless, or rather psychologically wrong, to expect anyone boldly and directly to confess his crime. . . . We must smooth the way, render the task easy". Gross, H., Criminal Investigation (1907) 120.

knows the whereabouts of an instrument or article which might have some connection with the crime, instead of merely asking, "Do you have such-and-such?" or "Do you know where such-and-such is?", it is much better to assume in the question that the subject does have, or does know the location of the object being sought. The effectiveness of this approach is well illustrated by the following described case. In the course of an interrogation of a suspect in a rape-murder case, the interrogator received the impression that, regardless of the question as to the suspect's guilt or innocence, he was a sex deviant. The interrogator's previous experience in the interrogation of sex deviants of various sorts brought to mind the possibility that this suspect, like so many others of his class, may have been keeping a diary of his sex affairs and practices. Since such an instrument might be of some value in the interrogation, the interrogator was interested in finding out if one were in existence. Toward this end the interrogator asked the question, "Where is your diary?". The subject paused momentarily and then replied, "It's home—hidden underneath my desk". Officers dispatched to the subject's home discovered a diary replete with records of numerous daily sexual experiences, running the gamut from "struggles" with girls he had picked up in his car to sexual stimulations and ejaculations provoked by a rereading of the past acts previously recorded in the diary. (His "struggles" in many instances actually were rapes which, unfortunately, had never been reported to the police.) When confronted with these diary entries the subject readily admitted a long series of rapes, and although no entry had been made in the diary of the most recent experience, the rape-murder, the interrogator became more and more convinced, as the interrogation continued, that the subject was guilty of the principal crime under investigation. The subject was constantly reminded of the significance attending his previous offenses and particularly as regards one of them in which the modus operandi was quite similar to many aspects of the principal offense. Eventually the subject admitted his guilt of the rape-murder.

There is every reason to believe that in the foregoing case if the issue as to the diary had been brought up in any other way than by the question, "Where is your diary?", the subject probably would not have divulged its existence or its whereabouts, and the investigators would have been deprived of a very valuable means for eliciting the confession. Had the interrogator merely asked, "Do you have a diary?", the subject probably would have inferred that its existence was not already known and therefore denied that he had one. But with the question phrased in such a way as to imply a certainty of its existence, it became difficult for the subject to make a denial—because for all he knew the interrogator or other investigators might already be aware of its existence or actually have it in their possession.

Another possible application of this detail question technique is in cases where the interrogator seeks to establish the identity of an accomplice or of another person who is in some way connected with the offense under investigation. Rather than confine the inquiry to "Who is the person?", it is often much more effective to supplement or substitute with "piecemeal" questions, such as "What part of the city does he live in?" or "What's his first name?" In this way the questions appear rather innocuous and render the subject's task of giving the information much less difficult. And once some "piecemeal" information is obtained, the complete identification usually follows immediately thereafter.

"Non-Emotional Offenders"

Interrogation of Offenders Who Experience Little or No Feeling of Remorse, Mental Anguish, or Compunction as a Result of Their Criminal Acts; and Who, for This Reason, Are Only Partially Responsive to a Sympathetic Approach—Their Realistic Mental Attitude Demanding as a Prerequisite to Any Admission or Confession a Showing That Their Guilt Can Be (or Is) Established by Other and More Tangible Means

TYPICAL SUBJECTS: Persons who have committed crimes for mercenary gain (e.g., robbery, burglary, etc.), and particularly those offenders who are repeaters or recidivists.

In view of the premise upon which the classification of the second group of offenders is based, it becomes readily apparent that tactics and techniques A, B, and C, previously discussed with reference to the first group of offenders, are equally applicable to this second group now under consideration. (As will be recalled, these three interrogation methods pertained to the effectiveness of displaying an air of confidence in the subject's guilt and of pointing out to him the various factors and circumstances indicative of his guilt.) On the other hand, the Group 1 tactics and techniques which are based upon a sympathetic and friendly approach are usually not so effective in the interrogation of members of Group 2, although, as already stated, there are occasions when such methods can be utilized to good advantage even on this latter group, whose members are ordinarily more vulnerable to appeals to the logic of their situation.

Because of the fact that there is no sharp line of demarcation between these two groups of offenders, or between the sets of interrogation methods recommended for the one group or the other, the following described tactics and techniques will be labeled in alphabetical sequence to those already discussed.

J. POINT OUT THE FUTILITY OF RESISTANCE

In recommending that the interrogator point out to the subject the futility of his resistance we have in mind something more than merely calling the subject's attention to the facts and circumstances indicative of his guilt. With members of this second group of offenders the interrogator must make an effort not only to have the subject believe or realize that his guilt is detected (which ordinarily is sufficient for the first group), but that it is or can be established to such an extent that the case against him may be proved without the necessity of obtaining his admission of guilt. On occasions the technique may be applied more or less in the form of a challenge or dare to the subject to take his chances on the evidence already available against him.

The manner in which this technique can be utilized is illustrated by the following comments which the interrogator may make to the subject during the interview:

"In some other situation perhaps it might have been a good idea to try to lie your way out of it, but here the circumstances are different. You're sunk. There's no sense in bucking your head against a brick wall. There's no use trying to kid yourself or anybody else about it. You're in a crack, and a deep one at that; don't dig yourself in any deeper."

"The only thing left for you to do is tell the truth; then if you think you have a break coming to you, talk it over with the judge."

"You can keep on denying this if you want to. That's up to you. I don't care; I don't get a bonus for having you tell me the truth. You're old enough and you have enough intelligence to make your own decisions. I'm only giving you some food for thought and telling you what I'd do if I were in your shoes—or what I'd advise my own brother (or sister, etc.) to do if he (or she) were in your place right now."

Where more than one person participated in the commission or planning of the offense, talk with the subject somewhat as follows:

"You know as well as I do that in all these cases where two or more persons pull off a job like this, someone always ends up talking, and in this case it might as well be you. So let's get going before somebody leaves you holding the bag. Don't let the other fellow get his licks in first and put all the blame on you. You say your piece first, and then we can believe you. But if you wait until the other fellow has his say, no one's going to believe your story even when you do decide to tell the truth."

K. APPEAL TO THE SUBJECT'S PRIDE BY WELL-SELECTED FLATTERY, OR BY A CHALLENGE TO HIS HONOR

Although there are relatively few emotional appeals which may be made to a member of this group, an effective technique is one based either upon flattery or upon a challenge to the subject's honor.

With regard to the type of flattery the interrogator may use, the following expressions are illustrative:

"How is it that a clean-cut (intelligent, or educated, etc.) fellow like you ever got mixed up in an affair like this?"

"You're too attractive a woman to have to resort to methods like this to get along. In any other environment you'd find that many a respectable man would be delighted to have you as a wife. Tell me, how in the world did you ever get involved in a situation like this?"

It is surprising at times to observe how remarks of this nature will quickly serve to place the subject in a frame of mind whereby he or she seems impelled to attempt to answer the interrogator's flattering question, even at the expense of an admission of guilt.

In cases involving juvenile or young adult "hit-and-run" motorists who succeed in outdistancing and eluding pursuing police, but who are at a later date apprehended and questioned, police interrogators may obtain fruitful results from such flattering remarks as: "You boys really gave the coppers a chase; they tell me that they have never seen anyone take corners on two wheels as you fellows did that night". One writer upon the subject of criminal interrogation mentions an example where a young police officer obtained a confession by expressing interest and admiration in the toughness and daring adventures of the subject.[106] The same writer discusses a case where the identity of the actual offender was obtained from a suspect who was accused of bungling the job and not performing it with his usual skill. Rather than lose "prestige" the subject chose to disclose the information he possessed regarding the perpetrator of the offense.[107]

When interrogating a person of low social status, it is advisable to address him or her as "Mr." or "Miss", rather than use the first name. On the other hand, however, it is usually better to address a person of high social or professional status by his or her first name, or by his or her last name without attaching the "Mr." or "Miss". The advantages in this practice are as follows: The first type is flattered and acquires a feeling of satisfaction and dignity from such unaccustomed courtesy. By according the subject this consideration the examiner enhances the effectiveness of whatever he

[106] See Kidd, W. R., Police Interrogation (1940) 115.
[107] *Ibid*, p. 111.

says or does thereafter. As regards the second type, the addressing by first name or by last name only (without the accustomed "Mr." or "Miss") has the effect of dispelling the subject's usual feeling of superiority and independence. He is made to realize that the examiner is in command of the present situation.

It is occasionally helpful to appeal to the subject's loyalty to a group of persons or to an organization whose reputation and honor have been jeopardized by the subject's unlawful behavior. For instance, an appeal may be made in the name of the subject's church, his lodge, or any other organization or group to which the subject appears to have some loyalty or allegiance.

Another form of appeal to the subject's pride by challenging his honor consists of calling into question his possible lack of manliness in not telling the truth about his offense. For instance, the interrogator may inquire, "Haven't you got guts enough—and aren't you man enough—to admit you made a mistake?" Or (in instances where there are co-offenders), "You're not yellow, are you? Can it be that you're afraid of the other fellows?"[168]

L. POINT OUT TO THE SUBJECT THE GRAVE CONSEQUENCES AND FUTILITY OF A CONTINUATION OF HIS OFFENSIVE BEHAVIOR

During the course of their unlawful careers many criminal offenders experience fleeting moments of a desire or intention to reform. While in such a mood—which at times manifests itself during an offender's periods of failure, that is, when he is accused or under arrest, and when thus brought face to face with the stark realities on the debit side of his activities—he becomes quite vulnerable to comments regarding the future consequences and futility of a continuation of his criminal behavior. This is particularly true where the offense is not of the most serious sort and when the offender is not too well seasoned by a long series of offenses and police experiences; for then he might be convinced (momentarily, anyway) that for his own sake it is a "good thing" that he was caught "early in the game", since this

[168] In the interrogation of co-offenders it is well to anticipate and counteract the feeling of honor and loyalty a subject may possess with regard to his fellow participants. Toward this end the interrogator should speak somewhat as follows: "In asking you to tell me the truth I'm not trying to use you as a stool pigeon or to get you to squeal on anybody. I merely want you to tell the truth and to take your share of blame along with the others. And that's the difference between a stool pigeon or a squealer and a person in your position. You are not holding your hand out for any dirty money to sell someone down the river, and I'm not jingling any gold before your eyes. To the contrary, by assuming your share of the blame you put yourself above any blame from anyone. So don't let any false notion of honor stand between you and the truth".

experience may serve to avoid much more trouble for him later on. In the course of his discussion—for instance in a larceny case—the interrogator may say: "You know what will happen to you if you keep this up, don't you? This time you've taken a relatively small amount of money; next time it will be more, and then you'll do it more often. You'll finally decide it's easier and more exciting to get what you're looking for at the point of a gun. You'll begin packing a rod. Then someday you'll get excited and pull the trigger when the muzzle's resting against somebody's belly. You'll run away and try to hide out from the police. You'll get caught. There'll be a trial, and when it's all over, despite the efforts of your parents and relatives who in the meantime have probably spent their last dime in trying to save your neck, you'll either have to spend the rest of your life in the penitentiary or else sit down on the hot seat and have a lot of electricity shot through your body until your life's been snuffed out. Listen, fellow, take may advice; now's the time to put the brakes on—before it's too late".

It is also advisable, whenever possible, to point out the relative insignificance of the offense in terms of how much worse it might have been. For instance, in a robbery case the interrogator may say to the subject: "This could have been a lot worse. You might have shot and killed someone while pulling off this stick-up. Then you would really be up against it. Instead of being in for only taking money away from somebody, you might be facing the electric chair". Such comments tend to make the subject believe he is rather fortunate in having escaped more serious difficulty. Once in that frame of mind he becomes less reluctant to admit his offense.

M. WHERE UNSUCCESSFUL IN OBTAINING A CONFESSION REGARDING THE OFFENSE IN QUESTION, SEEK (FOR USE AS A "WEDGE") AN ADMISSION ABOUT SOME OTHER OFFENSE OF A RELATIVELY MINOR NATURE

When the more or less direct efforts to secure a confession have failed, the interrogator may back off and try a rather devious route leading to the same final result. He may temporarily abandon any discussion of the principal offense and seek to obtain an admission about some other offense of a relatively minor nature—which then can be used as a "wedge" in eliciting a confession of the principal offense.

As a typical illustration of the effectiveness of this technique, let us take the case of a bank embezzler who persists in denying the theft of a sum of five thousand dollars. The chances are very good that at some time during the course of his employment he has found and kept a dime or a quarter or a dollar which rightfully belonged either to the bank or to one of its customers; or he may have taken a small "overage" (e.g., an unaccountable surplus in his cash at the end of the day's work). In any event, there very likely will be some such irregularity in his background; and it is usually a rather simple matter to get him to admit at least one of them. Toward this end the following line of questioning is quite effective: "You're very much disturbed and bothered about something concerning your work. If it isn't the five thousand dollars, what is it? Is it some other little irregularity which under the present circumstances gives you a feeling of guilt, even with regard to the larger sum we're looking for? Whatever it is, tell me about it. The main thing we're interested in is the five thousand, so if it's something else that's bothering you, get if off your chest and then forget about it. What is it, some small change you pocketed several years ago when you were new on the job? Some small 'overage'? Or some coin you found on the floor of the cage?"

The subject may, and probably will, start off by admitting the theft of ten cents or a dollar, "several years ago". But once he makes such a statement the interrogator has him "on the run" so to speak. The subject then can be told that there must be something else because he still does not display the relieved expression of a man who has just told the whole truth. Shortly thereafter he may state that he "just remembered" that he took another small sum of money on another occasion. Again the interrogator may state that on the basis of his experience in many other cases, he can tell that there is still something else bothering the subject. Eventually the subject may raise his admissions to a much higher figure than that originally stated. Finally, as a result of the interrogator's patient questioning, the subject may find himself caught in a very tight web of his own spinning; and in an effort to have himself believed he keeps adding to the previously admitted acts until he ultimately realizes the futility of persisting in a denial of his theft of the principal sum, the five thousand dollars.

The utilization of this technique of obtaining minor admissions for use as "wedges" in securing more important admissions has brought about the solution of many embezzlement cases, particularly in banking institutions.

N. WHEN CO-OFFENDERS ARE BEING INTERROGATED—AND THE PREVIOUSLY DESCRIBED TECHNIQUES HAVE BEEN FOUND TO BE INEFFECTIVE—"PLAY ONE AGAINST THE OTHER"

When two or more persons have collaborated in the commission of a criminal offense and are later apprehended for questioning, there is usually a constant fear on the part of each participant that some one of them will "talk". Individually they all may feel confident of their own ability to evade detection and to "stand up" under the police interrogation, but no one seems to experience a comparable degree of confidence with regard to the co-offender's ability or even willingness to do so. Uppermost in their minds is the possibility that one of them will confess in an effort to obtain special consideration for himself.

This fear and mutual distrust among co-offenders can be made the basis for a very effective interrogation technique known as "playing one against the other". But since it consists largely of a bluff on the part of the interrogator, it should be reserved as a last resort, to be used only after other possible techniques have failed to produce the desired result.

As previously stated with reference to the technique of pointing out the futility of resistance, the interrogator should always indicate to co-offenders, at the very outset of the interrogation, the strong probability that eventually some one of them is going to "talk". The interrogator's early comments to this effect (as discussed in Technique J) constitute a desirable build-up for the subsequent utilization of this technique.

There are, in general, two principal methods which may be used in playing one offender against another. The interrogator may merely *intimate* to one offender that the other has confessed, or else he may actually *tell* him so.

One form of intimation may consist of the practice of taking one subject into the interrogation room immediately after he has seen the other leave and then telling him: "This other fellow is trying to straighten himself out; how about you? Or do you want to let this thing stand as it is? Now I'm not going to tell you what I positively know about your part in this job. I don't want to put the words in your mouth and then have you nod your head in agreement. I want to see if you have what it takes to tell the truth. I want to hear your story—straight from your own lips".

The following procedure has been successfully employed in intimating to one subject that his accomplice has confessed:

After subject ⚥1 has been unsuccessfully interrogated, he is returned to the reception room occupied by a secretary who is engaged in carrying on her usual secretarial duties; then subject ⚥2 is taken to the interrogation room. If likewise unsuccessful in this second interrogation, the interrogator returns to the receiving room and instructs the secretary to "come in the back with your pencil and notebook". This instruction is given within hearing distance of subject ⚥1, but in such a natural manner that it does not appear to be an act performed for his benefit. The secretary then proceeds to sharpen her pencil, turn back some pages of her stenographic pad—all within the observation of subject ⚥1—and then departs in the direction of the interrogation room. After thus absenting herself for a period of time which would ordinarily be required for the actual taking of a confession, she returns to the reception room and begins typing shorthand notes presumably taken during the period of her absence. After several minutes she pauses and inquires of an officer seated near subject ⚥1, "How does this man (referring to subject ⚥1) spell his last name? (or if the name is a simple one, then the inquiry is directed to his exact address, etc.). After receiving the information she continues with her typing. About this time the interrogator appears and escorts subject #1 to the interrogation room (now vacated by subject #2 who has been taken to another room). After subject #1 is seated, the interrogator says, "Well, what have *you* got to say for yourself?" At this point the subject is very apt to confess, being under the impression that his co-offender already has done so.

Whenever the more direct bluff is attempted—that is, whenever the subject is actually told that his co-offender has confessed—the interrogator must be careful not to make any statement, purporting to come from the co-offender, which the person to whom it is related will recognize as an inaccuracy and therefore as a wild guess and a bluff on the part of the interrogator. Once the interrogator makes such a mistake the entire bluff is exposed and then it becomes useless to continue with the act of playing one against the other. Moreover, the interrogator himself is then exposed as a trickster and thereafter there is very little he can do to regain the trust and confidence of his subject. Therefore, unless from his own independent knowledge the interrogator is quite certain of the accuracy of any detail of the offense which he intends to offer to one subject as representing a statement made by his co-offender, it is better to confine his remarks to generalities only.[109]

The following described case is an excellent illustration of the advisibility of having some basis for any statement offered to one offender by way of proof that his co-offender has confessed. Several years ago one of the writers was interrogating two boys (brothers) who were suspected of committing a series of burglaries. For some time both of them persisted in their denials of any of the offenses, including the particular offense which brought about their arrest and which was the chief object of the present interrogation. Finally the younger one of the boys made an admission concerning one of the burglaries. He stated that he had assisted the other offender, his older brother, in throwing into a river some of the loot from a burglary. Equipped with this bit of information the investigator resumed his interrogation of the other subject, this time with a view to making him believe that his younger brother had made a complete confession of all the burglaries. The subject was told, "Well, your kid brother has told us everything; now let's see if you can straighten yourself out?" Since the subject seemed unimpressed and skeptical of what the interrogator had said, he was then told, "Just to show you I'm not kidding, how about that job when you and your

[109] It is interesting to note the instruction which was issued to the Spanish inquisitors regarding this technique: "The inquisitor must be careful not to enter into any details that might betray his ignorance to the accused. Let him keep to generalities". Sabatini, R., *Torquemada and the Spanish Inquisition* 176.

younger brother unloaded the brass metal in the river when things got too hot for you?" Thereupon the subject smiled and said, "You're bluffing; my brother didn't say that because it isn't true". Feeling quite confident that the younger boy was telling the truth about the brass disposal job, the interrogator decided to have him repeat the statement in the presence of the older boy. This was done, and the two boys then began to argue over who was telling the truth. However, soon thereafter the younger boy stated that he was mistaken about this particular job—adding that he had his brother confused with another boy whom he named and identified as his confederate in the theft of the brass. Nevertheless, he did implicate his own brother in several other burglaries. When confronted with such admissions the older boy also acknowledged his guilt.

In this case the boy to whom the interrogator had transmitted the incorrect information had every reason in the world to believe it was a bluff. Quite naturally he was not influenced by such a statement, and the same would be true in any case where an interrogator was inaccurate in his guess as to some detail offered as proof of the fact that a co-offender had already confessed.

An exception to the foregoing precautionary measure is to be made in a case where one of the offenders is definitely known to have played a secondary rôle in the commission of the offense. In such a case the subject may be told that the other offender has put the blame on him—for the planning of the offense, or for the actual shooting, etc. At the same time the interrogator may add: "I don't think this is so, but that's what he says. If it's not the truth, then you let us have the truth". In this way the interrogator avoids any danger to his bluff, since he concedes the possibility of the statement being a falsehood.

Interrogation of Suspects Whose Guilt is Doubtful or Uncertain

There are, in general, three courses or approaches available to an interrogator who is confronted with the task of interrogating a suspect whose guilt is doubtful or uncertain: (1) from the very outset of the interrogation he may treat the subject as though the subject were actually considered guilty of the offense in question: (2) he may immediately treat the subject as though the subject were actually considered innocent of the offense; or (3) he may assume a neutral position and refrain from making any statements or implications one way or the other until such time as the subject discloses some information or indications pointing either to his innocence or his guilt. What are the advantages and disadvantages attending each one of these three possible approaches?

The first approach, consisting of an implication or accusation of guilt, possesses the desirable element of surprise, and by pursuing this course the interrogator may on occasions successfully "shock" his subject into a confession in the event he is the guilty person. But this approach has two definite disadvantages: (a) if a guilty subject does not immediately succumb to the surprise or shock presented by the accusation or implication, he is thereby placed on his guard during the remainder of the interview, and if he eventually senses the fact that the approach is nothing more than a bluff, he is that much more fortified, psychologically, to continue his resistance; and (b) if the subject is innocent, he may become so confused and excited as a result of the guilt implication or accusation that it will be more difficult for the interrogator to ascertain the fact of the subject's innocence, or even to obtain possible clues or helpful information which the subject might otherwise be in a position to disclose.

The second approach, consisting of an implication or statement of a belief in the subject's innocence, possesses two distinct advantages, but these are offset to some extent by an attending disadvantage. The advantages may be stated as follows: (a) the interrogator's statement or implication of a belief in the subject's innocence will undoubtedly place an innocent subject at greater ease, and, as a result, the fact of his innocence may become more readily apparent to the interrogator; moreover, under such circumstances the interrogator can more successfully elicit whatever pertinent information or clues the subject may be in a position to divulge; (b) if the subject is actually guilty, this approach may cause him to lower his guard: he may become less cautious or even careless in his answers and in his conversation—as a result of which he is more apt to make a remark or contradiction that will not only make evident the fact of his guilt but which also can be used as a wedge for eliciting a confession. On the other hand, however, there is a disadvantage attending this approach when used on a guilty subject. Once an interrogator has committed himself as a believer in the subject's innocence, he must more or less confine his inquiries to those based upon an assumption of innocence, for to do otherwise would tend to destroy the very relationship or rapport which he seeks to establish by this approach. In other words, he is handicapped to the extent that he cannot freely adjust his methods and questioning to meet the subject's changing attitudes or inconsistencies. This is not an insurmountable difficulty, of course, but nevertheless, it is a possible disadvantage which the interrogator should consider before embarking upon this particular course.

The third approach, based upon a neutral position in which the interrogator refrains from making any commitments or implications as to the subject's innocence or guilt, obviously possesses neither the advantages nor the disadvantages of the other two. For this very reason, therefore, it may be considered the best approach to use in the average case where the interrogator's study and observation of his subject has given no encouraging indication that the subject might be particularly vulnerable to either one of the other two approaches.

Since the first approach is based upon an assumption of guilt, it calls for the immediate application of tactics and techniques designed to elicit an admission or confession. On the other hand, the second and third approaches require that the interrogator's efforts be directed immediately toward the detection of possible deception. As a matter of fact, if the first approach fails to produce the desired result, then even in that case the interrogator's problem becomes very much the same as that involved in the other two instances—the detection of deception.

It is not often possible to merely look at a person and determine whether or not he is lying (and guilty) or telling the truth (and innocent). Something more is necessary. The subject must be questioned and engaged in conversation in order to permit the interrogator to study the subject's behavior and conduct, to search for significant remarks or contradictions in the subject's statements, and to check his statements in the light of known facts or circumstances. The following described techniques are submitted as useful aids toward the end of providing an interrogator with such an opportunity. (Here again the alphabetical sequence of these interrogation methods has been preserved because of the fact that on occasions some of the following techniques may be of value in the interrogation of the previously described group of subjects, and vice versa).

O. ASK THE SUBJECT IF HE KNOWS WHY HE HAS BEEN BROUGHT IN FOR QUESTIONING

If up to the time of his interview the subject has not been informed of its purpose (either by the investigators or arresting officers, or by others), it is well for the interrogator to inquire of the subject, "Do you know why you are here?"

A guilty person who is asked such a question as this is immediately placed in a vulnerable defensive position. If he pleads ignorance when the circumstances clearly indicate his awareness of the purpose of the interrogation, that fact alone becomes of considerable importance to the interrogator, both for its diagnostic value as well as for its effect upon the subject's resistance when it is called to his attention as an indication of his guilt. On the other hand, if he admits knowing why he is being interrogated, he still may be kept on the defensive either by his own feeling of a necessity to offer an immediate explanation of his pretended innocence or, in the event he does not offer an unsolicited explanation, by an additional question such as, "Well, what do you know about (the offense)?" By thus being required to immediately defend himself, a guilty person may at the very outset of the interrogation make some significant remark or exhibit certain symptoms of guilt which otherwise might not have been so readily provoked.

If the subject happens to be innocent or ignorant of the particular offense under investigation but yet guilty of another offense, or in possession of pertinent information concerning such other offense, a "do you know why you are here" question may result in a lead to the solution of the latter offense. For instance, a reply of "Yes, you think I had something to do with the—job" (referring to the unsuspected offense) would obviously prompt the interrogator to make further inquiries about it. Information gained in this unexpected manner has led to the solution of cases which otherwise might have escaped the interrogator's attention.

Since this technique provides the interrogator with the foregoing advantages when dealing with subjects who are either guilty or concealing information, and since no disadvantage is encountered in using it on an innocent person, it is recommended as an effective method for beginning an interview with a suspect whose guilt is doubtful or uncertain.

P. OBTAIN FROM THE SUBJECT DETAILED INFORMATION ABOUT HIS ACTIVITIES
   BEFORE, AT THE TIME OF, AND AFTER THE OFFENSE IN QUESTION

Lawyers occasionally use a technique similar to this one in the cross examination of a witness whose testimony they seek to discredit by showing that although the witness' memory of his activities prior to and since the event in question is very bad (or very good, if such be the case), his memory of occurrences at the time when the offense was committed is, by comparison, unreasonably good (or unreasonably bad, as the case may be)—and therefore an apparent indication of untruthful testimony. In like manner a criminal interrogator may obtain indications of a subject's guilt or innocence, but the technique also opens up a number of other opportunities as well.

In employing this technique some interrogators not only seek detailed information covering the time just before the offense in question, but also delve into the subject's past history, in order to get what may be termed "background"; that is, information as to the subject's place of birth, his education, work, etc., all of which affords the interrogator a better opportunity to study or "size-up" his subject. In the average case, of course, it may not be necessary to go back much further than a few hours or days preceding the offense, but there are occasions when it is helpful to obtain information about the subject and his activities over a longer period of time. In any event, it is well for the interrogator to gradually lead his subject up to the day and time of the offense and then let him continue beyond that point, covering whatever subsequent period the investigator deems desirable.

Test the Validity of the Subject's Alibi

Unquestionably, the best way to check an alibi is by actual investigation methods. In other words, if a subject states that he was at a certain place during the time the offense was being committed elsewhere, the best way to determine whether or not he is telling the truth is to have an investigator go to the place stated by the subject and obtain information or evidence which will either substantiate or disprove the subject's contention. There are occasions, however, when this procedure is not feasible or even possible, and, therefore, reliance must sometimes be placed upon interrogation methods alone.

As previously suggested, one way to test the validity of a subject's alibi is to consider it in the light of his account of activities prior to and since the offense. A recollection of considerable detail as to activities before and after the offense, in contrast to an absence of a similar quality of recollection for the period of the offense may very well signify an effort to deceive; and calling this to the attention of the subject may facilitate a break in his resistance. In like manner, a significant and helpful disclosure may result from the contrast between a recollection of considerable detail at the time of the offense and the lack of it with regard to before and after occurrences. Moreover, a third situation might arise, to the ultimate advantage of the interrogator. A subject, while falsifying a detailed alibi, may realize the need for a comparable recollection of before and after activities and proceed to manufacture a set of before and after details which may be easily recognized as false and proved to be such by known facts already in the possession of the interrogator or else discovered by subsequent investigation.

Whenever a subject submits an alibi couched in such general terms as "I was out riding in my car the evening this crime was committed", it is advisable for the interrogator to have the subject relate all his activities during the period covered by the alibi, to name the places visited, or to state the route traveled, and also to give the approximate time for each activity or when each place was visited or each route traveled. In other words, suppose the crime was committed at 8 p.m., and the subject states he was riding in his car from 7 to 9 p.m. He should then be asked to trace the route he took, name the places he visited, and give the time at which he arrived or left. In this manner, he may be placed in a position of being unable to account for the full period from 7 to 9, or else find it necessary to offer fictitious details easily detected and provable as false.

Another method for testing an alibi—particularly as regards juveniles or young adult offenders—consists in asking the subject if he observed a certain occurrence which supposedly happened at the place mentioned in his alibi and during the time the subject alleges he was present. Thinking that the interrogator is referring to an actual occurrence, the subject may acknowledge his observation of it and thereby expose his deceit and guilt. For instance, the subject may state as his alibi that he was taking a walk along the lake shore at the time of the offense. He then may be asked in a rather curious and forceful manner: "This is a coincidence. My wife and I happened to be doing the same thing that evening. Did you see all the excitement on the shore when the kid was saved from drowning by the lifeguard"? An admission that he observed such a fictitious occurrence certainly would constitute an indication of deception and guilt, to say nothing of its value to the interrogator in his efforts to elicit a confession.

Some interrogators follow the practice of pausing at this stage of the interrogation to have a subject's detailed alibi statement reduced to writing and signed by him. Then, if the interrogator's subsequent efforts are unproductive of any specific indications of guilt or innocence, another statement regarding the alibi is obtained. This second statement is compared with the first one. If both statements agree in their various details, that fact is considered indicative of truthtelling, since few liars are able to remember all the details of a previous lie. On the other hand, however, if inconsistencies are present they can be called to the subject's attention and used as the basis for obtaining a confession.

Q. ASK THE SUBJECT TO RELATE ALL HE KNOWS ABOUT THE OCCURRENCE THE VICTIM, AND POSSIBLE SUSPECTS

In the early stages of the interrogation it is usually advisable to ask a few general questions regarding the subject's knowledge of the occurrence, the victim, possible suspects, etc. If the subject is innocent he is thereby given an opportunity to divulge possibly helpful information which otherwise might not be disclosed if his discussion were restricted to answering specific questions. On the other hand, if guilty, he is placed in a defensive position similar to that described with reference to Technique O, whereupon he may make a remark signifying his guilt, or a comment suggestive of a certain line of specific questioning, which lead might not have manifested itself except for this form of general questioning.

R. WERE CERTAIN FACTS SUGGESTIVE OF THE SUBJECT'S GUILT ARE KNOWN, ASK HIM ABOUT THEM RATHER CASUALLY AND IN A MANNER AS THOUGH THE REAL FACTS WERE NOT ALREADY KNOWN

The principal purpose of this technique is to afford the subject an opportunity to lie if he sees fit to do so. His answer will thus furnish a very good indication of his possible guilt or innocence; and if he is guilty, his position becomes very vulnerable when confronted with the facts possessed by the interrogator.

Rather than tell the subject a known fact and ask for an explanation, it is much more advantageous first to determine whether or not he will lie about the fact itself. Suppose, therefore, that in a robbery case the investigation disclosed that shortly after the robbery the subject made a substantial payment on his car, or paid off a large debt, or deposited money in a bank under a fictitious name. In such a case, instead of calling the occurrence to the subject's attention and asking for his explanation, the interrogator should casually inquire somewhat as follows: "Except for your salary (or other usual income) have you come into possession of any other money recently"? If he readily admits he has, and offers a satisfactory explanation of it, such a disclosure may serve to exonerate him from further suspicion. On the other hand, however, a lie to the question will be a strong indication of his possible guilt, and at the same time it will constitute a very valuable weapon for the interrogator to use in his efforts toward obtaining a confession.

For another illustration of the application of this technique, consider the case of a car owner suspected in a hit-and-run accident who tells the investigators that his car had been stolen from a place where he parked it prior to the accident. His car keys are found in the abandoned car. Under such circumstances an interrogator should inquire of the owner-suspect "You took the keys out of your car when you parked it, didn't you"? A reply of "yes" (which interrogators report to be the usual answer) will afford an opportunity to quickly break down the subject's entire story.

Although a lie under the foregoing conditions and circumstances usually may be considered indicative of guilt, the interrogator should realize, of course, that this is not always the case, since there may be some other motive for the lie than concealment of guilt. For instance, there have been many occasions when innocent persons have created much inconvenience and difficulty for both themselves and the police by lying about some phase of the investigation because they feared that a truthful answer might attract suspicion. And the same has been true of innocent persons lying as to their whereabouts at the time of a crime, as to their acquaintance with certain persons, or as to the possession of certain money, etc., because of an attempt to conceal some totally irrelevant indiscretion or embarrassing circumstance. Moreover, the lie may be told for the purpose of concealing another criminal offense. Nevertheless, taking into consideration these various other possibilities, the interrogator may often utilize this technique to a decided advantage.

8. AT VARIOUS INTERVALS ASK THE SUBJECT CERTAIN PERTINENT QUESTIONS IN A MANNER AS THOUGH THE CORRECT ANSWERS WERE ALREADY KNOWN

This technique, the converse of the previous one, is designed to elicit truthful information from a subject by creating the impression that the correct answer to a question is already known and that the interrogator is only interested in determining whether or not the subject is willing to tell the truth.

The answering of questions which imply the expected answers is the most common method of applying this technique (e.g., "You knew John Jones, didn't you"?). Another method, and a very effective one, consists of the prefacing of a selected question (not bearing directly upon the issue of the subject's guilt or innocence) with the statement, *"Think carefully before you answer this next question"*—an admonition which is apt to provoke a truthful reply even from a guilty subject, because of his fear that the truth is already known.

Whenever the desired acknowledgment does not result from the use of the "think carefully" warning, it is sometimes effective for the interrogator to express his skepticism about the reply given by stating "Are you *sure* about that"? In this way an opportunity is afforded a lying subject to reconsider the possible risk he incurs by not telling the truth about a fact which seems to be already known to the interrogator.

General Suggestions Regarding the Interrogation of Suspects and Offenders

In addition to the previously described interrogation principles, methods, and procedures, there are various other aspects of criminal interrogation worthy of consideration. They are here submitted as "general suggestions".

BE PATIENT AND PERSISTENT

Although there are occasions when a subject will respond immediately to some one or more of the tactics and techniques previously described, as a general rule more time is required to bring the interrogation to a successful conclusion. In one case the interrogation may last half an hour; in another case two hours—or even longer. During this period the interrogator's task is somewhat akin to that of a hunter stalking his game. Each must patiently maneuver himself or his quarry into a position from which the desired objective may be attained; and in the same manner that the hunter may lose his game by a noisy dash through the brush, so can the interrogator fail in his efforts by not exercising the proper degree of patience.

An interrogator should never lose sight of the fact that, after all, it is asking a great deal of a person to confess a crime which may mean the deprivation of his life or liberty; and there is no reason why we should expect him to confess without some degree of hesitation and resistance. Particularly is this true in cases where there is little or no other evidence of guilt apart from a possible confession itself.

Once a subject senses the fact that his interrogator is about to abandon his efforts the subject is thereby encouraged to continue his resistance. It is highly essential, therefore, that not only must the interrogator exercise considerable patience, but he must also carefully conceal whatever discouragement he may actually experience during the course of the interrogation.

Another prime requisite for a successful interrogation is persistency. In this respect the following rule of thumb is a helpful one for an interrogator to follow: *never conclude an interrogation at the time when you feel discouraged and ready to give up, but continue for a little while longer—if only for five or ten minutes.* The writers have observed many instances where the subject's resistance broke just at the very time when the interrogator himself was about ready to abandon his efforts.

THINK IN TERMS OF WHAT YOU MIGHT DO OR SAY, OR HOW YOU WOULD REACT, IF YOU WERE THE SUBJECT UNDER INTERROGATION

Place yourself "in the other fellow's shoes". By doing so, the interrogator may meet with success comparable to that attained by the farmer in the story of the lost mule. It seemed that several persons had searched long and laboriously for a lost mule, but with no success. Finally a searcher who had made the least manual effort of all returned with the missing animal. When questioned as to the secret of his success he replied: "Well, sir, I just thought to myself 'if I were a mule where would I go'; that's where I went, and there was the mule".

IF A SUBJECT REFUSES TO DISCUSS THE MATTER UNDER INVESTIGATION, CONCEDE TO HIM THE RIGHT TO REMAIN SILENT, AND THEN PROCEED TO POINT OUT THE INCRIMINATING SIGNIFICANCE OF HIS REFUSAL

The most effective way to deal with a subject who refuses to discuss the matter under investigation is to concede to him the right to remain silent. This usually has a very undermining effect. First of all, he is thereby disappointed in his expectation of the interrogator's resentment towards his claim of the constitutional privilege to remain silent. Secondly, a concession of this right impresses the subject with the apparent fairness of his interrogator.

After this psychological conditioning, the interrogator should then proceed to point out to the subject the incriminating significance of his refusal to talk. The following comments have been found to be very effective: "Certainly you have a legal right to remain silent. That's your privilege and no one will try to take it away from you. If that's the way you want to leave this it's all right with me. But let me ask you this. Suppose you were in my shoes and I were in yours and you called me in to ask me about this matter and I told you 'I don't want to answer any of your questions'.

You would think I had something to hide, and you'd be right in thinking that. That's exactly what I'll have to think about you, and so will everybody else. So if you have nothing to hide, let's sit here and talk this whole thing over".

After the subject has been talked to in this manner, the interrogator should then immediately ask the subject some innocuous questions which have no bearing whatsoever on the matter under investigation. For instance, the interrogator may inquire of the subject, "How long have you lived in this city"?, "Where are you working"?, "How long have you worked there"? As a rule the subject will answer such questions and then gradually the examiner may start in with questions pertaining to the offense under investigation. Except for the career criminal, there are very few persons who will persist in their initial refusal to talk after the interrogator has handled the situation in this suggested manner.

MAKE NO PROMISES WHEN ASKED, "WHAT WILL HAPPEN TO ME IF I TELL YOU THE TRUTH"?

Whenever a subject under interrogation makes such an inquiry as, "What will happen to me if I tell you the truth?" or "Do you think I'll go to jail if I confess?", the examiner should under no circumstances advise the subject of the consequences or hold out any inducement whatsoever. Any such reply would nullify the validity of the confession that may follow. Moreover, the interrogator should realize that whenever a subject raises a question of that sort, he is thereby beginning his confession. For these two reasons, therefore, the interrogator's reply should be somewhat as follows: "I'm not in a position to tell you what will happen if you tell the truth. That's up to a judge or someone else. I can't make any promises to you. I'm only here to find out the truth. If you think you have a 'break' coming to you, you'll have to ask the judge or someone else about that. My advice to you, however, is to tell the truth, and then if you think you have some consideration coming to you, take that up with the judge. If I wanted to, of course, I could deceive you by making a promise which I couldn't keep, or one which it would be unfair for me to make. But I'm not going to do that. That's not my way of doing business. It's up to you to make up your mind". These latter comments, displaying an apparent disinterest in any statement the subject is about to make, and also indicating a sense of fair play on the part of the interrogator, are invariably effective. Moreover, if later on the offender retracts his confession on the ground that it was forced from him, or obtained as a result of promises and inducements, the interrogator can in all sincerity relate the foregoing comments to good advantage.

The Preparation and Signing of the Written Confession

Experience has indicated that a large percentage of confessed criminals subsequently deny their guilt and either allege that no confession was ever made or else contend that it was obtained by force, duress, or other unlawful means. It is of the utmost importance, therefore, that the confession be reduced to writing and signed at the earliest possible moment, and that certain procedures be followed in its preparation in order to safeguard it against unwarranted attacks upon its validity at the time of trial.[110]

FORM OF CONFESSION

As a general rule the question and answer type of confession is to be preferred over the narrative form. For one reason it permits the incorporation of all the essential details in their most logical sequence. Then, too, if any part of it is later considered objectionable by the trial court, that part may be omitted or stricken out without affecting the confession as a whole.

In the event a stenographer is not readily available—and it appears that there may be a delay of several hours before the confession can be reduced to writing—the interrogator should write it himself, or else have the offender do so. In such instances the narrative form confession may suffice. The important thing is to get the offender's signature affixed to a written confession of some sort—at the earliest possible opportunity. Then, if later on circumstances permit the procurement of a typewritten question and answer form confession the latter may be substituted for the former. But if for some reason or other the more formal confession is unobtainable, the less formal document may still serve the purpose, though perhaps not so well as may have been desired.

Many good cases have been lost because an interrogator assumed that the next morning would be time enough to have a confession written and signed, only to find that in the meantime the offender had changed his mind about admitting his guilt. It is a safe practice, therefore, to lose no more time than is absolutely necessary in having it signed.

THE CONFESSOR'S OWN LANGUAGE

In the preparation of the written confession no attempt should be made to improve the language used by the subject himself. It should represent his confession *as he tells it*, and unless it does, a judge or jury may be reluctant to believe that a defendant whose education may have ended at the third grade spoke the language of a college graduate.

[110] For reasons subsequently discussed (*infra* p. 228), the writers are of the view that signed, written confessions are to be preferred over wire or tape recordings.

AVOIDANCE OF LEADING QUESTIONS

A confession in which the interrogator has done most of the talking, and the subject has confessed largely through "yes" or "no" answers, is not nearly so convincing and effective as one in which the interrogator plays the minor part and the subject plays the leading rôle of both informer and confessor. It is highly important, therefore, that the interrogator let the subject supply his own details of the occurrence and to this end the interrogator should avoid or at least minimize the use of leading questions.

To illustrate the point, suppose a subject is in the process of confessing a murder in which it is a known fact that the gun involved in the crime was thrown away under a certain house. The confessor has been giving various details of the crime and the interrogator is about to inquire regarding the disposal of the gun. At this stage some interrogators say: "Then you threw the gun under the house, didn't you"?—a question calling merely for a "yes" answer. But it is far more convincing to a court or jury to have the gun details appear in answer to a non-leading question such as "Then what did you do with the gun"?—a question calling for detailed information from the confessor himself.[111]

In addition to the foregoing advantages attending non-leading questions, there is another factor to be considered. Occasionally an interrogator will encounter a situation where subsequent to the confession he will become skeptical as to its validity—particularly where there is some suspicion that the confessor is a pathological liar and may be absolutely innocent of the crime to which he has confessed.[112] In such instances the interrogator will find considerable comfort in being able to evaluate the confession in the light of certain known facts; and this he can ordinarily do unless during the interrogation he disclosed such facts to the subject in the form of leading questions. In other words, in the above stated hypothetical case-situation regarding the gun under the house, an interrogator who had asked the subject what he did with the gun, and was told "I threw it under the house" (where the gun was actually found), is in a far more desirable position than the now skeptical interrogator who had told the subject "Then you threw the gun under the house, didn't you"? and merely received a "yes" answer.

[111] The practical importance of avoiding leading question is well illustrated by the United States Supreme Court case of Lyons v. Oklahoma, 322 U. S. 596 (1943), in which the Court, in sustaining the admissability of a confession, placed considerable significance in the fact that "The answers to the questions, as transcribed by a stenographer, contain statements correcting and supplementing the questioner's information and do not appear to be mere supine attempts to give the desired response to leading questions". (p. 605.)

[112] For further comments and references regarding pathological liars see *supra* p. 78.

PERSONAL HISTORY QUESTIONS

At his trial the offender may attack the validity of a confession by alleging that he only stated what he was told to say—that the interrogator "put the words into my mouth". An excellent precautionary measure to effectively meet such a defense is the practice of incorporating in the confession a number of more or less irrelevant questions calling for answers that only the offender himself would know. For instance he may be asked the date and place of his birth, his mother's maiden name, etc. With such questions and answers included in the confession, the prosecution may call this fact to the attention of the court or jury, as indications that the offender volunteered the information contained in his confession and was not merely accommodating the interrogator by repeating what he was told to say.

INTENTIONAL ERRORS FOR CORRECTION BY THE CONFESSOR HIMSELF

For much the same reasons that personal history data are incorporated into the confession, it is a good practice to purposely arrange for the presence on each page of the confession of one or two errors, such as an incorrect name of a person or street, which will be subject to later correction by the confessor when the document is read by or to him. Any such corrections, of course, should be in the confessor's own handwriting, accompanied by his initials or signature in the margin alongside the corrections. When confronted at his trial with a confession bearing corrections of this nature, the confessor will encounter considerable difficulty in denying that he read the document before signing it.

READING AND SIGNING OF CONFESSION

It is advisable for the interrogator to read the written confession aloud as the confessor follows the written document word for word. When the previously described intentional errors are reached, the subject himself will usually call them to the interrogator's attention; to play safe, however, the interrogator should keep the errors in mind and raise a question as to them in the event the subject neglects to do so.

In addition to the placing of initials or signatures alongside corrections, the subject should be requested to place his "O.K.", followed by his initials or signature, at the bottom of each page after the contents have been read by or to him. Then, at the end of the confession, it is well to have the offender write out, in his own hand, some such statement as the following: "I have read this statement of mine and it is the truth. I made it of my own free will, without any threats or promises having been made to me by anyone".[113] After this should appear his signature.

[113] In the event a legally permissible promise is made, then, of course, the statement should contain the exception. For example, if a promise not to divulge the con-

WARNING

The confession need not contain any statement regarding a warning of constitutional rights. No such warning is required except, by statute, in the State of Texas, and by a specific provision in the United States Code of Military Justice with respect to military offenses.[114]

WITNESSES

In most instances where the offender does not object to the oral confession being reduced to writing he will readily sign it in the presence of one or more witnesses in addition to the interrogator himself. There are some occasions, however, when a hesitating and wavering confessor may balk at the signing if other persons, and particularly uniformed police officers, enter the room for the obvious purpose of witnessing the signature. In such instances it may be advisable to have the confession signed only in the interrogator's presence. Then, a few minutes later, in the presence of other witnesses, the interrogator may elicit an identification of the signature and an acknowledgment of the validity of the confession itself.

As a matter of fact, however, a written confession need not be signed by any witnesses. All that is required is to have some one person authenticate it—someone to testify he saw the defendant sign it. For greater effectiveness, of course, the authenticating witness should also be the one to establish the fact that the accused made the confession and that the written document was read to him as he himself followed the written contents. All this testimony can best be supplied by the interrogator himself.

As regards all these various considerations regarding written confessions, the fact should be borne in mind that an oral confession is as admissible in evidence as a written one, the only difference being the greater weight and credibility usually given to the written, signed confession.[115]

PRESERVATION OF STENOGRAPHIC NOTES

Although a confession written and signed as previously outlined will be difficult to attack in court, there may be occasions when it will become necessary to refute certain objections to it by calling as a witness the stenographer who prepared the typewritten copy from her shorthand notes. The only way this can be done, of course, is to have the stenographer read to the court and jury the original shorthand notes. It is advisable, therefore,

---

fession to the newspapers was actually made, the statement should conclude with the words "except that Mr. — promised me he would not give this information to the newspapers". (For a discussion of the type of promises which will not nullify a confession, see *infra* p. 219.)

[114] See *infra* p. 223.
[115] See *infra* p. 227.

that these notes be preserved until the case has been finally disposed of in court.

At the time of trial, usually several months after the confession, an interrogator may be cross-examined at considerable length regarding the conditions and circumstances under which the confession was obtained. To meet such a contingency, he should never rely solely upon his memory. It is desirable, therefore, to keep notes regarding such matters as the time when the interrogation was begun and ended, the time when the confession was signed, the names of the persons who witnessed the signing, and also information as to the general condition of the interrogation room, particularly with reference to its lighting arrangements and approximate temperature.

A CONFESSION IS NOT THE END OF THE INVESTIGATION

Many investigators have the impression that once a confession has been obtained the investigation is ended. But seldom if ever is this true.

A confession that is unsubstantiated by other evidence is far less effective at the trial than one which has been investigated and subjected to verification or supporting evidence. For instance, assume that a confessed murderer has told when and where he purchased the knife he used in the killing, and that he identified a gas station where he washed his bloody hands, and that he told of a chance meeting he had with an acquaintance as he left the gas station. There should then be an immediate investigation regarding the purchase of the knife. If the seller remembers the transaction, he should be asked to give a signed statement about it. This will serve to insure his cooperation at the time of trial and minimize the risk of his possible appearance as a witness for the defense to deny any such transaction. For similar reasons interviews should be had with, and statements obtained from, the gas station attendants and the defendant's acquaintance. A confession thus supported and substantiated will be far more valuable than the bare document itself.

The Interrogation of Witnesses and Other Prospective Informants

The basic principles underlying the previously described techniques for interrogating suspects and offenders are, in general, equally applicable to cases involving the interrogation of witnesses and other prospective informants.

The search for and the interview of witnesses at the crime scene itself call for the employment of proper psychological techniques to much the same extent as does the interrogation of witnesses or informants who are located later and questioned at a place other than the scene of the crime. An excellent illustration of the proper method of an interrogation of witnesses at a crime scene is the one appearing below from the *Accident Investigation Manual* published by the Northwestern University Traffic Institute. Although it describes an automobile accident investigation, the principles there developed are equally applicable to a murder case or any other type of offense.

"Some officers seem never to be able to find witnesses; others have little difficulty. One officer in the former category would shoulder his way through a crowd. 'Did anybody see this accident?' he would shout. 'How about you?' 'How about you?' He would all but push the people about. Naturally, he found very few witnesses. In reporting back to his partner he would say, 'there weren't any witnesses. I went through the crowd four times asking everybody, but nobody saw the accident'. An adroit officer uses his head rather than his lung power. He goes about the job quietly. Perhaps he spots a talkative woman—at least one such person is to be found at most accidents. 'How do you do, madam', he says, 'did I understand you to say that you saw this accident?' 'Why, no, officer', she replies, probably feeling flattered that he singled her out, 'I didn't see it, but that man in the straw hat over there was telling me all about it. He was right here when it happened.' In approaching the man, the officer is very courteous but just a little more brisk and businesslike. He plans his question carefully. He does not say, 'did you see this accident'? but rather, 'pardon me, sir, would you mind telling me what you saw in connection with this accident?' This officer seldom has difficulty in finding witnesses.

"He listens carefully to their accounts of the accident. Then, if they are willing to write out a statement, he provides them with notebook and pencil and asks them to sign what they write. If they will not write the statement, he writes it, reads it to them aloud, then has them sign it. If they refuse to sign, he does not insist; they are still his witnesses and he wants their good will when they appear on the stand in the trial, if a trial follows.

"In brief, the good investigator usually seeks his witnesses indirectly. He finds somebody who knows that somebody else saw the accident. Getting the witness' name if possible, he addresses him by it. He is quiet and courteous. In requesting the witness to write and sign a statement or merely to sign it, he puts his question positively, not negatively. Instead of saying, won't you sign this, please?' he hands the pencil to the person and says, 'sign here, if you don't mind. It will make our investigation complete'. If the witness does not want to sign, the officer is cheerful, not resentful".[116]

[116] P. 171–172, *Accident Investigation Manual*, published by the Northwestern University Traffic Institute (1946). The author of the chapter of the manual in which the above quotation appears is the Institute's Director, Colonel Franklin M. Kreml.

Although a criminal interrogator ordinarily will not experience much difficulty in obtaining information from witnesses to a crime or from persons in possession of information derived from some other source, there are instances when a witness or other prospective informant will attempt to withhold whatever information he may have concerning another's guilt. In the interrogation of such subjects the following suggestions should assist the interrogator in obtaining the desired information.[117]

A. ASSURE THE WILLING BUT FEARFUL WITNESS OR OTHER PROSPECTIVE INFORMANT THAT HE WILL NOT BE HARMED BY THE OFFENDER OR HIS RELATIVES OR FRIENDS, AND THAT HE WILL RECEIVE POLICE PROTECTION IN THE EVENT SUCH PROTECTION BECOMES NECESSARY

It is quite natural that under certain conditions and circumstances a witness or other prospective informant might be desirous of assisting the police but yet be restrained from doing so because of his fear of retaliation at the hands of the offender or his relatives or friends. In such instances it is advisable to give the subject the following assurances:

(1) That retaliation is an extremely rare occurrence where the witness or informant is acting in good faith and without any selfish motive, such as receiving pay for his information, seeking personal revenge on the offender, etc. In this connection it is well to ask the subject if he knows of any case where an honest court witness, or an honest policeman or prosecuting attorney, was ever subsequently harmed by the offender or by someone else acting in the offender's behalf.

(2) That (where circumstances permit—e.g., where court testimony from the subject may not be necessary) the information he gives will be kept confidential and that therefore the offender and others will never know of the subject's cooperation with the police.

(3) That if it becomes necessary for him to testify in court, his previous cooperation will not be disclosed by the police, and since he will be subpoenaed as a witness he can always justify his act of testifying on the ground that he was ordered to do so by the court.

(4) That an adequate police guard will be assigned to the subject if he so desires, or if such protection is deemed necessary.

Along with the foregoing attempts to secure the proper degree of cooperation from a subject of this type, it is advisable to point out to him the fact that the interrogator is asking no more of him than he himself would expect of another person in the event the subject or some member of his family were the one against whom the offense was committed. More-

---

[117] No consideration is given to the investigator's problem regarding the police informer or "stool pigeon", for the reason that the handling of an informer or "stool pigeon" is essentially a matter of investigation rather than interrogation.

over, it is well to impress upon the subject his obligations, as a citizen of the community, to render such cooperation to the police.

In the event none of the foregoing suggestions suffice to elicit the desired information, the willing but fearful witness or other prospective informant may be treated as an actual suspect, in the manner described under the following technique (B). Ordinarily, however, resort to the latter method is unnecessary.

B. WHENEVER A WITNESS OR OTHER PROSPECTIVE INFORMANT REFUSES TO COOPERATE BECAUSE HE IS DELIBERATELY PROTECTING THE OFFENDER'S INTERESTS, OR BECAUSE HE IS ANTI-SOCIAL OR ANTI-POLICE IN HIS ATTI-TUDE, ACCUSE HIM OF THE OFFENSE AND PROCEED TO INTERROGATE HIM AS THOUGH HE WERE ACTUALLY CONSIDERED TO BE THE OFFENDER HIMSELF

Occasionally it is possible to break the bond of loyalty between a subject and the offender he is attempting to protect, by convincing the subject of disloyalty on the part of the offender. For instance, in the interrogation of a subject who is the wife, sweetheart, or mistress of the offender, she may be told that the offender is unfaithful to her and in love with another woman (whose true or fictitious name should be given); and by this method the subject may be induced to change her attitude toward the interrogator's request for helpful information. It is also possible, on occasions, to change a subject's anti-social or anti-police attitude by patiently pointing out to him the unreasonableness and unsoundness of his views. Ordinarily, however, some more effective measures are necessary.

There is one consideration which a subject of this type is likely to place above all others, and that is the protection of his own interest and welfare. When all other methods have failed, therefore, the interrogator should accuse the subject of committing the crime (or of being implicated in it in some way) and proceed to interrogate him as though he were in fact considered to be the guilty individual. A witness or other prospective informant, thus faced with the possibility of a trial or conviction for a crime he did not commit, will sooner or later be impelled to abandon his efforts in the offender's behalf or in support of his anti-social or anti-police attitudes.

Ethics of Criminal Interrogation

As the reader will soon observe—in the discussion of "The Law Concerning Criminal Interrogations"—the interrogation methods which are described in this text are legally proper and permissible. Nevertheless, even though the methods are legal, some readers may feel that certain of them are unethical and unfair to the subject who is being questioned. Let us pause briefly, therefore, to consider the criticisms which may arise concerning the ethical aspects of interrogation and to weigh the validity of these objections.

With none of the interrogation methods herein described do we revert to the medieval proposition that a confession must be obtained at all costs so as to obviate the necessity, and perhaps extra effort, of gathering other forms of evidence. Not for one minute do the writers intend or suggest that the police abandon or lessen their efforts as criminal investigators in favor of the practice of depending upon criminal interrogations for crime solutions and legal evidence. Moreover, such a shift of emphasis is highly improbable, first, because a confession which is unsubstantiated by confirmatory evidence lacks the weight in the eyes of the courts of a confession substantiated by independent evidence and, second, because without proper preliminary investigation the chances of obtaining a confession are greatly reduced. Nevertheless, the fact still remains that in certain instances the only alternative is to obtain evidence of guilt by a criminal interrogation, for in all communities many offenses are committed in such a manner or under such conditions and circumstances that the best investigative practices alone will not produce the solution. Consequently, there is, and perhaps always will be, a necessity for the practice of conducting interrogations. Therefore, it is to the best public interest that criminal interrogations be conducted in the most effective manner consistent with legal requirements and prohibitions.

Although it must be conceded that a few of these interrogation methods are, in a certain sense of the word, "unfair" to the person under interrogation, it can be stated with the utmost confidence that *none of the methods are apt to induce an innocent person to confess a crime he did not commit.* On the other hand, of course, they do serve the valuable purpose of bringing criminal offenders to the bar of justice, and thus prohibiting a continuance of their criminal careers. It is the writers' opinion that these facts should be carefully weighed when criticizing the ethics of any criminal interrogation technique, and such facts are of the utmost importance when consideration is given to the seriousness of the offenses which may be involved. (For example, consider for the moment the murderer, the rapist, or the criminal who commits armed robbery, as well as many other such offenders, who in many instances, except for interrogation and ultimate confession, might otherwise be allowed to remain at large and to commit similar or more serious crimes.)

In dealing with most criminal offenders, it is impractical and futile merely to give them a pencil and paper and trust that their conscience will impel them to confess. By and large their crimes are the result of some selfish motive and that same self-interest is not easily removed. Something more is required, and at times the interrogator must deal with a criminal offender in a somewhat lower moral plane than that upon which ethical, law-abiding citizens are expected to conduct their everyday affairs. That plane, in the interest of innocent suspects, has been wisely restricted—and in the writers' opinion, sufficiently restricted—in that only those interrogation methods, including both the "fair" as well as the "unfair", will be tolerated which will not cause an innocent person to confess a crime for which he is not guilty.[118]

Furthermore, police officers untrained and ill-equipped to conduct proper and effective interrogations are inclined to resort to physical abuse, threats, and promises to attain their objectives. In the interest of a reduction of such practices, which admittedly produce occasional miscarriages of justice and also tend to destroy an officer's self-respect, the interrogation techniques herein described should serve a very useful purpose.

Criminal Interrogation Specialists

There is as great a need for specialization in the field of criminal interrogation as there is for specialization in any other phase of criminal investigation or police administration. Within every police department or other investigating agency, some one person or group of persons should be assigned the function of interrogating criminal suspects. It should be the responsibility of persons who are specially qualified and specially trained for the purpose. A department or agency that established such a practice will solve more crimes and account for more convictions than another organization which entrusts this task to any investigator who happens to be involved in the case arrest or investigation.

[118] For an extended discussion of the reasons justifying the employment of "unethical" practices in criminal interrogations, see Inbau, "The Confession Dilemma in the United States Supreme Court," 43 Ill. L. Rev. 442 (1948).

THE LAW CONCERNING CRIMINAL CONFESSIONS

A criminal interrogator should always remember that it is his function not only to obtain a confession from a guilty subject, but also to obtain one which meets all the necessary legal requirements—so that it can be used as evidence at the trial of the accused. For this reason, familiarity with the law concerning criminal interrogations is in many respects equally as important as a mastery of the psychological tactics and techniques employed in eliciting the confession.

I

What are the General Principles Governing the Admissibility of a Confession?

The cruelty and injustice that resulted from the early practices of extorting confessions from accused persons by tearing their bodies apart on a rack, or by inflicting other forms of torture, eventually led to the development of certain precautionary rules regarding the admissibility of confessions.[119] The basic rules declared that before a confession could be used against an accused person it must be shown to represent a *voluntary* acknowledgment of guilt, or else it must have been obtained under conditions or circumstances which could not reasonably be considered as rendering it *untrustworthy*.

Although legal scholars differ somewhat as to which is the historically accurate test—the test of voluntariness or the test of trustworthiness—as a practical matter it seemed to make little difference which of these two tests was applied. In other words, the type of force, threat, or promise that would be considered sufficient to render a confession involuntary (by a court applying the test of voluntariness) would in all probability be declared sufficient to render a confession untrustworthy (by a court applying the test of trustworthiness); likewise, an untrustworthy confession would seldom be a voluntary one.[120]

The voluntary-trustworthy test of confession admissibility prevailed in

---

[119] Wigmore, *Evidence* (1940) §§822, 865, 2266.

[120] The late Dean Wigmore, in his treatise on *Evidence*, condemned the test of voluntariness as historically incorrect as well as inadequate. He contended that those who sponsor the test of voluntariness do so under the erroneous impression that there is an association between the confession rule and the privilege against self-incrimination, whereas the fact is that in point of time the origin of the confession rule and the privilege are widely separated. (The confession rule was enunciated about one hundred years after the recognition of the privilege against self-incrimination.) Moreover, the privilege against self-incrimination was designed to cover only statements in court under process as a witness, whereas the confession rule was intended to cover statements both in court and out. See Wigmore, *Evidence* (1940) §§823–827; 2266).

On the other hand, Professor McCormick and others find a kinship between the confession rule and the privilege against self-incrimination, and they see in the test

both federal and state courts until 1943–44, at which time the United States Supreme Court laid down a much more restrictive test in federal cases, and it also modified the conventional test in state cases.[121]

THE GENERAL TEST IN FEDERAL CASES

Since the United States Supreme Court has an inherent supervisory power over lower federal courts and federal law-enforcement officers, it was privileged, without specific legislative authorization, to impose whatever standards it desired regarding confession admissibility in federal cases. This it did in 1943, after having had presented to it for review several earlier cases involving interrogation practices which no self-respecting police officer could condone.[122] Although these cases were from state courts, most of the Supreme Court Justices apparently assumed that the interrogation practices there disclosed were universally employed in federal as well as state investigations. The Court then embarked upon its crusade to end or at least reduce the extent of such practices. It struck its first hard blow in the 1943 case of *McNabb v. United States*.[123] This case involved an investigation into the killing of an agent of the Alcohol Tax Unit of the Bureau of Internal Revenue. Five members of the McNabb family were arrested as suspects

---

of voluntariness an indication that the rules restricting the use of confessions are prompted by a desire to protect the subject against torture, as well as by a desire to safeguard the trustworthiness of the evidence. For an excellent discussion of the relative merits of these two views, see McCormick, "The Scope of Privilege in the Law of Evidence" (1938) 16 Texas L. Rev. 447 at pp. 452–457. Also see McCormick's very interesting article "Some Problems and Developments in the Admissibility of Confessions" (1946) 24 Texas L. Rev. 239; and Morgan, "The Privilege against Self-Incrimination" (1949) 34 Minn. L. Rev. 1.

For a concise discussion of the history and policy of the privilege against self-incrimination and of its relationship to the confession rule, see Inbau, *Self-Incrimination: What Can An Accused Person Be Compelled to Do?* (1950) at pp. 3–9.

[121] Prior to 1943 the practice of the Supreme Court in both federal and state cases was to determine from the trial court record whether the jury acted reasonably in holding that the defendant's confession had not been "forced" out of him, or, stated somewhat differently, "had not been obtained in a manner which rendered it untrustworthy". If the Supreme Court decided that the evidence clearly indicated force, and therefore untrustworthiness, the due process clause of either the Fifth or Fourteenth Amendment would be invoked and the case reversed. On the other hand, however, if the record did not clearly disclose coercion or untrustworthiness, the court would accept as final the trial court's finding that the confession was voluntary or trustworthy. Wilson v. United States, 162 U.S. 613 (1896); and Brown v. Mississippi, 297 U.S. 278 (1936)—the first state court confession case to be decided by the United States Supreme Court.

After abandoning this test of confession admissibility during the period from 1943 to 1949, the Court began to return to it. On June 15, 1953, the return was completed by the decision in Stein v. N. Y., *infra* note 146.

[122] Chambers v. Florida, 309 U.S. 227 (1940); White v. Texas, 310 U.S. 530 (1940); Ward v. Texas, 316 U.S. 547 (1942).

[123] 318 U.S. 332 (1943).

and questioned regarding the killing. Several hours after the last McNabb was arrested he confessed, upon being told that his brothers accused him of firing the fatal shot. Later on two others confessed their implication in the crime. A federal court trial resulted in a verdict of guilty, and the defendants ultimately appealed to the United States Supreme Court, alleging that the confessions were improperly admitted into evidence. The Government contended that the confessions were voluntarily given and therefore properly admitted.

Ordinarily an issue of the sort raised in the *McNabb* appeal would have been resolved on the basis of a "due process" inquiry. Here, however, the Court conceded that since the defendants had not been threatened, abused, or otherwise coerced, there was no problem of constitutional law respecting the confessions and their admissibility; but the Court then stated that its reviewing power in federal cases was not confined to the ascertainment of constitutional validity. Mr. Justice Frankfurter, in speaking for the majority of the Justices, said that "judicial supervision of the administration of criminal justice in the federal courts implies the duty of establishing and maintaining civilized standards of procedure and evidence," and that such standards "are not satisfied merely by observance of those minimal historic safeguards . . . summarized as 'due process of law'."[124] Justice Frankfurter then proceeded to state that the McNabb brothers had been put in "barren cells" and kept them there for many hours of "unremitting questioning", instead of being taken "before a United States commissioner or a judicial officer, as the law requires, in order to determine the sufficiency of the justification for their detention".[125] Because of this supposed infraction of the law by the officers, the Court held that the confessions obtained during the delay in arraignment (i.e., "preliminary hearing") should not have been admitted in evidence, and the convictions were accordingly set aside. The Court considered the officers' conduct a "flagrant disregard" of federal laws and expressed the view that if the convictions were upheld the Court would become an accomplice to the wilful disobedience of the law; and that although Congress had not explicitly forbidden the use of evidence so procured, if the courts permitted such evidence to stand they would stultify the policy which Congress enacted into law. In opposition to this view, Mr. Justice Reed in his dissent objected to "broadening the possibilities of defendants escaping punishment by these more vigorous technical requirements in the administration of justice". "If these confessions are otherwise voluntary", said Justice Reed, "civilized standards . . . are not advanced by setting aside these judgments because of acts of omission which are not shown to have tended toward coercing the admission".[126]

[124] 318 U S. 332 at p. 340 (1943).
[125] 318 U.S. 332 at p. 344–345 (1943).
[126] 318 U.S. 332 at p. 349 (1943). The majority of the Court may have been affected by a consideration of the federal rule regarding the nullification of evidence seized in

A rather amazing feature of the *McNabb* case is the fact that the defendants actually had been arraigned promptly, but the trial court record did not disclose the arraignment and the Supreme Court erroneously assumed that no arraignment had occurred until after the confessions had been obtained.[127] Moreover, the fact of actual arraignment was even called to the Court's attention in the Government's petition for a rehearing, but to no avail.[128] A retrial of the case resulted in a second conviction which was affirmed by the Circuit Court of Appeals and the case ended there.[129]

In addition to the Court's mistaken interpretation of the factual situation in the *McNabb* case, the federal statute relied upon by the Court as embodying a policy which it thought an affirmance of the case would "stultify" was actually enacted for distinctly other reasons than the one assumed by the Court. Its legislative history reveals that the sole purpose of the act (passed in 1893) was to suppress a practice whereby federal commissioners and marshals were cheating the Government in the matter of fees and mileage expense charges. The issue of interrogation practices and confessions was entirely without Congressional consideration.[130]

Despite the many criticisms leveled at the *McNabb* decision, the "civilized standards" rule which the Court laid down in that case still stands.[131]

---

violation of a constitutional mandate. In the *McNabb* case situation, however, there was no violation of a constitutional prohibition but only a statutory one. Even assuming, therefore, that the federal rule excluding illegally obtained evidence is a good one, the same quality of argument cannot be voiced regarding the indirect enforcement of statutory provisions.

[127] See Circuit Court of Appeals' decision affirming the conviction of the McNabbs upon their second trial: 142 Fed. (2d) 904 (1944).

[128] 319 U.S. 784 (1942); also, *supra* note 127, and 90 Cong. Rec. 9199 (1944).

[129] See *supra* note 127.

[130] For a detailed discussion of the legislative history of this act as well as of similar federal legislation, see Inbau, "The Confession Dilemma in the United States Supreme Court" (1948) 43 Ill. L. Rev. 442, at pp. 455–459.

[131] At a meeting of the American Bar Association soon after the *McNabb* decision the Association voted overwhelmingly against the incorporation in the Federal Rules of Criminal Procedure of a proposed rule which in effect would have perpetuated the *McNabb* case decision as a rule of court. The proposed rule was deleted from the draft of rules finally presented to the Supreme Court by the drafting committee. (The Supreme Court's apparent tacit approval of the rejection did not, of course, remove the effect of the *McNabb* decision itself.)

For further evidence of the general disapproval of the *McNabb* case rule, see: Hearings Before Subcommittee 2 of the Committee on the Judiciary, House of Representatives, 78 Cong., 1st Sess., on H.R. 3690 (1944) 11–17; A Statement by the Committee on Bill of Rights of the American Bar Association on H.R. 3690 (1944) 42; 90 Cong. Rec. 9366, 9368 (1944). Also see Waite, "Police Regulation by Rules of Evidence" (1944) 42 Mich. L. Rev. 679, 688–692. Moreover, a bill known as the Hobbs bill was introduced in Congress to nullify the effect of the *McNabb* case. It passed the House at three different sessions and was voted upon favorably by the Senate Judiciary Committee. The bill progressed no further, however, because some of its supporters thought that legislation was no longer necessary after the Supreme

The latest re-affirmance of the rule, however, was by a 5–4 decision, in *Upshaw v. United States*.[132] In the *Upshaw* case the defendant was arrested at 2:00 o'clock on Friday morning and questioned briefly concerning the theft for which he was arrested. He was again questioned on two occasions that same morning (at about 9:00 a.m. and 11:00 a.m.), and twice again later on during the day (at about 5:00 p.m. and 7:00 p.m.). On Saturday morning, after a sixth interrogation (at about 9:00 a.m.) he admitted his guilt. On none of these occasions was he questioned by more than one officer, and no session lasted longer than thirty minutes. It was not until Monday morning, however, that the accused was taken before a committing magistrate for arraignment. This delay was considered "unnecessary" by the Supreme Court and the "civilized standards" rule of the *McNabb* case was applied in reversing Upshaw's conviction. Here in the *Upshaw* case the majority of the Supreme Court made its position clear that they still meant what was said in the *McNabb* case.

As the *McNabb-Upshaw* rule now stands, therefore, if a confession is obtained during a period of "unnecessary delay" in taking an arrested person before a federal commissioner for arraignment, the confession cannot be used in a federal case against the accused regardless of its otherwise independent quality of voluntariness or trustworthiness.[133] At the present time, this rule is subject only to the following qualifications:

1. The "unnecessary delay" must occur before rather than after the confession. In other words if a confession is obtained immediately after an arrest, a subsequent "unnecessary delay" in arraignment will not destroy the confession's validity.[134]

2. If a federal commissioner is unavailable, as at night or over a weekend or other holiday, the delay in arraignment then becomes a necessary one and a valid confession may be obtained during the period pending a commissioner's availability.[135]

3. If an arrested person has been properly arraigned on one charge, he may be questioned regarding another offense and a confession to the latter

---

Court's decision in Mitchell v. United States, 322 U.S. 65 (1944), which was erroneously interpreted as representing a substantial modification of the extreme position taken in the *McNabb* case.

[132] 335 U.S. 410 (1948).

[133] Rule 5 of the present Federal Rules of Criminal Procedure, which uses the term "unnecessary delay", supersedes the various statutory provisions which contained such language as "immediately" or "forthwith".

[134] Mitchell v. United States, 322 U.S. 65 (1944). In this case the defendant confessed promptly after his arrest but eight days elapsed before he was taken before a federal commissioner for arraignment. The Supreme Court held that the illegality of the subsequent detention did not retroactively change the circumstances under which the confession was made.

[135] Garner v. United States, 174 F. (2d) 499 (1949); cert. den., 337 U.S. 945 (1949). In Patterson v. United States, 183 Fed. (2d) 687 (1950), the court held that the defendant had the burden of showing the availability of a federal commissioner before

will be unaffected by the fact that he was not arraigned on that particular charge also.[136]

THE GENERAL TEST IN STATE CASES

One year after the United States Supreme Court promulgated its "civilized standards" doctrine for federal cases, a somewhat similar attempt was made to impose a higher, "civilized" standard of investigative practices upon state law enforcement officers. Lacking the inherent supervisory power that it could exercise in federal matters, the Supreme Court simply followed the expedient of enlarging its conception of the "due process" requirement of the Fourteenth Amendment. Instead of merely requiring that confessions be voluntary or trustworthy, the Court now insisted that they should be free of any "inherent coercion". It laid down that rule in the case of *Ashcraft v. Tennessee*.[137]

In the *Ashcraft* case the defendant had been taken late one afternoon to a morgue where he identified as his wife the body of a woman who had been beaten to death. From the morgue Ashcraft was escorted to the county jail and questioned for several hours, after which he was released without having been placed under formal arrest. Nine days later he was arrested and taken to jail for further questioning. He was interrogated intermittently for 28 hours, whereupon he told the officers a Negro named Ware had killed his wife. Ware, who had not been suspected previously, was

he could complain about an unnecessary delay in arraignment. The general holding in the case was to the effect that once the government made a *prima facie* showing that the confession was voluntary, the defendant carried the burden of proving a violation of the arraignment rule.

[136] United States v. Carignan, 342 U.S. 36 (1951). Although the Supreme Court reversed the conviction in this case on other grounds, the majority of the Justices were of the opinion that the *McNabb* case rule had not been violated because of the defendant's lawful detention on the first charge. "We decline", reads the majority opinion, "to extend the *McNabb* fixed rule of exclusion to statements to police or wardens concerning other crimes while prisoners are legally in detention on criminal charges". (p. 45.)

A minority of the Court (Justices Douglas, Black, and Frankfurter) apparently are fearful of deliberate police evasion of the *McNabb* rule by arresting and properly arraigning a person on one charge for the primary purpose of interrogating him about another, more important offense. The minority opinion states: "Arraignment for one crime gives some protection. But when it is a pretense or used as the device for breaking the will of the prisoner on long, relentless, or repeated questionings, it is abhorrent. We should free the federal system of that disreputable practice which has honeycombed the municipal police system in this country. We should make illegal such a perversion of a 'legal' detention". (p. 46.) For similar views regarding the use of "Material Witness" statutes to legalize the detention and extensive interrogation of suspects, see 17 U. of Chicago L. Rev. 706 (1950) and 24 Temple L.Q. 232 (1950).

See also Tyler v. United States, 193 Fed. (2d) 24 (1951), where the defendant, who had been properly arraigned on one charge, was delivered by his jailor to police officers and then taken elsewhere in the city for a lie-detector test regarding another crime. The defendant's confession regarding the latter offense was held to have been properly admitted into evidence.

[137] 322 U.S. 143 (1944).

arrested and he promptly admitted the killing, stating further that Ashcraft had hired him to do it. Ashcraft was confronted with Ware's confession and the interrogation continued for another 8 hours, at the end of which time Ashcraft admitted his guilt but refused to sign a written confession. He repeated his admission of guilt to two business men and to his own family physician, who were called in to witness the confession. The doctor also examined Ashcraft and found him free from any signs of physical abuse. His oral confession was admitted in evidence and his conviction in the trial court was affirmed by the Supreme Court of Tennessee. Upon appeal to the United States Supreme Court, however, that Court, in a six to three decision, reversed the conviction on the ground that the holding of Ashcraft incommunicado, without sleep or rest, for 36 hours of interrogation, was "inherently coercive" and a violation of the "due process" of law provision of the Fourteenth Amendment.

In its consideration of the *Ashcraft* case the majority of the Court made what appears to be an abstract psychological appraisal of a thirty-six hour interrogation and decided that an interrogation of that duration was "inherently coercive", for which reason the confession would be held inadmissible regardless of the effect of the police practices upon the particular defendant and regardless of the otherwise trustworthiness of the confession.

The principal objection of the *Ashcraft* case has been directed not so much to the result in the particular case, but to the general rule laid down in the majority opinion. For instance, in his dissenting opinion in the *Ashcraft* case, Justice Jackson severely criticized the majority opinion for excluding a confession "on an irrebuttable presumption that custody and examination 'are inherently coercive' if of some unspecified duration within thirty-six hours". In his analysis of the case, Justice Jackson expresses the view that "despite the 'inherent coerciveness' of the circumstances of Ashcraft's examination, the confession when made was delivered free, and voluntary in the sense in which that term is used in criminal law".

In further criticism of the majority opinion of the Court, Justice Jackson said: "The Court bases its decision on the premise that custody and examination of a prisoner for thirty-six hours is 'inherently coercive'. Of course it is. And so is custody and examination for one hour. Arrest itself is inherently coercive, and so is detention. When not justified, infliction of such indignities upon the person is actionable as a tort. Of course such acts put pressure upon the prisoner to answer questions, to answer them truthfully, and to confess if guilty. . . . If the constitutional admissibility of a confession is no longer to be measured by the mental state of the individual confessor but by a general doctrine dependent on the clock, it should be capable of statement in definite terms. If thirty-six hours is more than is permissible, what about 24? or 12? or 6? or 1? All are 'inherently coercive'."

For several years following the *Ashcraft* case it appeared that the growing restrictions on state interrogation practices would soon eliminate the opportunity for effective interrogation of criminal suspects. This possibility seemed quite imminent after the 5 to 4 decision in *Haley v. Ohio*,[188] a 1948 case in which a reversal was ordered for the conviction of a 15 year old Negro defendant who had been questioned for five hours by several police officers "in relays of one or two each". The majority opinion stated that in any case where the undisputed evidence "suggested" that coercion was used the conviction would be reversed "even though without the confession there might have been sufficient evidence for submission to the jury". On June 27, 1949, however, the Supreme Court decided three state confession cases, in which there were some indications that the Court, or a majority of its members anyway, was prepared to relax the demands previously imposed by the Court upon state interrogators.

In the three 1949 cases of *Watts v. Indiana*,[189] *Turner v. Pennsylvania*,[140] and *Harris v. South Carolina*,[141] each of the defendants had been subjected to extensive interrogations over a period of several days and by relays of police officers. By a 6–3 decision in the *Watts* case, and a 5–4 decision in the *Turner* and *Harris* cases, the Supreme Court reversed the convictions. In each case four members of the majority—Justices Douglas, Frankfurter, Murphy, and Rutledge—found fault not only with the length of the interrogation and the relay method of questioning, but also with (a) the failure to take the defendants before a committing magistrate for a preliminary hearing, (b) The absence of "friendly or professional aid" at the time of their interrogation, and (c) the neglect to advise the defendants of their constitutional rights. One of the four, Justice Douglas, even went so far as to favor the outlawing of any confession, however freely given, if it is obtained during a period of custody between arrest and arraignment.[142] The encouraging indications previously mentioned as being evidenced in these cases are obviously not present in the attitudes expressed by the aforementioned justices. They are found, however, in the dissenting opinions of Chief Justice Vinson and Justices Burton, Jackson, and Reed, who rather clearly indicated that they thought the test of a confession's admis-

---

[138] 332 U.S. 596 (1948).

[139] 338 U.S. 49 (1949).

[140] 338 U.S. 62 (1949).

[141] 338 U.S. 68 (1949).

[142] 338 U.S. at p. 57. Also see Justice Jackson's reference to Justice Douglas' concurring opinion. Justice Jackson said: "A concurring opinion . . . goes to the very limit and seems to declare for outlawing any confession, however freely given, if obtained during a period of custody between arrest and arraignment—which, in practice, means all of them." (338 U.S. at p. 58.)

Justice Douglas reiterated this same view in his dissenting opinion in Stroble v. California, 343 U.S. 181 (1952), where he stated: "The practice of obtaining confessions prior to arraignment breeds the third degree and the inquisition. As long as it remains lawful for the police to hold persons incommunicado, coerced confessions will infect criminal trials in violation of the commands of due process of law".

sibility should be its trustworthiness.[143] "Checked with external evidence", the confessions were considered "inherently believable", and "not shaken as to truth by anything that occurred at the trial". Justice Jackson, who authored the dissenting opinions in two of the cases, pointed right to the crux of the whole confession problem when he stated that all three crimes were unwitnessed, and that there was no way to solve them without taking suspects into custody for questioning. He added that there were only these alternatives: "to close the books on crime and forget it", or to take suspects into custody for questioning—"a grave choice for a society in which two-thirds of the murders already are closed out as insoluble". He further commented that if the Constitution required the Supreme Court to hold that a state may not take into custody and question one suspected reasonably of an unwitnessed murder, "the people of this country must discipline themselves to seeing their police stand by helplessly while those suspected of murder prowl about unmolested".

With four of the Justices thinking in terms of "trustworthiness" as a test of confession admissibility in the *Watts*, *Turner*, and *Harris* cases, it seemed that the Court had definitely begun to return from the extreme position it had reached in the cases decided between 1943 and 1949. Another indication of that fact was the appointment to the court of former Attorney General Tom Clark and Federal District Judge Sherman Minton to succeed Justices Murphy and Rutledge who had voted so consistently to restrict the interrogation opportunities and practices of both federal and state law enforcement officers.

The decisions of the court since 1949 have definitely confirmed the expectations which were suggested by the *Watts*, *Turner*, and *Harris* cases and the appointments of Justices Clark and Minton shortly thereafter. In the very recent state confession cases of *Gallegos v. Nebraska*[144] and *Stroble v. California*,[145] the majority of the Court is once again testing a confes-

[143] Justice Black's reasons for a reversal of the *Watts*, *Turner*, and *Harris* cases also seemed to offer some encouragement for the future. In these three cases he was apparently more persuaded by the "inherent coerciveness" of the extensive, relay interrogation practices rather than by the other considerations relied upon by his other colleagues who voted for a reversal of the convictions. In more recent cases, however, Justice Black seems much closer to the strict views which Justice Douglas has been expressing. See the dissenting opinions of Justices Black and Douglas in Gallegos v. Nebraska, 342 U.S. 55 (1951) and in Agoston v. Pennsylvania, 340 U.S. 844 (1950).

Justice Frankfurter, although the author of the "civilized standards" rule for federal officers (in the *McNabb* case), generally looks for more basic consideration in state cases. See his dissent in the *Ashcraft* case, *supra* note 137, and his concurrence in the decisions affirming the convictions in Lyons v. Oklahoma, 322 U.S. 596 (1944), and Gallegos v. Nebraska, 342 U.S. 55 (1951).

[144] 342 U.S. 55 (1951).
[145] 343 U.S. 181 (1952).

sion's admissibility by its "voluntariness", and confining its own due process determination to "facts undisputed by the state". The Court has also definitely set aside the proposals to categorically outlaw a state confession obtained during a period of delay in taking an arrested person before a committing magistrate for a preliminary hearing or arraignment. Such a delay is only a factor to be considered along with all the other evidence in a case determining whether the confession is a voluntary-trustworthy one.

In addition to its return to the voluntary-trustworthy test of confession admissibility, the Supreme Court has also repudiated what it had said in the *Haley* case, and in several other cases, about the inherent invalidity of any conviction in which a coerced confession had been used. It will be recalled that in the *Haley* case a 5–4 majority of the Court said that a conviction must be reversed even though without the coerced confession there might have been sufficient evidence to support the verdict. On June 15, 1953, however, in the case of *Stein v. New York*,[146] Justice Jackson, speaking for six members of the Court, labeled as *dicta* the statements to that effect which had been made in the *Haley* case and in several other confession cases. The *Stein* case held that a state court conviction which was supportable by other evidence would stand even though a coerced confession had been used at the trial.

Defense counsel in the *Stein* case had requested a jury instruction to the effect that if the jury found the confession to have been coerced they must return a verdict of acquittal. The trial judge's refusal to give this instruction was held to be proper. The majority of the Supreme Court expressed the view that "coerced confessions are not more stained with illegality than other evidence obtained in violation of law". The majority opinion also made the point that the Fourteenth Amendment of the United States Constitution is not a rigid exclusionary rule of evidence but only a guarantee against convictions upon untrustworthy evidence.

The sum total significance of the most recent United States Supreme Court decisions may be summarized by the following statement with which the majority of the Court concluded its opinion in the *Stein* case: "The people of the State are also entitled to due process of law".

The Court appears to have definitely abandoned the *Ashcraft* case "inherent coercion" test of confession admissibility. In other words, instead of making an abstract psychological appraisal of the facts and circumstances involved in the interrogation of the accused, the Court definitely announced in the *Stein* case that it would examine the confession and the events leading up to the confession and determine whether or not the police interrogation procedure had a coercive effect *on the particular person making the confession*. The Court stated that the limitations to be prescribed in

[146] 21 Law Week 4469 (June 16, 1953).

any case would depend upon "a weighing of the circumstances of pressure against the power of resistance of the person confessing." In other words, said the Court, "what would be overpowering to the weak of will or mind might be utterly ineffective against the experienced criminal".

The Court's opinion in the *Stein* case also quite clearly indicated that there is nothing inherently wrong about a lengthy interrogation.[147] It does appear, however, that during a lengthy interrogation time must be taken out for eating, drinking, and rest. As to just what is required will depend upon the particular case. The interrogator will have to exercise his own discretion as to what is reasonable under the circumstances.

Until the *Stein* case the Supreme Court seemed to view an interrogation by several interrogators operating in relays as an inherently coercive practice. The *Stein* case opinion, however, does not consider the practice so inherently oppressive as to necessarily "overwhelm the suspect's power of resistance". Relay questioning, of course, will always be a factor for consideration in determining the voluntariness or trustworthiness of a confession, but it will not automatically render a confession inadmissible as evidence. Nevertheless, the better interrogation practice, for legal as well as psychological considerations, is to avoid relay interrogations and entrust the task of a criminal interrogation to one, or at most two, interrogators.

II

What Is the Legal Status in State Courts of a Confession Obtained after Neglect or Failure to Promptly Take an Accused Person before a Committing Magistrate, as Provided by Statute?

Practically every state has a statute which requires arresting officers to take arrested persons before a committing magistrate "without unnecessary delay", or "immediately", or "forthwith".[148] Similar provisions, as previously stated, are found in federal statutes[149] and also in the Federal Rules of Criminal Procedure.[150]

Although originally the statutory provisions in England regarding the preliminary examination of arrested persons by justices of the peace were for the benefit of the prosecution (as a means for obtaining further evidence against the accused), the primary purpose of present day statutory pro-

---

[147] Also, to this same effect, see State v. Folkes, 174 Ore. 568, 150 Pac. (2d) 17 (1944) and Commonwealth v. Shupp, 365 Pa. 439, 75 Atl. (2d) 587 (1950).

[148] See listing of the state statutes in McNabb v. United States, 318 U.S. 332 (1943) at p. 342 f.n. 7.

[149] See the various federal statutes and a discussion of their legislative history in Inbau, "The Confession Dilemma in the United States Supreme Court" (1948) 43 Ill. L. Rev. 442 at pp. 455–459.

[150] Rule 5.

visions regarding preliminary hearings is to determine whether the known evidence against the accused is sufficient to justify further proceedings against him.[151] It is intended to obviate the annoyance and expense of a defense in any further proceeding unless there is sufficient evidence to indicate at least the probability that the accused is guilty. If the examining magistrate concludes that there is insufficient evidence to justify further proceedings, he discharges the accused from custody. On the other hand, if the evidence disclosed by the prosecution indicates that a conviction might reasonably result, the accused is held for trial or temporarily released on bond.

Until the United States Supreme Court decision in *McNabb v. United States*,[152] there was no doubt regarding the validity of a confession which had been obtained during a period of delay in taking the accused before a committing magistrate for a preliminary hearing.[153] At most, the delay in violation of a statutory provision regarding an early hearing before a committing magistrate was only one factor to consider in determining the voluntariness or trustworthiness of the confession.[154] The only direct consequence of the violation was a possible civil action against the arresting officer or perhaps disciplinary action against him by his commanding officer.[155] In the *McNabb* case, however, the Supreme Court held that a confession obtained during a period of "unnecessary delay" in arraignment (i.e., "a preliminary hearing") was inadmissible as evidence regardless of its voluntariness or trustworthiness. The Court specifically stated that it was establishing this rule in the exercise of its supervisory power over lower federal courts and federal officers, rather than by reason of its constitutional power to safeguard "due process". Since no such supervisory power existed as regards state courts or state officers, the states were at liberty to accept or reject the *McNabb* case principle. They have uniformly and consistently refused to apply the same principle in state cases.

In one of the early state cases in which defense counsel urged the application of the *McNabb* case principle, the Supreme Court of Oregon expressed the view that "adherence to such a rule would place unnecessary obstacles in the way of the detection of crime and result in the acquittal of many a guilty man". In another case the Supreme Court of Connecticut said it

[151] Orfield, *Criminal Procedure from Arrest to Appeal* (1947) 53–59, 72–75.
[152] *Supra* note 123.
[153] State v. Alex, 265 N.Y. 192, 192 N.E. 289 (1934). Also see Cahill v. People, 111 Colo. 29, 137 Pac. (2d) (1943), which was decided a few days after the *McNabb* case, but apparently without knowledge of the Supreme Court decision; and People v. Devine, 46 Calif. 46 (1873).
[154] People v. Mummiani, 258 N.Y. 394, 180 N.E. 94 (1932). The same is true, of course, since the *McNabb* case: Stroble v. California, 343 U.S. 181 (1952).
[155] Madsen v. Hutchison, 49 Idaho 358, 290 Pac. 208 (1930).

was not unmindful of the judicial and ethical standards involved in the *McNabb* case, but considered that "society, as well as the defendant, is entitled to equal protection of the law and to due process of law".[156] Similar views have been expressed, or are implicit, in the many state decisions rejecting the *McNabb* case principle.[157]

III

What Are the Types of "Force" or "Abuse" that Will Render a Confession Involuntary or Untrustworthy?

Even before the 1943–49 series of restrictive United States Supreme Court decisions, all courts, federal and state, were in general agreement

[156] State v. Folkes, 174 Ore. 568, 150 Pac. (2d) 17 (1944); State v. Zukanskas, 132 Conn. 450, 45 Atl. (2d) 289 (1945).

[157] The decisions, listed in state alphabetical order are: *Alabama:* Ingram v. State, 252 Ala. 497, 42 So. (2d) 36 (1949); *Arkansas:* State v. Browning, 206 Ark. 791, 178 S.W. (2d) 77 (1944), Perkins v. State, 217 Ark. 252, 230 S.W. (2d) 1 (1950); *Colorado:* Downey v. People, 121 Colo. 307, 215 Pac. (2d) 892 (1950); *Connecticut:* State v. Zukanskas, 132 Conn. 450, 45 Atl. (2d) 289 (1945), State v. Guastamachio, 137 Conn. 179, 75 Atl. (2d) 429 (1950); *Florida:* Finley v. State, 153 Fla. 394, 14 So. (2d) 844 (1943); *Georgia:* Russell v. State, 196 Ga. 275, 26 S.E. (2d) 528 (1943); *Illinois:* People v. McFarland, 386 Ill. 122, 53 N.E. (2d) 884 (1944), People v. Lazenby, 403 Ill. 95, 85 N.E. (2d) 660 (1949); *Indiana:* Willennar v. State, 228 Ind. 248, 91 N.E. (2d) 178 (1950). Although this case involved the admissibility of the results of an alcoholic intoxication test given during a period of delay in taking the defendant before a committing magistrate, the court specifically rejected the McNabb rule contention. Presumably the same ruling would hold regarding confession admissibility. *Kansas:* State v. Smith, 158 Kans. 645, 149 Pac. (2d) 600 (1944); *Mississippi:* Winston v. State, 209 Miss. 799, 48 So. (2d) 513 (1950); *Missouri:* State v. Sanford, 354 Mo. 1012, 193 S.W. (2d) 35 (1946) (The dissenting opinion in this case made the interesting point that the court was acting with obvious inconsistency in view of Missouri's general rule against the use of illegally seized evidence), State v. Lee, 361 Mo. 163, 233 S.W. (2d) 666 (1950); *Nevada:* State v. Boudreau, 214 Pac. (2d) 135 (1950), State v. Williams, 219 Pac. (2d) 184 (1950); *New Jersey:* State v. Pierce, 4 N.J. 252, 72 Atl. (2d) 305 (1950), State v. Bunk, 4 N.J. 461, 73 Atl. (2d) 249 (1950); *New York:* People v. Perez, 300 N.Y. 208, 90 N.E. (2d) 40 (1949); *North Carolina:* State v. Brown, 233 N.C. 202, 63 S.E. (2d) 99 (1951); *North Dakota:* State v. Nagel, 75 N.D. 495, 28 N.W. (2d) 665 (1947); *Ohio:* State v. Lawder, 147 Ohio 530, 72 N.E. (2d) 785 (1946); *Oklahoma:* Fry v. State, 78 Okla. Cr. R. 299, 147 Pac. (2d) 803 (1944), Hendrickson v. State, 229 Pac. (2d) 196 (1951); *Oregon:* State v. Folkes, 174 Ore. 568, 150 Pac. (2d) 17 (1944); *Pennsylvania:* Commonwealth v. Johnson, 365 Pa. 303, 74 Atl. (2d) 144 (1950) (reversed on appeal on other grounds, 340 U.S. 881 (1950)), Commonwealth v. Agoston, 364 Pa. 464, 72 Atl. (2d) 575 (1950), cert. den. 340 U.S. 844 (1950); *Tennessee:* McGhee v. State, 183 Tenn. 26, 189 S.W. (2d) 826 (1945); *Texas:* Dimery v. State, 240 S.W. (2d) 293 (1951), but compare Cavazos v. State, 146 Tex. Cr. R. 144, 172 S.W. (2d) 348 (1948), which purported to follow the McNabb case principle. The Cavazos case was not cited or discussed in the Dimery case. See 28 Tex. L. Rev. 114; *Utah:* Mares v. Hill, 222 Pac. (2d) 811 (1950), State v. Gardner, 230 Pac. (2d) 559 (1951); *Washington:* State v. Winters, 39 Wash.

upon one rule—that the police use of any form of *direct physical abuse*, or the threat of such force or abuse, for the purpose of obtaining a confession will render a resulting confession inadmissible in evidence.[158] It matters not whether the abuse was in the form of a beating with the proverbial rubber hose or with the interrogator's open hands; the legal result of inadmissibility was the same.[159] The basic reason for the rule of exclusion seems to be the well founded presumption that the infliction or threat of physical abuse is very apt to make an innocent person confess.[160]

Differences in court opinions have arisen, however, as to the effect of charges of *indirect physical abuse*[161]; and still greater differences are to be observed in cases involving what might be termed *psychological abuse*.[162]

(2d) 545, 236 Pac. (2d) 1038 (1951); *Wisconsin:* State v. Babiek, 258 Wis. 290, 45 N.W. (2d) 660 (1951). Also see, for *Hawaii*, Territory v. Young, 37 Hawaii 189 (1945).

The right of a state court to reject the *McNabb* case principle was reiterated by the U. S. Supreme Court in the June 15, 1953 decision of Stein v. N. Y., *supra* note 146.

[158] Wigmore, *Evidence* (1940) §851: "If physical violence is used . . . the confession is plainly inadmissible. But if no physical violence, or threat of it is used, both the moral and legal question become quite different".

[159] Rowe v. State, 98 Fla. 98, 123 So. 523 (1929); State v. Myers, 312 Mo. 91, 278 S.W. 715 (1925). For a collection of cases involving a variety of forms of direct physical abuse see McCormick, C. T., "Some Problems and Developments in the Admissibility of Confessions" (1946) 24 Texas L. Rev. 239, at p. 241–242; also 43 Harv. L. Rev. 617 (1930).

The one general exception to this principle is to be found in those cases where the confession occurred a considerable time later, when the coercive effect of the abuse had disappeared. See the *Lisenba* case, *supra* note 166. Also, see discussion *infra* pp. 220–222.

[160] Self-inflicted wounds, or injuries which the accused sustained from his crime victim or adversary or which were necessarily administered in effecting his arrest will not preclude the admission of a confession otherwise properly obtained. Comm. v. Lundin, 326 Mass. 551, 95 N.E. (2d) 661 (1950).

[161] State v. McNeal, 237 S.W. 738 (Mo. 1922) (a convict 'trusty' in solitary confinement in cell for ten days before confession; confession approved); State v. McCullum, 18 Wash. 394, 51 Pac. 1044 (1897) (accused confined in dark cell for several days prior to confession; confession excluded); Osborn v. People, 83 Colo. 4, 262 Pac. 892 (1927) (confinement in dark empty cell for 4 or 5 hours; confession admitted); People v. Jones, 402 Ill. 231, 83 N.E. (2d) 579 (1949) (while in jail the accused was put on meager food ration for a week, and he was also deprived of cigarettes and blankets; confession excluded). The mere fact that handcuffs or leg irons were on the accused during his interrogation will not render a confession involuntary: State v. Joseph, 217 La. 175, 46 So. (2d) 118 (1950); Le Moore v. United States, 180 Fed. (2d) 49 (1950).

[162] State v. Doyle, 146 La. 973, 84 So. 315 (1920) (accused interrogated 45 out of the 53 hours between arrest and confession; confession admitted); Clafin v. State, 154 Kans. 452, 119 Pac. (2d) 540 (1941) ("When a twenty-one year old youth is held in a hotel room for 16½ hours by a number of police officers . . . 'to induce him to make an admission', such an act is a form of coercion and grossly offends against the most sacred principles of our American way of life").

The underlying distinction between the latter forms of "pressure" and actual direct physical abuse seems to be this: that whereas relatively few innocent persons will withstand a severe beating, or even a mild one which carries the implication of greater pain and suffering later on, the effects of alleged indirect physical abuse, such as a temporary denial of food, or sleep, or physical comforts to innocent persons are not so predictable; and the same holds true for alleged psychological abuse such as lengthy interrogation (unaccompanied, of course, by the aforementioned forms of indirect physical abuse). In other words, the danger of false confessions is generally considered to be inherent in all instances of direct physical abuse, and consequently it was categorically outlawed. As regards the other two types of questionable practices, however, the danger is ordinarily viewed as not quite so real, and in such instances the courts seemingly preferred to examine *all the surrounding circumstances* in the case and determine therefrom the probable effect of the alleged abuse *upon the particular defendant.*[163]

Excellent illustrations of the type of physical and psychological abuses which have, and which should, render a confession inadmissible, are to be found in two United States Supreme Court cases decided in 1940. These two cases, *Chambers v. Florida*,[164] and *White v. Texas*,[165] as well as the other Supreme Court decisions during the period from 1940 to 1943, are again of

---

[163] In support of the foregoing conclusions regarding the underlying considerations involved in the numerous state court confession cases, see Justice Jackson's dissenting opinion in the Ashcraft case, 322 U.S. at p. 160, in which he said: "American courts hold almost universally and very properly that a confession obtained during or shortly after the confessor has been subjected to brutality, torture, beating, starvation, or physical pain of any kind is *prima facie* 'involuntary'."

"When, however, we consider a confession obtained by questioning, even if persistent and prolonged, we are in a different field. Interrogation *per se* is not, while violence *per se* is, an outlaw".

Also see similar views by Justice Jackson in the majority opinion of the court in the 1953 case of Stein v. N. Y., 21 Law Week 4469 (June 16, 1953).

Also see: Williams v. State, 22 So. (2d) 821 (Fla., 1945) (A confession is not rendered invalid simply because the defendant was at the time in custody . . . or the examination protracted, or conducted by a person of superior physique or mentality, but the voluntariness must be determined from all these circumstances considered together); State v. Layton, 174 Ore. 217, 148 Pac. (2d) 522 (1944) (The fact that prior to his confession the defendant, a 'large, healthy young man', spent all night in a chair, sleeping only part of the time, did not nullify his murder confession); and State v. Meyer, 293 Mo. 108, 238 S.W. 457 (1922) ("whether a confession is voluntary or involuntary depends upon the character, age, sex, disposition and past experience of the accused".)

[164] 309 U.S. 227 (1940).

[165] 310 U.S. 530 (1940).

particular interest and significance now that the Supreme Court has re-established the voluntary-trustworthy test of confession admissibility.

In the *Chambers* case, the defendants (Negroes accused of murdering a respected white member of the community) were kept in jail for a week and interrogated every day for many hours—to such an extent that the sheriff, according to his own testimony, was too tired to continue at night —and then an all-night session was finally held, during which time the subjects were interrogated in the presence of a number of persons, including police officers and several private citizens. The first written confession obtained that night was rejected by the prosecuting attorney who there-upon informed the interrogators not to call him from his home again until they had secured "something worthwhile". Subsequently the interrogators obtained confessions which were considered satisfactory. At their trial the defendants were convicted, and the convictions were sustained by the Su-preme Court of Florida. When the case was appealed to the United States Supreme Court, however, it was reversed on the ground that the use of the confessions thus obtained had deprived the defendants of due process of law.

In the *White* case, a Negro farm hand who had been arrested on a rape charge was confined to jail for about a week, taken into the woods on several nights and interrogated there "because the jail was too crowded", and then just prior to his confession he had been interrogated in a locked elevator for four hours. Upon these facts the United States Supreme Court held that the defendant had been deprived of the due process of law guaran-teed by the Constitution of the United States, and therefore the Texas Court of Criminal Appeals was held to be in error in upholding the admis-sibility of the confession.

In reversing the *Chambers* and *White* cases, the Court spoke only in terms of violations of "due process", and did not discuss the specific reasons for the decisions. It may reasonably be inferred, however, that the Court was thinking in terms of the untrustworthiness of the confessions. At any rate, in its very next confession case, *Lisenba v. California*,[166] decided in 1941, the Court specifically stated that "the aim of the rule that a confes-sion is inadmissible unless it is voluntarily made is to exclude false evi-dence", and that "tests are invoked to determine whether the inducement to speak was such that there is a fair risk the confession is false". It appears, therefore, that in these 1940–41 decisions the Supreme Court was examining all the surrounding circumstances in the case and determining the probable

[166] 314 U.S. 219 (1941). In the interim, however, the Court reversed two other state court confession cases, upon the authority of the *Chambers* case, but in neither case did the court render a written opinion. See Canty v. Alabama, 309 U.S. 629 (1940) and Vernon v. Alabama 313 U.S. 547 (1941).

effect upon the particular defendant. If the Court concluded that the indirect physical abuse or psychological abuse was likely to produce a confession even if the defendant were innocent, then the State Court conviction would be reversed because of a violation of "due process".

In applying the trustworthiness test in the *Chambers* and *White* cases, the Supreme Court was unquestionably justified in reversing the state court decisions. Applying the same test in the *Lisenba* case, the Court concluded that despite a number of abuses and even outright violations of state laws, the police practices, when viewed in the light of all the circumstances of the particular case, were unlikely to induce a false confession. Here, however, for the first time in a state court confession case, the Supreme Court was divided, with two justices dissenting and of the opinion that the confession used in the state trial was not "free and voluntary" and that the conviction should therefore be reversed. The *Lisenba* case involved the following facts: The defendant was arrested upon a charge of having murdered his wife by rendering her unconscious with liquor, placing her foot in a box containing rattlesnakes and then drowning her in a fish pond to give the appearance of accidental death in order that he might collect on an accident insurance policy. He was not taken before a committing magistrate as required by statute, nor was he incarcerated in the county jail as required by statute. He was also held incommunicado for about twenty-four hours and subjected to incessant questioning, during which period he was also slapped once by an interrogator. Twelve days later, after being confronted with the confession of an accomplice, and interrogated again for approximately twelve hours, the defendant confessed. At his trial, the defendant conceded that no threats, promises or beatings immediately preceded his confession, but he contended that he still suffered from the pain and memory of the abuse administered to him shortly after his arrest. Although the majority of the Supreme Court condemned the police practices employed in the case, it stated that the evidence of the illegality of the police activity and the abuse involved in the case were relevant only insofar as they had any bearing on the reliability of the confession. In other words, the majority of the Court was of the opinion that if upon consideration of all the circumstances in the case, and the probable effect upon the particular defendant, the confession appeared to be trustworthy, then it was usable against the defendant.[167]

Apart from the dissenting opinion of the two justices in the *Lisenba* case, that case furnished another clue of an approaching change in the Court's view of the confession rule. In the majority opinion itself, there

[167] Although direct physical abuse was involved in this case, it occurred twelve days before the confession. Otherwise, the general rule previously stated regarding such abuse may have been invoked to nullify the confession.

were several statements concerning the desirability of preventing "fundamental unfairness" in using certain kinds of evidence, *even if accurate and reliable.*

Not long after the *Lisenba* case the Court was again confronted with another case, *Ward v. Texas,*[168] which was quite similar upon its facts to the *Chambers* and *White* cases previously discussed. Here, too, was a Negro defendant who had been subjected to a series of indirect physical and psychological abuses (and perhaps even direct physical abuse), which were of such a nature as to warrant any unbiased court in excluding the resulting confession, and the Supreme Court was unanimous in its decision for a reversal. As in the *Lisenba* case, the Court again condemned several illegal police practices, such as transporting the suspect from three or four different counties in order to evade a *habeas corpus* order; and once more the Court gave a clue as to coming events.

A reading of the undisputed evidence pertaining to the police abuses and illegal practices involved in the *Chambers, White,* and *Ward* cases will itself furnish some explanation for the restrictive rules which the Court was soon to impose upon law enforcement officers. In every one of these cases the law enforcement agencies had employed interrogation practices which no self-respecting officer can conscientiously defend. They were particularly revolting to a court which by the very nature of its position in our judicial system was only occasionally called upon to review criminal cases, especially state court cases. They should also be condemned by all state courts, and, since interrogation practices of this type do render a resulting confession involuntary or untrustworthy, a reviewing court should have no hesitation in reversing convictions which rest upon such confessions.

IV

What Constitutes a Threat Within the Meaning of the Confession Rule?

In determining what statements or conduct of the interrogator amount to threats within the meaning of the confession rule, the following test is perhaps as helpful as any:

Was that which the interrogator said or did of such a nature that the subject reasonably thought he was placed in sufficient danger—of his life or physical suffering—so as to cause him to make a false confession?

Applying this test, an interrogator will find no difficulty in concluding (and the courts so hold) that a confession is inadmissible in evidence if obtained as a result of telling a subject that unless he confesses he will be

[168] 316 U.S. 547 (1942).

hanged,[169] shot,[170] or thrown to a mob outside the jail[171]; or as a result of administering the "third degree" to a fellow suspect while in the subject's presence.[172] The test also seems broad enough to render inadmissible a confession obtained as a result of a statement that unless the subject confesses he will be sent to the penitentiary for a series of more serious offenses.[173]

On the other hand, however, it is not improper for an interrogator merely to ask a question rather roughly,[174] to assume in his various questions that the subject is guilty,[175] to merely express his impatience with the subject's alleged lying,[176] to tell a subject that the investigators will secure, or already have secured, the necessary proof to convict him anyway,[177] or to tell him that if he so desires he can "stick to his story" and run the risk of being convicted and executed.[178] Also, the mere fact that the interrogator is armed, or that an officer had pointed a pistol at the subject when he was arrested, does not affect the validity of a confession.[179]

Advising or imploring a subject to "tell the truth" is never considered objectionable.[180] Some difficulties occasionally arise, however, when the

[169] Reason v. State, 94 Miss. 290, 48 So. 820 (1909). In Edwards v. State, 194 Md. 387, 71 Atl. (2d) 487 (1950), the interrogator kept making a "hangman's knot" with a piece of rope as he talked to the defendant. This was considered a threat, especially in view of the defendant's further testimony that the interrogator said that a mob might hang the defendant if he were released.

[170] Rollins v. State, 18 Ala. App., 354, 92 So. 35 (1922).

[171] People v. Sweetin, 325 Ill. 245, 156 N.E. 354 (1927).

[172] People v. Flores, 15 Cal. App. (2d) 385, 59 Pac. (2d) 517 (1936).

[173] State v. Miller, 68 Wash. 239, 122 Pac. 1066 (1912); State v. Harvey, 145 Wash. 161, 259 Pac. 21 (1927).

[174] Anderson v. State, 133 Wis. 601, 114 N.W. 112 (1907).

[175] People v. Fitzgerald, 322 Ill. 54, 152 N.E. 542 (1926).

[176] Dame v. State, 191 Ark. 1107, 89 S.W. (2d) 610 (1936). The interrogator's impatience even to the extent of swearing at the subject has been held insufficient to nullify a confession. State v. Dehart, 242 Wis. 562, 8 N.W. (2d) 360 (1943). Also, upon this point, see Buschy v. People, 73 Colo. 472, 216 Pac. 519 (1923), and the second *McNabb* case, 142 Fed. (2d) 904 (1944).

[177] State v. Johnson, 137 S.C. 7, 133 S.E. 823 (1926); People v. Castello, 194 Cal. 595, 229 Pac. 855 (1924).

[178] State v. Donovan, 40 Dela. 257, 8 Atl. (2d) 876 (1939). Also see People v. Hubbell, 128 P. (2d) 579 (Calif., 1942), in which the court held that telling a subject accused of a sex offense against a child that thirty children would be used as witnesses for the prosecution did not vitiate the confession made thereafter.

[179] State v. Thomas, 161 La. 1010, 109 So. 819 (1926); State v. Hart, 292 Mo. 74, 237 S.W. 473 (1922).

[180] People v. Randazzio, 194 N.Y. 147, 87 N.E. 112 (1909); State v. Caldwell, 212 N.C. 484, 193 S.E. 716 (1937). See note in 37 Mich. L. Rev. 315 (1938) for citation to additional cases.

One state, by statue, provides that "The fact that a confession shall have been

interrogator uses such language as "it would be better for you to confess", "you had better confess", "it would be better for you to tell the truth", or "you had better tell the truth".[181]

A number of courts have held that such statements as "you had better confess" or "it would be better for you to confess" constitute threats or promises which will nullify a confession. Some courts have gone so far as to hold that the same rule applies even when the subject is told "it would be better to tell (or you had better tell) *the truth*".[182] There are many cases, however, in which the courts have taken a more liberal view, particularly as regards the latter type of expressions.[183] Nevertheless, it is well for the interrogator to play safe and avoid the use of expressions involving the words "you had better . . ." or "it is better . . ."[184]

---

made under a spiritual exhortation . . . shall not exclude it". Georgia Code (1933), Ch. 38, §412.

[181] For a discussion of the distinctions between a mere adjuration to tell the truth, and telling the subject "it is better to tell the truth", or "it is better to confess", see Edwardson v. State, 255 Ala. 246, 51 So. (2d) 233 (1950). Also see State v. Robinson, 215 La. 974, 41 So. (2d) 848 (1949), where the statement "you had better confess" was preceded by "Boy, I have got you in the palm of my hand".

[182] See in particular the following cases, which have disapproved the use of any form of expressions such as those above mentioned: Biscoe v. State, 67 Md. 6, 8 Atl. 571 (1887); Edwards v. State, 194 Md. 387, 71 Atl. (2d) 487 (1950); West v. U.S., 20 D.C. App. 347 (1902); State v. Nagle, 25 R.I. 105, 54 Atl. 1063 (1903); State v. Dobbs, 148 Md. 34, 129 Atl. 275 (1925); People v. Leavitt, 100 Cal. App. 93, 279 Pac. 1056 (1929).

[183] Hintz v. State, 125 Wis. 405, 104 N.W. 110 (1905); State v. Gee Jon, 46 Nev. 418, 211 Pac. 676 (1923); State v. Mayle, 108 W. Va. 681, 152 S.E. 633 (1930); State v. Meyers, 202 N.C. 351, 162 S.E. 764 (1932); Hicks v. State, 178 Ga. 561, 173 S.E. 395 (1934); State v. Tharp, 234 Mo. 46, 64 S.W. (2d) 249 (1933); State v. Wickman, 39 N.M. 198, 43 Pac. (2d) 933 (1935); Comm. v. Mabey, 299 Mass. 96, 12 N.E. (2d) 61 (1937); State v. Thompson, 227 N.C. 19, 40 S.E. (2d) 620 (1946); Territory v. Sumngat, 38 Hawaii 609 (1950); People v. Pugh, 409 Ill. 584, 100 N.E. (2d) 909 (1951). An interrogator's statement to a Negro subject that "the best thing that I think you can do is to get down on your knees and tell God about it" was approved in Smith v. State, 248 Ala. 363, 27 So. (2d) 495 (1946).

The most reasonable view, of course, is the one taken by the majority of courts, which examine the expression in the light of all the other conditions and circumstances in the case. For instance, in People v. Ardelean, 368 Ill. 276, 13 N.E. (2d) 976 (1938), the court even tolerated the expression "it would be better for you to talk and if you don't it would be too bad", because, said the court, "if sufficient facts are proved showing that a statement of guilt was freely made, a trial court may admit it in evidence, although there may be some evidence of threats or promises". Also see Murphy v. U.S., 285 Fed. 801, certiorari denied 261 U.S. 617 (1923), and State v. Wickman, 39 N.M. 198, 43 Pac. (2d) 933 (1935).

[184] For a general discussion of the law regarding such expressions see Wigmore, *Evidence* (1940) §§832, 838.

V
What Promises Are Prohibited by the Confession Rule?

There are certain types of promises that an interrogator is permitted to make, and there are others which are prohibited. The line of demarcation is usually determined by the following test: "Is the promise one that is likely to cause the subject to make a false confession"?

As a general rule, in order for a promise to invalidate a confession it must have reference to the subject's escape from punishment or the mitigation of his punishment. It is not sufficient if the promise merely offers the subject an opportunity for the gratification of his personal desires and comfort, or for the granting of a benefit to some third person.[185]

A promise to the subject that if he confesses he will be released from custody,[186] that he will not be prosecuted,[187] that he will be granted a pardon[188] or that he will receive a light sentence,[189] is usually held to invalidate a confession.[190] The same is true even though the interrogator merely states that he will do whatever he can to induce the proper authorities to grant such immunity or diminution of sentence.[191]

[185] State v. Williamson, 339 Mo. 1038, 99 S.W. (2d) 76 (1936); State v. Palko, 121 Conn. 669, 186 Atl. 657 (1936). Also see Stein v. N. Y., *supra* note 146.

The above statement, and those to follow, are all subject to the qualification that the promise must be one which the confessor reasonably believed was made by a person who could carry it out.

[186] Such promises have been held improper even when they refer only to a temporary release on bail: People v. Campbell, 359 Ill. 286, 194 N.E. 533 (1935); Clash v. State, 146 Miss. 811, 112 So. 370 (1927).

[187] People v. Vinci, 295 Ill. 419, 129 N.E. 193 (1920)..

[188] State v. Squires, 48 N.H. 364 (1869).

[189] State v. Livingston, 202 N.C. 809, 164 S.E. 337 (1932). In State v. Ellis, 207 La. 812, 22 So. (2d) 181 (1945), a written and signed confession was held inadmissible because of a statement in the document that "We have definite proof and if you will tell us it will be better for you. It will go easier on you". But see Lewis v. U.S., 74 Fed. (2d) 173 (1934), holding that a confession was admissible even though the defendant (an Indian) had been told that Indians usually "got off easier".

[190] But see a statute of the state of Washington, which provides as follows: "The confession of a defendant made under inducement, with all the circumstances, may be given as evidence against him, except when made under the influence of fear produced by threats; but a confession made under inducement is not sufficient to warrant a conviction without corroborating testimony". Rem. Rev. Stats. §2151. Applied and upheld in State v. Meyer, 37 Wash. (2d) 759, 226 Pac. (2d) 204 (1951), and State v. Winters, 39 Wash. (2d) 545, 236 Pac. (2d) 1038 (1951).

[191] People v. Martorano, 359 Ill. 258, 194 N.E. 505 (1935). In fact, an intimation of such assistance will also nullify a resulting confession. See Edwards v. State, 194 Md. 387, 71 Atl. (2d) 487 (1950), where the interrogator showed the accused a letter from a convict which stated: "Next time you get a smart guy . . . show him this letter, from another wise guy, and don't forget to tell him what it cost me for not listening to you".

Promising a subject who is accused of a number of crimes that if he will confess to one he will not be prosecuted for the others has been held to nullify a confession.[192] A promise to a parolee that if he confessed to a murder he would be returned to the neighboring state prison from which he was paroled has been held to constitute a promise of immunity and therefore an improper inducement.[193]

The courts have uniformly held that an interrogator's promise to keep the subject's confession a secret does not affect its validity.[194] In one state such a promise is rendered permissible by statute.[195]

Promises made *after* a confession has been received are held not to affect the validity of the confession, regardless of the nature of the promise.[196] There is a practical danger, however, in making a promise after a confession. Such a promise may be considered by the trial court or jury as corroboration of the defendant's contention that a promise was made to him *before* the confession. It is advisable, therefore, to refrain from making any promises whatsoever, even after the confession itself.

As previously stated, expressions such as "it would be better for you to confess" or "it would be better for you to tell the truth" have been interpreted by a few courts as constituting promises sufficient to invalidate a confession.[197] It is suggested, therefore, that the interrogator avoid the risk incurred by the use of expressions of this nature.

[192] People v. Hurst, 36 Cal. App. (2d) 63, 96 Pac. (2d) 1003 (1939).

[193] State v. Williamson, 339 Mo. 1038, 99 S.W. (2d) 76 (1936). Regarding Missouri cases generally, see (1952) 20 Univ. of Kansas City L. Rev. 66.

[194] State v. Novak, 109 Iowa 717, 79 N.W. 465 (1899); Markley v. State, 173 Md. 309, 196 Atl. 95 (1938).

[195] Georgia Code (1933), Ch. 38, §412: "The fact that a confession shall have been made under a . . . promise of secrecy . . . shall not exclude it."

[196] State v. Moore, 124 Ore. 61, 262 Pac. 859 (1928); State v. Williamson, 343 Mo. 732, 123 S.W. (2d) 42 (1938); State v. Green, 210 La. 157, 26 So. (2d) 487 (1946). And a promise of a lighter penalty, made between the making of an oral confession and the signing of a substantially similar one does not necessarily render the written confession inadmissible, if upon a consideration of all the circumstances the confession appears trustworthy. State v. La Pean, 247 Wis. 302, 19 N.W. (2d) 289 (1945).

Upon a related question, as to the effect of force in securing the signature to the written confession upon the admissibility of the voluntary oral confession, see Gray v. Comm., 293 Ky. 833, 170 S.W. (2d) 870 (1943) (holding that the written confession was also admissible; but here the defendant admitted that his oral confession, which was the same as the written one, was voluntarily made).

[197] See cases cited *supra* notes 182 and 183. But *cf.* Penton v. State, 194 Ark. 503, 109 S.W. (2d) 131 (1937), where the sheriff told the accused that it would go well with him if he told the truth, and the court held that "this was merely an expression of opinion, and the statement was not coupled with innuendo or subtleties calculated to deceive the prisoner. Appellant was only advised to tell the truth".

VI

Under What Conditions and Circumstances May an Incriminating Statement Be Admitted in Evidence Even Though It Was Obtained by Force, Threats, or Objectionable Promises?

There are a number of state court decisions to the effect that if, in consequence of a confession otherwise invalid, a search is made and facts are discovered which confirm the confession in certain material respects, then the confirmed part of the confession is admissible as evidence.[198] For instance, if a confession is obtained from a burglary suspect by force and he tells where the stolen goods are hidden, that part of the confession locating the loot—but only that part —would be usable as evidence against the accused.[199]

The status of this rule regarding the use of a confirmed statement is rather uncertain at the present time. Although the "civilized standards" rule of the *McNabb* and *Upshaw* cases would seem to prohibit the use of any part of an illegally obtained confession in a federal case,[200] the United States Supreme Court may reach a different result in a state case. The Court's recent return to the voluntary-trustworthy test of confession admissibility in state cases is an indication in that direction.[201] Also indicative of that position is the Court's very recent repudiation of its former *Haley* case rule that a coerced confession would nullify a conviction even though the other evidence in the case was sufficient to support the jury's verdict.[202]

VII

Once Improper Interrogation Methods Have Been Used, Is It Possible, Later On, to Obtain a Valid Confession?

The fact that improper interrogation methods have been used to obtain a confession (which is thereby rendered valueless as legal evidence) does not

[198] State v. Garrison, 59 Ore. 440, 117 Pac. 657 (1911); Baughman v. Comm., 206 Ky. 441, 267 S.W. 231 (1924); Patton v. State, 29 So. (2d) 96 (Miss., 1947); Harris v. Comm., 301 Ky. 818, 193 S.W. (2d) 466 (1946); State v. Cocklin, 109 Vt. 207, 194 Atl. 378 (1937).

[199] In Texas there is a statutory provision to the effect that whenever any material part of a confession is substantiated by circumstantial evidence (finding the loot or body, etc.) the entire confession becomes admissible. §727, Tex. C.C.P. But the effect of this provision has been nullified because of a conflict with another Texas statute (§727a, C.C.P.) rendering illegally seized evidence inadmissible. Colley v. State, 158 S.W. (2d) 1014 (Tex. Cr. R., 1942).

[200] But see United States v. Bayer, 331 U.S. 532 (1947).

[201] See cases cited *supra* notes 144 and 145.

The Indiana Supreme Court in the second *Watts* case was apparently of that opinion. See Watts v. State, 229 Ind. 80, 95 N.E. (2d) 570 (1950).

[202] Stein v. N. Y., 21 U.S. Law Week 4469 (June 16, 1953).

preclude the possibility of subsequently obtaining from the same subject a valid and admissible confession.[203] And this is even possible in federal cases which are subject to the application of the Supreme Court's "civilized standards" rule of admissibility.[204]

When the prosecution attempts to introduce the second or later confession in evidence, it must assume the burden of showing that "the influence which induced the original confession had been removed and the confessing party was no longer dominated by such influence".[205] In other words, a presumption exists in favor of the accused that the previous objectionable influence has continued to exist.[206]

Whenever an interrogator is called upon to interview a subject who has been mistreated or threatened, he should be informed (and the conditions and circumstances surrounding the interview should so indicate) that no further mistreatment or threats will occur, and if a previous objectionable promise has been made it should be revoked in unmistakable terms. More-

[203] The usual position of the courts in such cases finds expression in Lyons v. Oklahoma, 322 U.S. 596 (1944), where the Court said: "If the relation between the earlier and later confession is not so close that one must say the facts of one control the character of the other, the inference is one for the triers of fact, and their conclusion, in such an uncertain situation, that the confession should be admitted as voluntary, cannot be a denial of due process". (*Ibid.* p. 603.) But according to the opinion of the dissenting justices, "It is inconceivable under these circumstances that the second confession was free from the coercive atmosphere that admittedly impregnated the first one". (*Ibid.* p. 606.) Also in accord with the view of the majority of the Court in the Lyons case: Lisenba v. California, 314 U.S. 219 (1941); U.S. v. Bayer, 331 U.S. 532 (1947); State v. Williamson, 343 Mo. 732, 123 S.W. (2d) 42 (1938); State v. Foster, 136 Ia. 527, 114 N.W. 36 (1907); U.S. ex vel. Weber v. Ragen, 176 Fed. (2d) 579 (1949), cent. den., 338 U.S. 809.

[204] U.S. v. Bayer, 331 U.S. 532 (1947).

[205] People v. Sweetin, 325 Ill. 245, 156 N.E. 354 (1927); People v. Jones, 24 Calif. (2d) 601, 150 Pac. (2d) 801 (1944); People v. Thomlison, 400 Ill. 555, 81 N.E. (2d) 434 (1948).

[206] Boudreaux v. State, 175 Miss. 625, 168 So. 621 (1936); State v. Henry, 196 La. 217, 198 So. 910 (1940); State v. Jugger, 217 La. 687, 47 So. (2d) 46 (1950); Barnes v. State, 199 Miss. 86, 23 So. (2d) 405 (1945); People v. La Coco, 406 Ill. 303, 94 N.E. (2d) 178 (1950)—to the effect that the first confession is the controlling one, the presumption being that the repetition is a product of the same coercive circumstances; Huntley v. State, 34 So. (2d) 216 (Ala. 1948). In the dissenting opinion in Malinski v. New York, 324 U.S. at p. 433, Justice Rutledge said: "The conclusion would seem doubtful in any case that a later confession could be entirely voluntary or uncoerced, where an earlier one had been compelled. A man once broken in will does not readily, if ever, recover from the breaking . . . No change in circumstances can wholly wipe out its effects upon himself or upon others". In the same case, Justice Murphy expressed the view, as a dissenting judge, that "Once an atmosphere of coercion or fear is created, subsequent confessions should automatically be invalidated unless there is proof beyond all reasonable doubt that such an atmosphere has been dispelled and that the accused has completely regained his free individual will".

over, none of the persons who previously abused or threatened him should be present at the second interview.[207] It is also desirable, as a precautionary measure in instances of this nature, to advise the subject of his privilege not to incriminate himself. (This advice, however, is not necessary in other types of cases not involving such previous objectionable features.[208]) Moreover, it is advisable to arrange for the witnessing of the subject's confession by one or more reputable persons, in whose presence the subject again should be assured of his safe and proper treatment.

VIII

Is It Permissible to Use Trickery or Deception in Obtaining a Confession?

Thus far the courts have uniformly held that the validity of a confession is unaffected by the fact that it was obtained by the use of trickery or deception on the part of the interrogator. This rule, however, is subject to the exception that the trick or deception must not be of such a nature as to be likely to produce an untrue confession.[209]

In interrogating two criminal suspects an interrogator may "play one against the other", and a confession resulting from such a trick is competent legal evidence.[210] He may also deceive the offender by showing him a fake telegram purporting to be a report from another police department stating that the offender's accomplice has confessed and implicated the subject under interrogation.[211] A valid confession also may be obtained by deceiving the subject into believing that his fingerprints were found at the scene of the crime.[212]

An investigator may pose as a fellow prisoner or as a friend of a suspect, and a confession obtained as a result of such trickery is competent evidence at the trial of the accused.[213] Likewise, it is legally permissible for a police

[207] As an example of the necessity of having previous abusers absent, see Jones v. State, 184 Wis. 50, 198 N.W. 598 (1924).

[208] See *infra* p. 223. Also see Johnson v. State, 226 Ind. 179, 78 N.E. (2d) 158 (1948), where a warning was considered necessary because of prisoner's prior abusive treatment.

[209] Wigmore, *Evidence* (3d ed., 1940) §841. There is also another exception, laid down in a Michigan case, that the attorney-client privilege will render incompetent a confession obtained by a person pretending to be the subject's attorney. See People v. Barker, 60 Mich. 277, 27 N.W. 539 (1886).

[210] Osborn v. People, 83 Colo. 4, 262 Pac. 892 (1927); State v. Palko, 121 Conn. 669, 186 Atl. 657 (1936).

[211] Comm. v. Green, 302 Mass. 547, 20 N.E. (2d) 417 (1939).

[212] People v. Connelly, 195 Cal. 584, 234 Pac. 374 (1925); Lewis v. U.S., 74 Fed. (2d) 173 (1934).

[213] People v. White, 176 N.Y. 331, 68 N.E. 630 (1903).

officer to fake notes purporting to be from one prisoner to another and thereby eventually procure a statement in the handwriting of one of them admitting his guilt of the offense for which he was under arrest.[214]

The foregoing police practices are illustrations of the general rule that trickery and deception do not nullify a confession, regardless of the possible objection to such practices from a strictly moral viewpoint. To what extent federal officers may rely upon this seemingly well established rule is somewhat uncertain in view of the Supreme Court's "civilized standards" test of admissibility in federal cases. In state cases, however, there is considerably less likelihood of the Supreme Court disturbing state court precedents upon this point, particularly since the Court's recent return to the voluntary-trustworthy test of confession admissibility.

IX

Is It Necessary, before Obtaining a Confession, to Advise an Offender of His Constitutional Rights?

In the absence of a statute or rule of court specifically requiring a criminal interrogator to advise or warn an offender of his constitutional rights before obtaining his confession, it is unnecessary to do so.

By reason of a provision in the Uniform Code of Military Justice, an interrogator in the Armed Forces must issue such a warning.[215] In civilian investigations, however, apparently Texas is the only state which, by statute, makes a warning necessary.[216] It is not required in any other jurisdiction, although the fact that no warning was given may be taken into consideration by the trial judge and the jury in determining the volun-

[214] State v. Dingledine, 135 Ohio St. 251, 30 N.E. (2d) 660 (1939).

[215] Article 34.

[216] Art. 727, Code of Criminal Procedure, Vernon's Texas Statutes (1936): "The confession shall not be used if, at the time it was made, the defendant was in jail or other place of confinement, nor while he is in the custody of an officer, unless made in the voluntary statement of the accused, taken before an examining court in accordance with law, or be made in writing and signed by him; which written statement shall show that he has been warned by the person to whom the same is made: First, that he does not have to make any statement at all. Second, that any statement made may be used in evidence against him on his trial for the offense concerning which the confession is therein made; or, unless in connection with said confession, he makes statements of facts or circumstances that are found to be true, which conduce to establish his guilt, such as the finding of secreted or stolen property, or the instrument with which he states the offense was committed. If the defendant is unable to write his name, and signs the statement by making his mark, such statement shall not be admitted in evidence, unless it be witnessed by some person other than a peace officer, who shall sign the same as a witness". (An Act of 1907). As regards the effect of the conflict between this statute's provision with another statutory prohibition against the use of illegally seized evidence, see *supra* note 199.

tariness of a confession. Decisions to this effect have been rendered by the highest courts of approximately thirty states.[217] The Supreme Court of the

[217] *Arizona:* Wagner v. State, 43 Ariz. 560, 33 Pac. (2d) 602 (1934); *Arkansas:* Greenwood v. State, 107 Ark. 568, 156 S.W. 427 (1913); *California:* People v. Chan Chaun, 41 Cal. App. (2d) 586, 107 Pac. (2d) 455 (1940); People v. Triplett, 161 Pac. (2d) 397 (Calif. App., 1945); People v. Landry, 106 Calif. App. (2d)8, 234 Pac. (2d) 736 (1951); *Colorado:* Reagan v. People, 49 Colo. 316, 112 Pac. 785 (1911); Cahill v. People, 111 Colo. 29, 137 Pac. (2d) 673 (1943); *Connecticut:* State v. Guastamachio, 137 Conn. 179, 75 Atl. (2d) 429 (1950); *Florida:* Kearson v. State, 123 Fla. 324, 166 So. 832 (1336); Rollins v. State, 41 So. (2d) 885 (Fla., 1949); *Georgia:* McDowell v. State, 78 Ga. App. 116, 50 S.E. (2d) 633 (1948); *Illinois:* People v. Fahrner, 330 Ill. 516, 162 N.E. 133 (1928); People v. Shelton, 388 Ill. 56, 57 N.E. (2d) 473 (1944); People v. Weber, 401 Ill. 584, 83 N.E. (2d) 297 (1949); *Indiana:* Hawkins v. State, 219 Ind. 116, 37 N.E. (2d) 79 (1941); Marshall v. State, 227 Ind. 1, 83 N.E. (2d) 763 (1949), but see Johnson v. State, 226 Ind. 179, 78 N.E. (2d) 158 (1948), where a warning was considered necessary because of prior abusive treatment; *Iowa:* State v. Mikesh, 227 Iowa 640, 288 N.W. 606 (1939); *Kansas:* State v. Criger, 151 Kans. 176, 98 Pac. (2d) 133 (1940), but see State v. Seward, 163 Kans. 136, 181 Pac. (2d) 478 (1947), where the court expressed the view that a 17 year old defendant should have been advised of his constitutional rights before handwriting specimens were obtained from him. In this case, however, the court was apparently greatly affected by the youthfulness of the accused, and the court's view regarding the warning in this case should be considered in the light of its previous *Criger* case decision; *Louisiana:* State v. Burks, 196 La. 374, 199 So. 220 (1940); State v. Holmes, 205 La. 730, 18 So. (2d) 40 (1944); State v. Alleman, 218 La. 821, 51 So. (2d) 83 (1950); *Massachusetts:* Comm. v. Mabey, 299 Mass. 96, 12 N.E. (2d) 61 (1938); Comm. v. Lundin, 326 Mass. 551, 95 N.E. (2d) 661 (1950); *Mississippi:* Newell v. State, 209 Miss. 653, 48 So. (2d) 332 (1950); *Missouri:* State v. Hoskins, 327 Mo. 313, 36 S.W. (2d) 909 (1931); State v. Tillett, 233 S.W. (2d) 690 (Mo. 1950); *Nebraska:* Bush v. State, 112 Neb 384, 199 N.W. 792 (1924); *Nevada:* State v. Gambetta, 66 Nev. 317, 208 Pac. (2d) 1059 (1949); *New Mexico:* State v. Archuleta, 29 N.M. 25, 217 Pac. 619 (1923), State v. Walker, 50 N.M. 132, 172 Pac. (2d) 588 (1946); *New Jersey:* State v. Pierce, 4 N.J. 252, 72 Atl. (2d) 305 (1950), State v. Bunk, 4 N.J. 461, 73 Atl. (2d) 249 (1950); *New Mexico:* State v. Archuleta, 29 N.M. 25, 217 Pac. 619 (1923), State v. Caro, 55 N.M. 176, 228 Pac. (2d) 957 (1950); *New York:* People v. Radazzio, 194 N.Y. 147, 87 N.E. 112 (1909), but see People v. Leyna, 302 N.Y. 353, 98 N.E. (2d) 553 (1951) to the effect that if a privileged communication between a doctor and a patient are used to obtain a confession, then the accused must be warned of his self-incrimination privilege; *North Carolina:* State v. Grier, 203 N.C. 586, 166 S.E. 595 (1932), State v. Lord, 225 N.C. 354, 34 S.E. (2d) 205 (1945), and also see State v. Matthews, 231 N.C. 617, 58 S.E. (2d) 625 (1950); *Oklahoma:* Tarkington v. State, 41 Okla. Cr. 423, 273 Pac. 1015 (1929), but see Fields v. State, 138 Pac. (2d) 124 (Okla. Cr., 1943), where the court said: "The fact that the defendant, 17 years of age, under arrest on a felony charge, in the absence of parent, guardian or counsel, was not advised of his constitutional right to refuse to answer questions that might incriminate him, should be considered as affecting the admissibility of any statement made by him purporting to be a confession of guilt".; *Oregon:* State v. Wilder, 98 Ore. 130, 193 Pac. 444 (1920), State v. Folkes, 174 Ore. 568, 150 Pac. (2d) 17 (1944), and also see State v. Leland, 190 Ore. 598, 227 Pac. (2d) 785 (1951); *Pennsylvania:* Comm. v. Dilsworth, 289 Pac. 498, 137 Atl. 683 (1927), but see Comm. v. Woong New, 354 Pa. 188,

United States reached a similar decision many years ago in a federal criminal case,[218] but that ruling must be considered in the light of the Court's present "civilized standards" rule for federal officers and lower federal courts. It is problematical, therefore, whether the Supreme Court will insist upon a warning in federal cases.[219] In state cases, however, the indications are that the Court will not insist upon a warning as an essential safeguard of due process.[220]

The constitutional provision that no person shall be compelled to be a witness against himself is considered by some courts of such force and effect as to require *a judicial tribunal* to advise an accused person of this privilege before his testimony can be heard; and the rule has been considered applicable not only to trial court proceedings but also to preliminary hearings and coroners' inquests.[221] However, if the accused is being interrogated by

---

47 Atl. (2d) 450 (1946), where the court condemned several police practices involved in the case, including the failure to warn the defendant, a Chinese, of his constitutional privilege; *Rhode Island:* State v. Gancarelli, 43 R.I. 374, 113 Atl. 5 (1921); *Utah:* State v. Karumai, 101 Utah 592, 126 Pac. (2d) 1047 (1942); *Vermont:* State v. Watson, 114 Vt. 543, 49 Atl. (2d) 174 (1946); *Virginia: dicta* to effect no warning necessary, Newberry v. Comm., 191 Va. 445, 61 S.E. (2d) 318 (1950); *West Virginia:* State v. Digman, 121 W. Va. 499, 5 S.E. (2d) 113 (1939); *Wisconsin:* Link v. State, 217 Wis. 582, 259 N.W. 428 (1935).

An exception to the general rule regarding warnings is to be found in cases where prior threats, force, or objectionable promises have been made, or where a previous improper confession has been obtained. In such instances a warning should be given —not because of any sanctimonious formality, but to indicate to the subject that the previous improper conditions and circumstances no longer exist. See Van Buren v. State, 24 Miss. 512 (1852), and the above cited Indiana case of Johnson v. State.

[218] Wilson v. United States, 162 U.S. 613 (1896). Also see lower federal court cases of Powers v. United States, 223 U.S. 303 (1912), U.S. v. Block, 88 Fed. (2d) 618, cert. den., 301 U.S. 690 (1937).

[219] The Court denied *certiorari* in a federal case where no warning had been given by federal interrogators. Cryne v. United States, 326 U.S. 727 (1945). But contrast that fact with the strong language in the *Haley, Watts, Turner,* and *Harris* cases.

[220] In the *Haley* case, 332 U.S. 596 (1948), the Court indicated that a warning was required for due process, but, as previously discussed (pp. 207–208), the court has greatly modified its general attitude in state cases since then. See Stein v. N. Y. *supra* note 146.

[221] Maki v. State, 18 Wyo. 481, 112 Prac. 334 (1911); McDonald v. State, 70 Fla. 250, 70 So. 24 (1915); State v. Meyer, 181 Iowa 440, 164 N.W. 794 (1917); Wood v. U.S., 128 Fed. (2d) 265 (1942).

In State v. Kotthoff, 177 Pac. (2d) 474 (Idaho, 1947), the court quoted at length from the *Maki* case, *supra,* and gives the impression that the warning required in the *Maki* case, as regards a judicial proceeding, is also applicable to police interrogations. But the court gave no specific consideration to this point and the decision is of dubious value as authority for a view in opposition to that taken by the cases cited in note 219, *supra.*

As for the reasons behind the requirement for the warning in judicial proceedings,

an investigator rather than by a judicial officer, no warning is necessary unless specifically required by statute or by rule of court.

X

Why Is It Desirable, from a Legal Standpoint, to Restrict the Number of Persons Present during an Interrogation?

The courts of at least one state (Illinois) have held that if the defense is raised at a criminal trial that a confession has been obtained under duress, the prosecution must, if practicable, produce as a witness each and every police officer or investigator who participated "in the hearing" or "in the procuring" of the confession.[222] Obviously there are many disadvantages, and even a very real danger to the prosecution's case, in being required to produce five or ten witnesses to establish the voluntary character of a confession. In the first place, considerable time and expense will be consumed

---

see State v. Gilman, 51 Me. 206, at p. 223 (1862): "The impressiveness of obligation and the solemnity of the occasion would have a tendency to wring from the party thus situated facts and circumstances which he is not bound to disclose, and therefore can in no just sense be said to be voluntary. As a general proposition this may be true, especially if the party is uninformed with regard to his rights"; and Bram v. U.S., 168 U.S. 532 (1897) at p. 550: "The reason upon which this rule rested undoubtedly was, that the mere fact of the magistrate's taking the statement, even though unaccompanied with an oath, might, unless he was cautioned, operate upon the mind of the prisoner to impel him involuntarily to speak".

Some state statutes specifically require the warning at preliminary examinations. See §4561 of the North Carolina Code (1939): "The magistrate shall then proceed to examine the prisoner in relation to the offense charged. Such examination shall not be on oath; and before it is commenced, the prisoner shall be informed by the magistrate of the charge made against him, and that he is at liberty to refuse to answer any question that may be put to him, and that his refusal to answer shall not be used to his prejudice in any state of the proceedings".

[222] "An inescapable duty rests upon the prosectuion . . . to bring in every police officer and every other person connected with taking the statements in order to ascertain whether they were forced by threats and physical violence". People v. Sloss, 412 Ill. 61, 104 N.E. (2d) 807 (1952). To the same effect: People v. La Coco, 406 Ill. 303, 94 N.E. (2d) 178 (1950); People v. Ickes, 370 Ill. 486, 19 N.E. (2d) 373 (1939); People v. Ardelean, 368 Ill. 274, 13 N.E. (2d) 976 (1938); People v. Ardenarczyk, 367 Ill. 534, 12 N.E. (2d) 2 (1937). But see People v. Jankowski, 391 Ill. 298, 63 N.E. (2d) 362 (1945), where the defendant testified that he did not remember making a confession and did not know what he signed, but claimed that a particular officer, whom he named, was the only one who had beaten him, which officer was produced as a witness for the prosecution and denied any abuse. The court held that under the circumstances it was unnecessary to call the other officers as witnesses.

Some other states have indicated an intention of establishing a similar rule. State v. Scarborough, 167 La. 484, 119 So. 523 (1929); State v. Lord, 42 N.M. 638, 84 Pac. (2d) 80 (1938); Holmes v. State, 51 So. (2d) 755 (1951). *Contra:* Logan v. State, 251 Ala. 441, 37 So. (2d) 753 (1948).

in producing the testimony of all police officers who were present when the confession was obtained. Secondly, the more witnesses there are to the event, the more likely there is to be a certain amount of inconsistency in their testimony as to the various details surrounding the confession—even though they all may be attempting to tell the absolute truth—and this inconsistency is very apt to lend credence to the allegations of duress.[223]

XI
Is an Oral Confession Competent Legal Evidence?

An oral confession is competent legal evidence, and it may be proved by anyone who heard it.[224]

For all practical purposes, of course, a written and signed confession has a decided advantage over one that is unwritten or unsigned. An offender who is confronted with a written and signed confession will have considerable difficulty convincing a judge or jury that he did not make the confession; but where the only proof of a confession is the word of another person or persons, then the offender is in a far better position to effectively deny the alleged confession. Nevertheless, they are both equally admissible as evidence, the only difference being this feature of the greater weight or credibility usually given to the written and signed confession.[225]

[223] As regards the effect of "relay" interrogations on a confession's admissibility see *supra* p. 208.

[224] State v. Lu Sing, 34 Mont. 31, 85 Pac. 521 (1906); State v. Coy, 140 Kan. 284, 36 Pac. (2d) 971 (1934); Douberly v. State, 184 Ga. 577, 192 S.E. 226 (1937); People v. Leving, 371 Ill. 448, 21 N.E. (2d) 391 (1939). Also see Evans v. U.S., 122 Fed. (2d) 461 (1941), where it was held that oral statements made by the accused, which he did not want incorporated into the written statement, were nevertheless admissible in evidence.

In Texas, by statute, a confession must be in writing and signed by the defendant before it is admissible in evidence. Tex. Code Crim. Proc. (1925), Art. 727.

[225] With respect to unsigned, written confessions, see State v. Dierlamm, 189 La. 544, 180 So. 135 (1938), where an unsigned confession, transcribed from shorthand notes, was admitted in evidence "in support of, and as part of the oral testimony" of a witness who heard the defendant so testify; also State v. Folkes, 174 Ore. 568, 150 Pac. (2d) 17 (1944), in which the court said: "Before an instrument can be deemed admissible as the written confession of the defendant, he must in some manner have acquiesed in the correctness of the writing itself. A writing not signed, or not thus approved by the defendant, is not per se his confession". Also see, upon this point, Mobley v. State, 227 Ind. 335, 85 N.E. (2d) 489 (1949); State v. Dietz, 5 N.J. Supp. 222, 68 Atl. (2d) 777 (1949); Needham v. State, 215 Ark. 935, 224 S.W. (2d) 785 (1949); People v. Kelly, 404 Ill. 281, 89 N.E. (2d) 27 (1949); State v. Saltzman, 241 Iowa 1373, 44 N.W. (2d) 24 (1950); State v. Cleveland, 6 N.J. 316, 78 Atl. (2d) 560 (1951); as to the application of the "best evidence" rule in situations of this sort, see Gordon v. State, 41 So. (2d) 611 (Colo., 1949). (Footnote continued next page.)

XII

Are Voice Recorded Confessions, and Sound Movie Confessions, Admissible as Evidence?

The point is well established, by a variety of state court decisions, that voice recorded confessions and sound movie confessions are admissible as evidence. All that is required as a prerequisite is the testimony of a witness who can authenticate the recording or movie—someone who can say, from first hand knowledge, that the recording or movie is an accurate reproduction of what transpired.[226]

Although such recordings and movies are admissible as evidence, before any police department or agency resorts to this method of confession preservation and proof, it is well to consider at least one practical disadvantage. If a recording or sound movie is made and used as evidence in any one case, the department or agency may find it necessary to do so in *all* comparable cases. Otherwise defense counsel in a subsequent case may very appropriately point out and effectively argue that no such procedure was followed in the present case—for the reason that his client's confession was obtained by force, threats, or other illegal means, which a recording or sound movie would have revealed.

XIII

In Cases Where a Subject Confesses Several Crimes, Is It Proper to Incorporate All of Them in One Written Confession?

It is a general rule of law that evidence is not admissible which shows or tends to show that the accused person committed another crime wholly independent of the one for which he is being tried.[227] However, there are exceptions to this general rule.

The prosecution may introduce evidence which shows or tends to show that the accused committed some other offense or offenses if such evidence tends to establish (1) the absence of mistake or accident—in other words, the guilty knowledge or aforethought—on the part of the accused when he committed the offense for which he is being tried; (2) the intent or motive

---

In Gray v. Comm., 293 Ky. 833, 170 S.W. (2d) 870 (1943), it was held that even though force was used in obtaining the defendant't signature to the confession, it was nevertheless competent evidence because the defendant admitted it to be an accurate account of his voluntary oral confession.

[226] State v. Alleman, 218 La. 821, 51 So. (2d) 83 (1950); Comm. v. Roller, 100 Pa. Sup. 125 (1930); People v. Hayes, 21 Calif. App. (2d) 320, 71 Pac. (2d) 321 (Cal. App., 1937); Williams v. State, 226 Pac. (2d) 989 (Okla., 1951); State v. Perkins, 355 Mo. 851, 198 S.W. (2d) 704 (1946).

[227] Hergenrother v. State, 215 Ind. 89, 18 N.E. 784 (1939).

with which the act was committed; (3) the identity of the accused; and (4) the scheme, plan, or system used in the commission of the offense.[228] Such evidence is also admissible where two or more crimes are inseparable parts of the one transaction.

A knowledge of the foregoing exceptions to the general rule regarding the admissibility of evidence concerning other crimes will prove helpful to an interrogator confronted with the problem of including or omitting references to them in a confession of the main offense under investigation. It is suggested, however, that except where the other offense or offenses can be considered as an inseparable part of the one transaction, it is perhaps safer to restrict the contents of the confession to the one offense. As to the other offenses, it is in order, of course, for the interrogator to take a separate confession for each one.

The practice of employing the question and answer form of confession in preference to the narrative form will obviate some of the difficulties which otherwise might be encountered because of the rule regarding the inadmissibility of other offenses, for in such instances the objectionable questions and answers may be stricken out and omitted when the confession is read to the jury, without seriously affecting the portions relating to the principal offense.

XIV

Under What Conditions and Circumstances May the Confession of One Defendant Be Used against a Co-Defendant, and What Procedure May an Interrogator Follow in Order to Lay the Foundation for the Use of a Confession for This Purpose?

Whenever a person is accused of a crime under conditions and circumstances which would normally bring forth a denial from an innocent person,

---

[228] The following provision of a Michigan statute states the rule in much the same way: "In any criminal case where the defendant's motive, intent, the absence of mistake or accident on his part, or the defendant's scheme, plan or system in doing an act, is material, any like act or other acts of the defendant which may tend to show his motive, intent, the absence of mistake or accident on his part, or the defendant's scheme, plan or system in doing the act in question , may be proved, whether they are contemporaneous with or prior or subsequent thereto, notwithstanding that such proof may show or tend to show the commission of another or prior or subsequent crime by the defendant". Mich. Stats. Ann. (1938), 28, 1050.

As illustrations of some of the exceptions outlined in the text above, see the following cases: People v. Lisenba, 14 Cal. App. (2d) 403, 94 Pac. (2d) 569 (1939), aff'd., 314 U.S. 219 (1941); People v. Anderson, 375 Ill. 163, 30 N.E. (2d) 648 (1940); Whitman v. State, 119 Ohio St. 285, 164 N.E. 51, 63 A.L.R. 595 (1928); State v. Palko, 122 Conn. 529, 191 Atl. 320 (1937); Banks v. State, 187 Ark. 962, 63 S.W. (2d) 518 (1933); People v. Collins, 195 Cal. 325, 233 Pac. 97 (1925).

and the accused remains silent, his failure to reply or deny is generally admissible in evidence as "an admission by silence".[229] Upon this general principle many courts have held that a confession of one person may be used against his accomplice if the accomplice, when first confronted with the confession, made no reply or otherwise failed to deny it.[230]

Since a confession of one offender cannot (because of the hearsay rule) be used against his accomplice unless the confessor himself so testifies in court, or unless the confession has been made in the presence of the accused *and he failed to deny it*, criminal interrogators may find it advisable on occasions to have the confessing offender confront and accuse his accomplice. Then, if no denial is made by the accomplice, the accusation and the fact of his silence may be used in many states as evidence pointing toward his guilt.[231]

[229] Comm. v. Vallone, 347 Pa. 419, 32 Atl. (2d) 889 (1943); State v. Portee, 200 N.C. 142, 156 S.E. 783, 80 A.L.R. 1220 (1931). Also see 4 Wigmore, *Evidence* (1940) §1072, and annotations in 115 A.L.R. 1510. For an illustration of the application of this principle in instances of replies of an equivocal nature, see Skidmore v. State, 59 Nev. 320, 92 Pac. (2d) 979 (1939), where the statement "you had better be careful what you say", made by the accused when confronted by a 5 year old sex victim, was held admissible as an admission of conduct (silence), since the accused's statement was not a direct, unequivocal denial of the accusation. The court further held that although the 5 year old was incompetent to testify, the sheriff could properly testify to her accusation and the accused's failure to deny.

Some courts, however, follow the rule that a person under arrest has a right to remain silent and his silence cannot be used against him as a tacit admission of guilt. Walker v. State, 156 Pac. (2d) 143 (Okla., 1945). For a general discussion of "admissions by silence" and the various ramifications of the rule, see Wigmore, *supra*. Also see (1941) 31 J. Criminal L. & Criminology 461; and (1948) 38 *Ibid.* 514 at p. 515.

[230] People v. Lehne, 359 Ill. 631, 195 N.E. 468 (1935); Clark v. State, 240 Ala. 65, 197 So. 23 (1940); Edwards v. State, 155 Fla. 550, 20 So. (2d) 916 (1945). In Comm. v. Brooks, 355 Pa. 551, 50 Atl. (2d) 325 (1947), the signing of a confession, as a witness, by one who was implicated by the confessor, constituted an admission because of his failure to deny or repudiate the accusation. There are some limitations upon the use of evidence of this sort, however. For instance, in People v. Simmons, 28 A.C. 715, 172 Pac. (2d) 18 (1946), the California court said that if the accused's previous responses to the police interrogators indicate that he has chosen a policy of silence, then his silence to the accusation cannot be used against him; and "the same ruling should be made if it appears that a great mass of extraneous hearsay matter will be placed before the jury through this device". See comment on the Simmons case, (1947) 35 Calif. L. Rev. 128 (1947). Another case disclosing limitations upon the admission by silence rule in cases involving accomplices, see People v. Kozlowski, 368 Ill. 124, 13 N.E. (2d) 174 (1938), in which the court refers to the general exceptions to the rule admitting such evidence: fear, legal advice, previous denials, etc.

[231] No attempt is made here to list the states adhering to one view or the other regarding the effect of silence to an accusation while under arrest, because even in states excluding such evidence no harm can result from an interrogator's practice

XV

What Is the Legal Distinction between an Admission and a Confession?

Whereas a confession is a direct acknowledgement of the truth of the guilty fact charged, or of some essential part of it, a so-called admission is an acknowledgement of a subordinate fact not directly involving guilt and not essential to the crime charged. Or, stated in somewhat different terms, a confession is an acknowledgment of the commission of the criminal act itself, whereas an admission is merely an acknowledgment of a fact or circumstance from which guilt can only be inferred.[232] A confession implies that the matter confessed constitutes a crime, but an admission, however incriminating it might be by inference, is a statement made without any intention of actually confessing guilt.[233]

The rules governing the admissibility of an admission are much less strict than those pertaining to confessions. For instance, the prosecution may introduce an admission in evidence without the necessity of first showing that it was made freely and voluntarily.[234] With regard to confessions, of course, the contrary rule prevails.[235]

---

of confronting one offender with his accomplice's accusation. In an excluding state the prosecution need only refrain from attempting to use such evidence. The mere fact of such confrontation is not objectionable.

[232] Wigmore, *Evidence* (1940) §821: "An acknowledgment *of a subordinate fact, not directly involving guilt*, or, in other words, not essential to the crime charged, is not a confession, because the supposed ground of untrustworthiness of confessions is that a strong motive impels the accused to expose and disclose his guilt as the price of purchasing immunity from present pain or subsequent punishment, and thus, by hypothesis, there must be some quality of guilt in the fact acknowledged". See Comm. v. Haywood, 247 Mass. 16, 141 N.E. 571 (1923); State v. Red, 53 Iowa 69, 4 N.W. 831 (1880).

[233] People v. Wynecoop, 359 Ill. 124, 194 N.E. 276 (1935).

[234] People v. Johnson, 203 Calif. 153, 263 Pac. 524 (1928); People v. Wynecoop, *supra* note 283.

[235] An attempt was made to take advantage of this admission-confession distinction in the retrial of the *Ashcraft* case and thereby get into evidence an oral statement that the defendant "knew who killed his wife". Although the state contended that this was an exculpatory statement, the Supreme Court considered it in the nature of a confession and again reversed the case. 327 U.S. 274 (1946). Although there was some indication in the *Ashcraft* case that there should be no distinction between the rules governing the admissibility of confessions and admissions, the recent *Stein* case opinion (*supra* note 146, footnote 5) indicates that the Supreme Court still adheres to the distinction. With regard to the opposite view of the same rule of admissibility governing both types of evidence, see People v. Reilly, 224 N. Y. 90, 120 N.E. 113.

———————

(Readers wishing to keep up to date regarding future developments in the law of confessions should consult the **Journal of Criminal Law, Criminology and Police Science,** *a bi-monthly publication of Northwestern University School of Law. A special effort is made in the Journal's sections on "Criminal Law Notes and Comments" and "Police Science Legal Abstracts" to discuss or abstract significant cases involving confessions and other subjects of particular interest to law enforcement officers.)*

———————

Appendix

History of the Polygraph

The following article, which appeared in the June 13, 1908 number of The British Medical Journal (vol. 1, p. 1411) describes a polygraph which was invented many years ago by Dr. James Mackenzie, a famous heart specialist. His instrument, although intended solely for medical purposes, is basically the same as the blood pressure-pulse and respiration recorders used today for lie detection purposes. The article is here produced in its entirety and exactly as it appeared in the 1908 British Medical Journal.

The Ink Polygraph

I exhibited at the meeting of the Medical Section of the British Medical Association in Toronto in 1906 a method of recording the movements of the circulation by means of an ink polygraph. I have not hitherto published a description of this method as there has been some difficulty in getting the instrument made, and the maker until lately has not been able to meet the demand for the instrument.

A long experience in taking graphic records of the movements of the circulation impressed me with the fact that there were many features in these movements which it was impossible to investigate satisfactorily by the methods in vogue. Changes in the heart's contraction that occurred at infrequent intervals, or in great variety, were apt to be overlooked, while the relationship of the respiration has never been satisfactorily worked out. There was a necessity, therefore, to devise a method by which tracings could be taken over a period of time of considerable duration. I conceived the idea that if a roll of paper could be unwound and levers could be made to inscribe the movements in ink, the end I had in view would be achieved.

I had considerable difficulties to overcome, but found a skilled helper in Mr. Shaw, who not only comprehended and appreciated my ideas, but constructed an instrument that carried them out. The case, *A*, in the accompanying figure contains the clockwork for the roller which unwinds the roll of paper, *D*, and also the separate clockwork which moves the time-marking pen; *B*, *B* are the two tambours, and *F*, *F* their levers, one of which is

233

represented raised, while the pen of the other is resting on the paper. The Writing pens are narrow grooved wires, one end fixed to the bottom of a small cistern at the free extremity of the lever. The other end of the grooved wire is adjusted barely to touch the paper. The ink is put into the tiny cistern, and it flows along the grooves of the pen-point by capillary attraction. If the pens are kept clean and the ink is free from dust, they serve their purpose most admirably and are ever ready for use.

As the radial pulse is the most serviceable of standards, a special method is employed to record it. A splint, C, somewhat like that belonging to a Jacquet sphygmograph, is fastened to the wrist in such a manner that the pad of the steel spring falls on the radial artery and is pressed down by an eccentric wheel, 18, until a suitable movement is transmitted to the spring

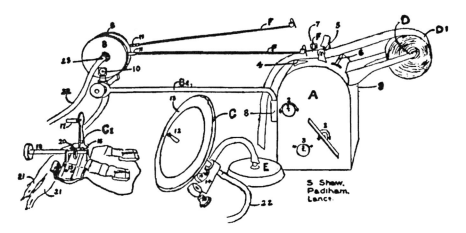

S Shaw.
Padiham.
Lancs.

by the artery; then the broad tambour, C, is fitted on to the splint so that the knob, 12, falls on the moving spring. This wrist tambour is connected to the tambour, B, by india-rubber tubing, $22, 22$, and the movements of the radial pulse are recorded by the lever, F. The shallow cup (receiver), E, is placed on the pulsation which it is desired to record, and the movement is conveyed to the lever, F, of the other tambour. In this way simultaneous with the radial pulse a record can be obtained of the apex-beat, carotid, jugular, or other pulses.

To record the respiratory movements a bag can be substituted for the receiver, E.

By turning the screw, 3, the rate at which the paper passes can be quickened or slowed at will. This is of the greatest use, for it often happens that in quickly succeeding events a wider interval may be required, whereas in recording respiratory movements a slow rate is best. As the time-marker registers one-fifth of a second and is driven by a separate clockwork, the rate of the recorded movements can always be ascertained with absolute accuracy.

It has been suggested that another tambour should be added to record three movements, and I have tried this, but I have practically discarded it, as, though it might be of use occasionally, it would complicate the apparatus unnecessarily. When making observations single-handed the two tambours are quite sufficient to occupy attention. With a little practice this apparatus can be used with the greatest facility. In the course of a few minutes the different movements can be recorded with the patient sitting up or in the recumbent position.

When the tambour is strapped to the wrist to take the radial pulse, one hand is always free to start the machine and to replenish the ink or regulate the rate, the other hand holding the receiver over the movement to be recorded.

The instrument is made by Mr. S. Shaw, instrument maker, Padiham, Lancashire.

This interesting historical information about the "Polygraph" came to our attention for the first time while reading an article entitled "The Search for the Truth" by William O. Gay, in a 1948 number of the English Police Journal (vol. 21, No. 4, at page 284). Mr. Gay, in his discussion of the use of lie-detectors in the United States, made the statement that "the Polygraph is really a modification of a device invented by Sir James Mackenzie, the famous heart specialist".

Index

CPSIA information can be obtained at www.ICGtesting.com
Printed in the USA
LVOW071440021212

309755LV00008B/123/P